Workbooks for Psychotherapists

Volume II:
*Listening
and
Formulating*

The Workbook Series . . .
by Robert Langs, M.D.

WORKBOOKS
FOR PSYCHOTHERAPISTS

Volume I:
Understanding Unconscious Communication

Volume II:
Listening and Formulating

Volume III:
Intervening and Validating

ABOUT THE AUTHOR

Robert Langs, M.D. is a classically trained psychoanalyst and program director
of the Lenox Hill Hospital Psychotherapy Program. He is Editor-in-Chief of *The
Yearbook of Psychoanalysis and Psychotherapy* and a practicing and supervis-
ing psychotherapist and psychoanalyst. Dr. Langs has written more than
twenty books for the profession on aspects of psychoanalysis and psychotherapeutic technique and on studies of the therapeutic interaction. His work
has specialized in studies of unconscious communication. Dr. Langs is also the
founder of The Society for Psychoanalytic Psychotherapy and lectures widely
in the United States and Europe.

Workbooks for Psychotherapists

Volume II:
*Listening
and
Formulating*

Robert Langs, M.D.

NEWCONCEPT
press, inc.

EMERSON, NEW JERSEY

NEWCONCEPT PRESS, INC.
EMERSON, NEW JERSEY 07630

**Library of Congress
Catalog Card Number 84—62354**

Library of Congress Cataloging in Publication Data

Langs, Robert, Date.
  Workbooks for psychotherapists.

  (The Workbook series / by Robert Langs)
  Contents: v. 1. Understanding unconscious
communication—v. 2. Listening and formulating
—v. 3. Intervening and validating.
  Includes bibliographies and indexes.
  1. Psychotherapist and patient—Problems,
exercises, etc. 2. Communication—Psychological
aspects—Problems, exercises, etc. 3. Sub-
consciousness—Problems, exercises. I. Title.
II. Series: Langs, Robert   . The
workbook series. [DNLM: 1. Communication—
examination questions. 2. Psychotherapy—
examination questions. WM 18 L285w]
RC480.8.L37 1985   616.89'14'076   84-62354
ISBN 0-931231-01-9 (pbk. : v. 1)

ISBN 0-931231-02-7
ISBN 0-931231-00-0 (series)

Printed in the United States of America

10 9 8 7 6 5 4 3 2

Contents

Preface

This is the second volume of a workbook series designed to foster a practical understanding and application of the *communicative approach* to psychotherapy. The communicative approach is based on two fundamental propositions: first, that there is a *stimulus-response interaction* occurring between patients and therapists in the psychotherapeutic arena; and second, that this interaction takes place at both *conscious and unconscious levels of communication*. Understanding both levels of this interaction progressively illuminates for a therapist the pertinent factors in a patient's madness or psychopathology (neurosis in its broadest possible sense). These propositions dictate a fundamental listening and formulating process by which the conscious and especially unconscious meanings and functions of the patient's communicative expressions can be detected, thus revealing the full implications of a patient's behaviors and associations. This method of illuminating the important unconscious facets of a patient's emotionally founded illness constitutes the essence of psychoanalytic understanding.

In the psychotherapeutic and psychoanalytic situations (the terms will generally be used interchangeably in the present work), issues of communication take precedence over all other levels of meaning and defense. Before problems of conflict, genetics, narcissism, form of psychopathology, and the like can be explored and dealt with in the treatment situation, it is essential to determine exactly what the patient is and is not expressing in the course of a session—and how well and how clearly. Thus, the fundamental listening process must come first.

Listening is by no means merely a cognitive task. Despite beliefs to the contrary, every psychotherapist is powerfully motivated to avoid the activated unconscious meanings of the material communicated by his or her patients. It therefore requires effort and self-mastery to engage fully in an insightful psychoanalytic or psychotherapeutic listening endeavor. Such work requires, in addition to education and training, both a significant measure of self-understanding and the resolution of the therapist's own madness.

It is the basic goal of the present volume to promote the active mastery of the listening-formulating process. The main vehicle for this endeavor will be the use of listening exercises, enabling the reader to participate in both listening and formulating.

The book is designed to be self-sufficient. In concise, near-outline form, the rationale for the communicative listening approach will be spelled out, followed by exercises in listening to the three basic components of the patient's material—*indicators* (expressions of patient-madness), *adaptive contexts* (the evocative stimuli for the patient's material, constituted by the therapist's interventions), and the patient's *direct and encoded responses* (in particular, the *derivative complex*, constituted first and foremost by the patient's disguised unconscious perceptions of the therapist's interventions). In a final section, complete sessions are offered as a means of integrating the knowledge gained to that point.

The first workbook of this series (Langs, in press-b) offers the clinician practice in understanding unconscious communication and presents the details of the basic decoding process in psychotherapy. The third workbook offers training in the technique of intervention. The present volume provides the tools for mastery of the fundamental listening and formulating process that is the foundation for sound psychoanalytic and psychotherapeutic practice.

Robert Langs, M.D.
New York City

I
THE
BASIC
LISTENING
PROCESS

1

Communication in Psychotherapy and Psychoanalysis

Human beings are adaptive organisms. An important part of adaptation involves communication, which takes place both consciously and unconsciously. Among the many psychobiological factors in madness (the term I use for the entire spectrum of emotionally founded human disorders), its role as a form of unconscious communication is of great importance. Madness essentially involves an attempt to adapt based on perceptions that conflict with one's conscious point of view. Such attempts take place indirectly, outside of consciousness, and may be expressed by way of emotional symptoms, psychosomatic disorders, personality disturbances, and the like. Among the various means of modifying such expressions of madness, an understanding of their unconscious basis in a fashion that permits conscious insight and a fresh means of adaptation is especially useful. A well-managed therapeutic relationship, setting, and hold, and the patient's consequent positive introjective identifications with the well-functioning therapist are also important background factors in this means of cure.

Cure through genuine insight can be achieved *only* by understanding the unconscious basis of madness. The other factors involved in a cure are not at the heart of the psychotherapeutic process. Essentially, patients communicate their indirect responses to the adaptive contexts represented by the therapist's interventions and the therapeutic situation through *displaced* and *disguised* (*symbolized*) expressions. These expressions convey meanings and functions outside of the patient's direct awareness—that is, by way of *unconscious communication*. A comprehensive listening process must therefore take into account the immediate stimuli for such unconscious expressions as well as the *encoded (derivative)* meanings involved.

In the therapeutic situation, the stimuli to which the patient is attempting to adapt, both consciously and unconsciously, are virtually always the interventions of the therapist. These stimuli contain both manifest and latent meanings, conscious and unconscious factors. As such, they determine and organize the patient's various responses. They evoke the patient's symptoms, and these symptoms can be understood because they reflect the patient's perceptions of and attempts to adapt to both the manifest and latent implications communicated by the therapist's interventions. In other words, the patient's responses to interventions in therapy reflect and give meaning to his or her madness. A basic element of the listening process accordingly involves a full comprehension of the manifest and indirect or encoded implications of every intervention made by a therapist.

THE NATURE OF THE STIMULUS

Very recent communicative studies have shown that once a patient enters psychotherapy, both symptomatic improvement and clinical remission are prompted mainly by the stimuli of the therapist's interventions. Although outside factors do indeed play a role, these are generally secondary to the transactions within treatment. This finding suggests (1) that the key interactive factor with respect to patient-madness is in the interpersonal relationship with the therapist, and (2) that the intrapsychic element is in some significant manner a response to this interaction.

The stimuli constituted by the therapist's interventions are called *adaptive contexts*, and the term is used from the vantage point of the patient. Synonyms for these stimuli include *adaptation-evoking contexts* and *intervention contexts*. It is essential to recognize that these adaptive contexts (as constituted by the intervention from the therapist) are the key organizers of the patient's communications and behaviors in psychotherapy.

In addition to realizing that all madness-related adaptive contexts derive from the therapist's efforts, it is also critical to comprehend the wide range of interventions used by therapists, and the existence not only of conscious but of very crucial unconscious meanings and functions to these interventions. The interventions of the therapist include: all aspects of his or her establishment of the setting, development, and management of the ground rules of therapy; silences and verbal interventions of all types; the therapist's self-revelations, including personal information obtained by the patient about the therapist from other sources; the therapist's active or implicit sanction of third-party involvement in the treatment; the prescription of medication; and anything else pertaining to or done by the therapist that has a bearing on the psychotherapeutic experience.

In substance, then, virtually everything that a therapist does or does not do constitutes the critical adaptive contexts for the patient's material in psychotherapy. Such contexts are loaded with latent implications and meanings, which are critical to the understanding of the patient's expressions.

THE PATIENT'S RESPONSES

There are several important dimensions to a patient's responses to the adaptive contexts constituted by the therapist's interventions. They may be classified as follows:

1. *The form or modality of the patient's responses: actions (behaviors), affects, images, and words.* There is a great difference, of course, in the consequences for both patient and therapist when a patient responds to an intervention through an extended series of behaviors, as opposed to responding with words, thoughts, and dreams. In keeping with our focus on the listening process, however, the significance of form in this particular context derives from the finding that actions and affects tend to be poor carriers of decodable unconscious meaning, whereas words (especially narratives and images) are potentially strong carriers of decipherable encoded meaning.

2. *Adaptive versus maladaptive responses.* A patient may respond to an intervention—whether traumatic or helpful—either adaptively and nonsymptomatically or, instead, in a maladaptive or symptomatic manner. A symptomatic response may include pathological behaviors, emotional symptoms, such as phobias, disturbances in affect, psychosomatic disorders, psychotic responses, and so forth. Maladaptive responses in the treatment situation generally involve certain, though not all, forms of gross behavioral resistance—inappropriate absences, lateness, silences, and the like.

For our purposes, the importance of distinguishing between adaptive and maladaptive responses lies in the fact that a nonsymptomatic response to an adaptive context is essentially healthy and does not call for an intervention from the therapist. In contrast, a symptomatic response may be termed a *therapeutic context* or *indicator* (a sign of disturbance and indication for intervention). A disturbed response is a manifest expression of patient-madness that requires interpretive understanding and, sometimes, a securing of the ground rules or frame (the total conditions of the treatment setting and relationship).

3. *Conscious versus unconscious expression.* The patient's responses to an adaptive context may involve behaviors and thoughts that can be directly understood, are manifest, and have consciously intended meanings and implications, but at the same time are serving as vehicles for unconscious expression. Clinical studies indicate that the manifest and conscious realm of experience cannot, by definition, in itself reveal the unconscious meaning and function of a symptomatic expression. The unconscious meanings and functions of a manifest expression are simply that—unconscious. They can be conveyed by the patient only through latent or encoded messages, whose meaning is not known to the patient consciously.

Freud (1900, 1908) used the word *derivative* for a manifest expression that contains a latent meaning. The term implies that the surface communication is *derived from* the underlying unconscious message—the raw perception or fantasy that is being disguised. The basic model was presented in *The Interpretation of Dreams* (Freud, 1900). This model may be summarized simply as follows:

a. The raw (undisguised) image of a stimulus unconsciously perceived by the individual is experienced as a danger situation, which creates anxiety. Therefore, the mind constructs a compromise between expression of the image and protection against it (defense).

b. This compromise is effected by subjecting the raw image to the *primary process mechanisms* of *displacement* and *symbolization (representation)*. Secondary use is made of *condensation, concern for representability,* and *secondary revision*. In this way, a raw, dangerous, *latent* image (in Freud's theory, the dream thought; communicative theory includes perceptions of and, more rarely, fantasies about the therapist) is transformed into a less-threatening *manifest* image—a derivative or element of manifest content.

c. In order to decipher the underlying meanings of a manifest element and arrive at its latent implications, it is necessary to undo the mechanisms of displacement and symbolization. This endeavor basically involves identifying the *theme* shared by the two levels of communication. The manifest image will have an important factor or a number of factors in common with the latent image.

It must be stressed that raw perceptions of others as well as raw inner fantasies are experienced as danger situations that create anxiety. These in turn lead automatically (unconsciously) to the use of the encoding or disguising process. The patient who communicates an encoded message is aware only of its manifest meanings, remaining unaware of those that are latent. In therapy, the activated latent meanings of a patient's disguised expressions have been stimulated by the adaptive contexts of the therapist's interventions. These disguised expressions encode the patient's raw perceptions of that context and the meanings those perceptions have for him or her. A proper decoding process must therefore rely on the use of adaptive contexts as the *decoding key* for the patient's derivative expressions. Only an awareness of what the patient has perceived can make clear the activated unconscious meanings of a patient's subsequent communications.

In brief, then: Patients in psychotherapy communicate at times through derivatives; these derivatives are stimulated by the manifest and latent meanings of the therapist's interventions (adaptive contexts); and they will reveal the unconscious meanings of a patient's madness—but only in light of the active stimuli involved. Derivatives do not exist as isolated intrapsychic encoded contents; rather, they are part of active adaptive and communicative responses to intervention contexts.

4. *Conscious and unconscious perceptions; conscious and unconscious fantasies.* As I have indicated, the most important and predominant meaning response to an adaptive context is constituted by encoded or unconscious perceptions of the therapist in light of his or her interventions. But the patient is, of course, perceiving and encoding *particular* unconscious aspects of an adaptive context, the selective factor being his or her madness (psychopathology). This does not imply either distortion or transference; these elements are absent at the *first level* of a patient's response (although they may be introduced subsequently). The patient's perceptions of the therapist's interventions are virtually always accurate—not only reliable, but often deeply sensitive. The derivative expressions they engender do not represent unconscious fantasies. Unconscious fantasies, rather, along with other dimensions of the patient's madness, lead him or her to select from the multiplicity of universal meanings communicated by an intervention those meanings that are pertinent and relevant to his or her needs and psychopathology.

It is the patient's tendency to perceive certain aspects of an adaptive context and not others, along with the meanings these perceptions have for him or her that will illuminate the dynamics and genetic history of the patient's madness. These factors are an inherent component of the patient's encoded expressions and are therefore available for interpretive understanding *in light of the adaptive context.*

Unconscious fantasies, then, are never the primary response of a patient to an intervention. They do, however, play a role in evoking interventions from a therapist, and they may determine a therapist's response to the patient's initial, veridical view of him or her. All listening must therefore begin with an awareness of the implications of the adaptive context of the therapist's interventions. And all understanding of derivatives must center on the patient's highly selective unconscious perceptions of the true meanings of these intervention contexts.

5. *Reactions to unconscious perceptions.* Once an unconscious perception registers outside of awareness, the patient may respond with behaviors, verbal-affective associations, conscious and unconscious memories, conscious and unconscious fan-

tasies, and efforts to help or harm the therapist. But before assigning any other meaning or function to these responses, all associations from a patient must first be decoded as valid unconscious perceptions of the therapist.

6. *Good (close) and poor (distant) derivatives.* The patient's communicative reactions may carry strong and clear encoded meaning (close derivatives) or be flat, empty, and either lacking in derivative implication or highly disguised (distant derivatives). The most important carriers of meaningful derivatives are stories, narratives, images, and dreams. Among the poor carriers of encoded meaning (primarily, as noted, meaning in terms of unconscious perceptions of the therapist) are manifest allusions to the therapist in treatment, intellectualizations, speculations, ruminations, symptoms, extended behaviors, and affects. Although each of these responses has other implications, their importance as conveyors of unconscious perceptions is usually minimal. The most notable exception is the rare session in which manifest communications about the therapist do indeed contain encoded and disguised perceptions of *other* aspects of his or her interventions.

SUMMARY

To summarize the main elements of the basic model of communication within the therapeutic interaction (see Appendix A):

1. The main stimulus for the patient's material is constituted by the therapist's interventions—adaptive contexts that have both manifest and latent implications.

2. The patient's main communicative response as it illuminates his or her madness, rendering material accessible for interpretation, is constituted by his or her selected and valid encoded perceptions of the implications of the therapist's efforts.

3. An adaptive context has both universal meanings and meanings that are personal and specific to the patient. Among these, the patient unconsciously selects for derivative expression the ones that are most pertinent to his or her illness. Conversely, the presence of encoded communications provides evidence that such perceptions are in fact being registered outside of the conscious awareness of the patient.

4. The unconscious meanings of the patient's derivative material can be determined only by using the implications of an adaptive context as a decoding key.

5. The best vehicles for derivative communication are narratives, images, memories, and dreams. All such material, however, must be decoded—that is, the effects of displacement and symbolization on the raw images from which the encoded messages are derived must be undone. This is the only way to determine the activated unconscious implications of the patient's encoded material. These efforts must be made consistently and exclusively in light of the specific stimuli of intervention contexts.

6. Among the other adaptive reactions to the therapist's interventions, any type of symptomatic response is especially important. Symptoms represent an immediate expression of the patient's madness as activated in the course of the therapeutic interaction by the interventions from the therapist. They serve as therapeutic contexts or indicators that lend themselves to interpretation.
As with encoded expressions, all efforts at understanding the unconscious factors

in symptomatic responses will require the identification of the adaptive context, as well as the recognition of the patient's encoded perceptions of that context's meanings. As I have stated, the meanings of an adaptive context are selectively perceived by a patient in terms of his or her own needs and related to his or her own madness. Only this type of interpretation will reveal the activated unconscious meanings of a symptom or personality disturbance in light of the ongoing therapeutic interaction. Further, only this type of interpretation will be followed by the revelation of fresh encoded material from the patient, which extends the interpretation in a unique and unexpected fashion. This revelation can be understood as a genuine psychoanalytic validation of a correct interpretation.

Such cognitive confirmation is supplemented by both interpersonal validation and conscious understanding. The former can be recognized in the emergence of positive and constructively functioning figures in the patient's material; these figures represent the patient's introjection of the well-functioning therapist. Conscious understanding permits the patient to work through an aspect of his or her madness and leads ultimately to an adaptive resolution of both madness and its symptoms.

2
The Elements
of Listening

The basic model of communication in therapy dictates a method of working with the patient's material that will sort out its various elements and permit the unconscious basis of the patient's illness to be understood in depth. As we have seen, it is necessary both to identify the stimulus for the patient's behaviors and associations, and to understand the conscious and unconscious implications of that stimulus. One must also identify the patient's reactions to the stimulus—most critically, the patient's symptomatic responses, because these will be the target for the therapist's intervention and the focus of interpretive work.

It is essential to remember that the patient is attempting to *adapt* to what he or she is perceiving in the therapeutic context. The sequence of interactions that take place between patient and therapist are actual (living) and immediate. When attempting to identify the nature of the unconscious perceptions and fantasies that form the basis of the patient's reactions, one must fully assess the stimulus or adaptive context for those reactions. One begins this assessment by concentrating on the therapist's evocative interventions. The patient's various responses are then studied for their communicative implications.

The patient's responses must be separated into two interrelated classes: symptomatic (including pathological resistances) and communicative. Technically speaking, symptomatic responses are communicative, but they reveal a minimal measure of their own unconscious implications; they are global and relatively nonspecific as carriers of encoded messages. But other communicative responses to the same stimulus, such as narratives and images, may be quite specific in their function as carriers of derivative or latent meanings. These messages can be readily decoded to reveal the unconscious implications of the adaptive context and, thus, the unconscious basis for the symptomatic response. This is why we make the distinction. A *symptomatic response* is an *indicator* or *therapeutic context*. A *derivative complex* is a network of *encoded messsages* that center primarily upon unconscious perceptions of the *adaptive context*—the unconscious implications of the therapist's interventions. These encoded messages, when properly decoded, reveal the unconscious basis for the manifest indicator.

Thus it is essential to treat a patient's associations as derivative communications. They will contain in encoded form the unconscious perceptions and fantasies that constitute the underlying basis for symptomatic reactions. In decoding this associative material, the therapist must engage in a true effort at undoing displacement and symbolization. One cannot simply read out the manifest content or make use of intellectualized inferences. The latter do not reflect the patient's intended and expressed unconscious meanings, but only the psychotherapist's need for defense against them. Unconscious meaning is available only through decoding efforts.

A stimulus sets off many levels of response in a patient. A symptom is only one element of the total conscious and unconscious reaction to an adaptive context. The derivative complex is another. There are also nonsymptomatic responses to intervention contexts, which in general, do not require interpretive intervention. All components of an adaptive response are organized and given meaning by the shape (conscious and unconscious implications) of the stimulus—the adaptive context of the therapist's interventions. An *interpretation*, then, serves to explain the unconscious basis of an indicator or therapeutic context (symptom) by identifying the adaptive context or stimulus that set it off, and by proceeding to delineate the implications of the patient's encoded or derivative material. This type of effort gradually results in a series of mini-analyses, whose accumulation constitutes a symptom-alleviating insightful psychotherapy.

IDENTIFYING THE COMPONENTS

The communicative model leads to a systematic and practical approach to material from a patient. In the course of a session, as the therapist listens to the patient's associations, he or she assigns each communicative segment to one or all of the three possible categories of implications or functions served by it: adaptive context, indicator, or derivative complex (unconscious preceptions and so forth). These assignments are shaped entirely by the nature of the patient's associations.

Two lines of thinking are going on in this effort: The first is an attempt to organize and understand the total constellation of the available material. To this end, the therapist is studying the implications of each active intervention context and from there tracing out the patient's symptomatic and communicative responses. The second serves to facilitate the intervening process—the therapist's interpretations and framework-management efforts. The therapist is focusing in this respect on the indicators (the patient's symptoms and resistances) as targets for intervention, that is, as the clinical disturbances, the therapeutic contexts, that are to be explained or interpreted to the patient in the session at hand.

The goal of interpretation is to provide the patient with an understanding of the unconscious meanings and functions of symptoms and resistances. The therapist should thus endeavor to target the most pressing indicators in a given hour. The first step in the process of clinical formulation must be to identify manifest allusions in the patient's material to symptoms and resistances that warrant intervention in that particular session.

When the therapist has determined which indicators are the most pressing, he or she moves to a consideration of the adaptive contexts that may have prompted them. This leads to a consideration of the derivative complex—the patient's disguised expression of perceptions of the therapist *in light* of those adaptive contexts, along with the patient's reactions to these perceptions.

An advantage of engaging in this particular sequence of thinking—of assigning meaning and function to each segment of the patient's communications and responses—is that the therapist progresses from identifying components that are manifest and directly represented in the patient's associations to a consideration of components that must be decoded for their latent implications. As a rule, indicators emerge as symptomatic responses described directly by the patient and as pathological resistances that are self-evident in the patient's behaviors or referred to manifestly in the patient's material. This direct display of or reference to the indicator is necessary before a therapist can target it as the focus of an interpretation. If the patient is not conscious of his or her symptomatic response or resistance, he or she will not be able to accept the fact that his or her other communicative responses explain the unconscious factors in the disturbance. The indicators must be actively portrayed and experienced by the patient in the session on a manifest level, or it is virtually impossible to interpret them to the patient.

Ideally, the second component of the communicative network, the adaptive context, also will be referred to by the patient on a manifest-content level. The best possible basis for a therapist's interpretation is a brief allusion to a prior intervention rather than an extended and preoccupied commentary on it. An allusion made in passing will provide a reference point for the balance of the material. The therapist can use it to demonstrate to the patient that he or she is indeed reacting to the conscious and unconscious implications of an intervention alluded to in his or her own material. An extended commentary will generally contain little encoded communication. It may be possible to use a good encoded representation of an adaptive context as the basis of an interpretation; but the fulcrum for an interpretation should always be a clear enough representation of the adaptive context that it can be established as the true stimulus for the patient's symptomatic and encoded reactions.

Beyond these two manifest representations—the indicator and the adaptive context that has prompted it—all else in a patient's material must be considered as possible encoded communication, expressing unconscious perceptions of the therapist in light of the implications carried by an adaptive context. One is searching for manifest themes in the patient's associations that indicate the expression of disguised latent perceptions. The therapist identifies the themes that bridge manifest and latent levels of communication by being aware of the implications generally carried by an activated adaptive context and looking for their possible representation in the patient's material.

In practical terms, then, as the patient is speaking and indicating feelings, the therapist is attempting to identify (1) manifestly represented symptoms and resistances, (2) direct allusions to his or her prior interventions, and (3) encoded themes that represent unconscious perceptions and other derivative responses to the prevailing adaptive contexts.

It is important to understand that unconscious meaning is conveyed by a patient in scattered fashion in the course of a therapy hour. It is the task of the therapist to identify these components and to synthesize them into an intervention modelled adaptationally on the stimulus-response paradigm (see Appendix B).

In substance, then, the listening–formulating process developed through the communicative approach is the only means by which the spiraling conscious and especially unconscious communicative interaction between patient and therapist—and its influence on the patient's intrapsychic life and madness–can be understood. If full comprehension of the patient's material were possible simply by listening to manifest content and deriving implications from evident meanings in the patient's associations, there would be no need for the more complicated communicative effort. But clinical studies have clearly shown that psychoanalytic validation does not follow interpretation formulated on the basis of the patient's manifest concerns and responses. True validation, true insight, and structural change are based on genuine adaptive understanding of *unconscious factors* in the patient's responses. Only communicative listening and interpretations generated on this basis can bring about these results.

Indicators

As a means of providing a brief overall perspective, we may define indicators or therapeutic contexts as expressions of the patient's madness communicated in a particular session. There are two main classes of indicators: (1) symptomatic expressions and (2) gross behavioral resistances. The first category comprises all emotionally founded symptoms, from psychosis to psychosomatic syndromes, including phobias, anxieties, depression, obsessions, personality disturbances, behavior disorders, and the like. In the second category are all evident resistances—obstacles to the therapeutic process—most of them efforts by the patient *to alter the basic ground rules of treatment*—silences, lateness, absences, wishes to terminate treatment, failure to pay for sessions, mistakes in payment, and so forth. It is essentially through these two means that patients express their madness in psychotherapy sessions.

Such expressions should be understood both as *indicators of psychopathology* and as *indications for intervening*. When they are strong—for example, a threat to terminate treatment or a suicidal symptom—they in a sense express a demand (a wish or need) that the therapist intervene at some point in the hour. Because they are the patient's way of manifesting an aspect of his or her madness in a given session, interpretations and management of the ground rules are directly pertinent to an activated aspect of the patient's emotional illness.

It must be recognized that even though the manifestation belongs to the patient, such expressions of psychopathology are *interactional products*, having inputs from both participants to treatment. The immediate stimuli for symptoms and resistances are the interventions of the therapist—the adaptive contexts. Symptoms and resistances are therefore efforts at adaptation. They may represent constructive endeavors quite in keeping with the unconscious implications of an intervention; or they may represent emotional maladaptation—a disturbed and distorted response to an intervention. In either case, they will reflect the patient's madness and so contain a pathological component to be understood and insightfully modified, thereby promoting sound adaptation and growth.

Adaptive Context

The interventions of the therapist are by far the most powerful stimuli for the vicissitudes of a patient's madness in the course of psychotherapy and psychoanalysis. Every communication from a therapist, if it in some way influences the patient and the treatment experience, constitutes an adaptive context. Thus, silence is an intervention, as is the physical setting of a psychotherapeutic experience. Every attempt at explanation by the therapist, every noninterpretive intervention, every management of a ground rule—whether its modification, maintenance, or rectification—is an adaptive or intervention context. The transactions between patient and therapist on the telephone before the first consultation involve adaptive contexts to the extent that the therapist is either silent or active. Any contact between the therapist and someone other than the patient (though known to the patient) is an adaptive context. Without exception, then, everything that a therapist does and does not do in respect to the psychotherapy of a particular patient is an adaptation-evoking context for the patient.

To clarify a common source of confusion, patients do at times consciously and unconsciously work over and respond to their own indicators—a symptom, an absence, or another form of gross behavioral resistance. But these indicators are not adaptation-evoking stimuli. They do not prompt a patient's further expression of madness, nor do they lead to conscious and unconscious communications that illuminate the underlying basis of a patient's psychopathology. Such stimuli lie always in the therapist's interventions. These interventions constitute the adaptive context for the patient, and the patient responds to an adaptive context through symptoms, resistances, and other communicative expressions. Every indicator has a prior adaptive context. The therapist's response to that indicator constitutes a fresh adaptive context, leading to subsequent indicators. Both the adaptive and the therapeutic contexts, then, are interactional products. Although the experience of a symptom or resistance belongs to the patient, and the experience of intervening belongs to the therapist, these experiences are always the consequence of contributions from both participants to therapy.

In general, the basic spheres of valid intervention are interpretation–reconstruction and management of the ground rules and psychotherapeutic frame. The distinction between those interventions that pertain to the ground rules and boundaries of psychotherapy and any other type of intervention (interpretive–reconstructive, noninterpretive, etc.) is critical. The therapist's management of the frame—that is, adherence to a ground rule when under pressure to deviate, a deviant-frame response, and so forth—will necessarily involve the core relationship between patient and therapist and the basic holding and containing qualities of the therapist's efforts. Thus, interventions that pertain to the ground rules of treatment always take precedence for the patient. It is the core relationship established by a secure frame that permits interpretive–reconstructive efforts to be made and to be effective.

In both interpretive–reconstructive and frame-management efforts, the conscious and especially unconscious implications of the adaptive context at hand are crucial. Interventions have both conscious and unconscious, manifest and latent properties; a therapist can come to terms with the complexities of any given intervention only by engaging in both a careful prospective analysis and a retrospective reevaluation. In the actual process of listening, the therapist is attending to the patient's material for direct allusions to his or her recent and important past interventions. In the absence of such allusions, the search is made for close and relatively easy to decipher derivative representations of those intervention contexts.

Most gross behavioral resistances will involve efforts by the patient to modify one or another ground rule of psychotherapy. This is the indicator—the target for intervention. Again, because the core relationship with the therapist is determined by his or her proper management of the frame, the vicissitudes of the patient's madness and of his or her derivative communications as they illuminate that madness are most meaningfully stimulated by ground rule issues. The antecedent adaptive context of pressures to deviate from a ground-rule is usually a frame-related intervention. This prior intervention will be alluded to in the patient's material, and the patient's derivative communications will indicate his or her pathologically selected encoded perceptions of the therapist in light of the implications of that intervention. The derivative complex may also contain disguised directives toward the rectification of the frame.

The therapist's response to the patient's conscious request or demand for deviation will constitute a fresh adaptive context for the patient. As implied, the patient's encoded material virtually never supports his or her conscious demand, but usually expresses an unconscious wish for maintenance of the frame. The therapist interprets in light of that encoded directive, thereby providing a meaningful holding response to the patient-indicator, accompanied by the crucial work of insight and understanding. It is cycles of this kind that lead to conflict resolution and adaptive change in the patient.

The Derivative Complex

Among the many responses a patient makes to an adaptive context, those that are encoded and derivative (outside of the patient's awareness) are most critical in illuminating the unconscious basis of an indicator—the segment of the patient's madness being expressed. Among these derivative reactions, those that constitute selected unconscious perceptions of the implications of the therapist's interventions are by far the most abundant and the most crucial. These unconscious perceptions generally precipitate a series of behavioral and communicative reactions based on their meaning to the patient. Once the selectively perceived meaning is recognized, these behavioral and communicative responses are relatively easy to identify and to formulate. The basic focus in listening and formulating, then, is a patient's encoded perceptions. Supplementary responses are used to complete one's understanding of the patient's material and behaviors.

Each adaptive context has a multiplicity of meanings and functions. In psychotherapy, a patient *unconsciously selects* those implications of the therapist's interventions that are most pertinent to his or her madness. Unconscious perception therefore results in unconscious images, which contain factors pertaining both to the therapist (in terms of the nature of the intervention context) and to the patient (in terms of what is selectively perceived and has meaning for him or her). As a consequence, any intervention that makes use of a particular derivative perception in order to give the patient insight into the nature of his or her immediate expressions of madness (symptoms/indicators) is perforce a statement about both the therapist and the patient. It reflects the madness or sanity of the prior adaptive context, and the madness (or sanity) that has determined the patient's selected unconscious perception of the context's implications.

Implicit in the fundamental listening–formulating process is the assumption that a significant contribution to the patient's madness is made by his or her unconscious introjective identifications with the therapist—as well as with other figures outside of treatment, especially those with whom the patient has interacted prior to the psychotherapeutic experience. This introjective aspect of emotional dysfunction has been amply demonstrated in mother-child interactions, but its implications for the psychotherapeutic interaction have been largely ignored.

The communicative model also takes into account the intrapsychic basis of madness. The patient selects from the multiplicity of meanings carried by an adaptive context those that are pertinent to his or her own needs. This process of selection relies upon the patient's already existing conscious and unconscious propensities—in particular, the patient's unconscious fantasies and memories, along with current pathological dynamics, self-needs, other need systems, and curative and harmful efforts directed toward the therapist.

In practical terms, then, the analysis of a patient's material for encoded or derivative expressions requires a search for selected perceptions of an intervention context registered within the patient outside of awareness. A therapist must be guided in this search by a knowledge of the universal and personal meanings of each major adaptive context for both patient and therapist and by their respective implications for the particular moment in a specific therapeutic interaction. These meanings will inform the patient's manifest material thematically, giving the therapist a link to the patient's latent or unconscious perceptions of the therapist with respect to his or her prior interventions.

As I indicated earlier, the communicative process of listening and formulating is more than a cognitive task. There are fundamental resistances in the therapist against identifying the patient's encoded perceptions of his or her interventions. This defensiveness holds true whether the patient's perceptions reflect valid or erroneous interventions. A valid interpretation mobilizes intense perceptions and fantasies within the patient, engendering powerful instinctual drive and idealization responses. Much of this is conveyed unconsciously by the patient in encoded form, and the therapist automatically reacts to the material as a danger situation. Thus, there is a fundamental dread of sound interpretation of active issues within the therapeutic interaction—a point brilliantly conceptualized as far back as 1934 by James Strachey, who cites Melanie Klein as the source of this insight. It should be recognized as well that a validated effort to secure the psychotherapeutic frame creates a similarly dangerous claustrum for both patient and therapist. Thus, a therapist may resist proper frame management because of its anxiety-provoking consequences.

When the adaptive context is constituted instead by an erroneous effort at understanding, a noninterpretive intervention, an inappropriate silence, or an errant deviation in the frame, the therapist dreads formulating the patient's encoded perceptions because they concentrate on the therapist's own madness and its implications. Fearful of the patient's recognition of this madness and of its unconscious meanings, therapists have tended to avoid formulations of the patient's valid unconscious perceptions. Nonetheless, it remains true that the patient's initial response to an erroneous intervention is the unconscious expression of selected perceptions of its meanings. Understanding such encoded perceptions is pivotal to understanding all other direct and derivative reactions to intervention contexts. Thus, the detection of encoded perceptions will be studied most carefully in this workbook.

It should be recognized that the stress on indicators, adaptive contexts, and derivative perceptions in this volume reflects the fact that problems in listening which are modifiable through teaching exercises are accessible only at the cognitive level. The listening–formulating process developed through the communicative approach will, of course, entail a therapist's use of empathy and intuition, the ability to establish temporary identifications with the patient and his or her objects, and all those human sensitivities normally inherent to sound and effective listening. A psychotherapist develops such resources largely through a personal psychotherapy and a constant and quiet appraisal of these mental instruments and their ongoing application in his or her therapeutic work. But the information gathered by means of these tools must be funneled ultimately into a cognitive schema that will permit the valid organization and understanding of the patient's scattered communications. Empathy must be extended to the patient's encoded as well as manifest expressions; intuition must be sensitively utilized to take into account unconscious and interactional factors.

Despite the cumbersome qualities of the communicative approach, with consistent practice, the tripartite schema proposed here becomes a highly sensitive therapeutic instrument. Indeed, once this approach is mastered, a therapist comes to realize that he or she is at a loss without the ability to assign segments of the patient's material to one (or all) of the three basic communicative categories. Listening of this kind soon becomes an essential and natural tool of comprehension without which a therapist can no longer function in truly effective fashion.

II
THE
THREE
COMPONENTS
OF LISTENING

3
Indicators

Indicators, or therapeutic contexts, are activated expressions of patient-madness. As already discussed, they take two major forms: symptoms (broadly defined) and gross behavioral resistances. Most often they appear manifestly in the patient's material and tend to do so early in a session. It is therefore relatively easy to identify them and to place them in the back of one's mind as the *target for intervening*—that is, as the manifestations of the patient's psychopathology that the therapist hopes to interpret in light of an activated adaptive context and derivative complex. Such indicators will emerge either in the patient's associations (e.g., a thought of terminating, a reference to an anxiety attack, an allusion to an interpersonal quarrel, a reference to an irrational act, the wish to cancel a session, etc.) or in the direct behaviors of the patient (e.g., absence from a prior session, lateness, silence, and the like). These symptoms and resistances should be treated as responses to prior interventions and in terms of the patient's own selected derivative perceptions—hence, as interactional products with contributions from both patient and therapist.

Indicators are part of the patient's experience, even though they are stimulated by the interventions of the therapist. They are *not* adaptive contexts, although patients sometimes react to their own symptoms and resistances. Such reactions generally tend to be manifest or to contain virtually no derivative meaning. The unconscious meaning of an indicator is revealed *only* when the prior adaptive context that has evoked its presence can be identified.

Most indicators do appear directly in the patient's associations, but occasionally they will be expressed indirectly or in encoded fashion. A patient may, for example, allude to a symptom in someone else that exists in the patient as well. Sometimes, when a patient has been absent or failed to pay the bill, an indirect representation of the indicator will appear in his or her material rather than a direct allusion to that situation. In general, unless an indicator has been manifestly stated, its meanings are difficult to interpret to a patient, but in exceptional instances, an encoded representation may be utilized.

On rare occasion, an interpersonal or life crisis may form an important patient-indicator. But in such cases, the patient's response is not symptomatic, so there is seldom a basis for interpretive intervention. Similarly, such outside traumas are almost never the stimulus for meaningful encoded communicative reactions; thus, they cannot serve as critical adaptive contexts in psychotherapy.

Indicators have a measure of power and importance. Certain symptoms, such as a panic attack or suicidal impulse, reflect a far greater need in the patient for intervention than do others, for example, a passing moment of anxiety or a two-minute lateness. The therapist should gauge the relative strength of an indicator, because those that are quite intense will call for immediate intervention, even with a minimum amount of useful communicative material—a well-represented adaptive context and a coalescing derivative complex (one that touches upon divergent encoded perceptions and their genetic repercussions for the patient). In the presence of mild indicators, there is less pressure on the therapist (less need in the patient) for intervention at the moment, and the therapist should thus wait until the communicative material is quite clear before attempting interpretation.

It is also of value to order the patient-indicators in terms of their importance. All gross behavioral resistances, because they involve efforts to modify the ground rules and framework of the treatment experience and relationship, are significant. If at all possible, such pressures to deviate or the actualization of a deviation by the patient warrants both an interpretive and rectifying or holding response from the therapist—efforts based on identifying the relevant adaptive context and derivative complex. Because only one or two indicators can be interpreted in a given session, it is well to focus on those that most seriously threaten the treatment situation itself and those that reflect the most intense symptoms within the patient.

To summarize the main principles of listening as applied to indicators:

1. Indicators or therapeutic contexts are expressions of the patient's madness that take the form of symptoms and gross behavioral resistances (breaks in the frame).

2. Indicators are usually represented in the patient's manifest associations or direct behaviors.

3. The therapist should identify indicators and keep them in the back of the mind as targets for intervention—interpretation and framework-management responses.

4. Indicators should be evaluated for the strength of the disturbance they reflect within the patient and the intensity of the patient's need for intervention. Those that are most powerful will require response from the therapist based on whatever material is available; those that are less powerful will call for intervention only if the communicative material permits.

5. All efforts by the patient to modify the ground rules of treatment are serious and significant indicators. Intense symptoms and interpersonal disorders, such as suicidal impulses and uncontrolled (mad) behaviors, are also high-level indicators.

6. Because each session can be an immediate and mini-analysis of a dimension of the patient's madness, it is critical to keep in mind manifestly represented indi-

cators as the expression of the patient's madness that will be subjected to interpretive understanding and framework-management response.

7. Although indicators are symptoms and actions experienced and expressed by the patient, they are also interactional products that have been stimulated by the adaptive contexts of the therapist's interventions. On the other hand, even though they often have adaptive value, it must be clear that indicators are nonetheless expressions of madness within the patient.

INDICATORS: EXERCISES

We move now to the work of identifying indicators in actual portions of psychotherapy sessions. The format will be as follows:

1. a presentation of clinical material, with questions pertinent to the material,

2. an opportunity for the reader to record his or her responses,

3. the formulations of the author.

The reader is strongly advised to *actively* participate in these exercises.

Exercise 3.1

The patient is a young woman in psychotherapy for episodes of depression. She is being seen by a male therapist in his private office on a once-weekly basis. She arrives for her session five minutes late.

> *Patient:* I'm very depressed again. I think of killing myself, but I really don't think I would do it. [Silence] I have an exam at school next week. Would it be possible to change my hour since the examination is at the same time? I was with my sister; she annoyed me. I felt a bit anxious with her. Sometimes she can be quite inane. I had a dream that a man was chasing after me.

What are the patient-indicators that can be identified in this excerpt? Classify them as symptomatic or gross resistances. Mark them as strong or weak. Indicate which are most important, and state the overall power of the indicators at this juncture in the session.

_____

_____

_____

_____

_____

_____

_____

_____

_____

_____

_____

_____

=======

Answer

In this rather typical session, several indicators appear at the beginning of the hour. They begin with a behavioral response and then are reflected manifestly in the patient's free associations. We may list them in order of appearance, although while actually listening to the patient, a therapist would also be inclined to group them together into the two main categories—symptoms and resistances. In this sequence, the indicators—signs of patient-madness—are:

1. The patient's lateness (a gross behavioral resistance—frame break; moderately strong).

2. The patient's depression and suicidal thoughts (symptoms; very strong).

3. The period of silence (gross behavioral resistance—frame break; weak because brief).

4. The request for a change in the hour (gross behavioral resistance—effort to alter the frame; moderately strong).

5. The patient's annoyance with her sister (this may be symptomatic or appropriate; weak).

6. The small measure of anxiety (symptomatic; weak).

It is to be noted in this analysis that a dream is *not* an indicator; it is neither a symptom nor a resistance, although it may be symptomatic if it occurs in the form of a nightmare. By and large, dreams tend to be good carriers of derivative expression. More rarely, they may contain within their manifest content an allusion to a symptom or resistance and, quite infrequently, may also allude directly to an adaptive context. Although many therapists believe that they are under an obligation to interpret the dreams of their patients, in the communicative approach a dream is treated in a manner similar to all other types of expression from a patient. Stating this conversely, all of the patient's associations, whatever form they take, are analyzed in a manner comparable to dream-analysis—as modified through communicative understanding and applied to the therapeutic interaction.

In terms of categories, the symptomatic therapeutic contexts or indicators include the patient's depression, suicidal thoughts, a small measure of anxiety, and possibly her annoyance with her sister—a point to be clarified by later associations. The gross behavioral resistances, each a modification of the ideal ground rules, include the patient's lateness, silence, and effort to change the hour.

The accumulation of a large number of indicators points to a strong need within the patient for intervention by the therapist—interpretive and/or framework-management responses carried out at the behest of the patient's encoded derivatives. The intensity of this need is reinforced by the suicidal reference, which warrants intervention if at all possible, and is further heightened by the appearance of three different frame issues, including two actual breaks in the frame: the lateness, modifying the ground rule of the 50-minute hour; the silence, altering the fundamental rule of free association; and the wish to change an hour, which would alter the fixed day and time of each session. Typically, the appearance of several ground-rule alterations and/or frame issues suggests the presence of an adaptive context constituted by a break in the frame by the therapist. Thus, when a therapist modifies the frame, the patient is likely to do so or to seek additional frame alterations on his or her own.

Among these indicators, the patient's suicidal thinking is the most prominent symptomatic expression; her request to change an hour is the most critical frame issue. It will be necessary, of course, for the therapist to verbalize an answer to the patient's request, but in principle, he should do so on the basis of the patient's subsequent derivative associations.

We have, then, identified the main indications of madness in this patient as the therapeutic contexts we hope to interpret and to respond to with suitable framework-management interventions.

Exercise 3.2

The patient is a young man in once-weekly psychotherapy with a woman psychotherapist. He suffers difficulty in concentrating on his job and anxiety when in the presence of women. He is being seen at a clinic and has not paid his bill for three months. He began a recent hour as follows:

> *Patient:*   Was it you that I saw on the street last Thursday? [Silence] Did you see me? [Silence] I don't know why you won't answer. Anyhow, I'm pretty sure it was you. I tried to catch your attention, but you didn't seem to see me. That night I had a terrible attack of abdominal cramps and diarrhea. On Saturday I had a terrible backache. I lay in bed and felt that everything was unreal. That night I dreamt that this woman was trying to seduce me. I got panicky and ran away from her. I decided I would never go near her apartment again since it all happened in her neighborhood. I didn't recognize her clearly, but it was a terrible nightmare. I really don't understand the dream. Oh, yes, I have my insurance form in my pocket. I'd like you to fill it out again. I visited my mother and she insisted on overstuffing me with her lousy burned chicken and a ton of cakes and sweets.

Name the indicators in this vignette, classifying them into categories (symptoms and resistances) and evaluating them for their strong or weak qualities. How strong is the need for intervention to this point in the session?

_____
_____
_____
_____
_____
_____
_____
_____
_____
_____
_____
_____

Answer

In general, we collect indicators as they appear in a session, one by one. At times, however, a therapist will be aware of a background indicator (a recent symptom or ongoing frame issue) to which the patient does not allude for the moment. In principle, the therapist does not introduce this particular therapeutic context when intervening, but waits for the patient to do so, indicating his or her readiness to explore its unconscious basis. The background indicators in this case are:

1. The clinic setting (implying a series of as yet undefined frame deviations; strong).

2. The patient not having paid his bill for three months (a gross behavioral resistance—frame break; strong).

The manifest indicators represented in order of their appearance are as follows:

3. The direct questions of the patient to the therapist (a gross behavioral resistance and attempt to disrupt the fundamental rule of free association; moderate).

4. The patient's silence (another gross behavioral resistance—frame deviation, a modification of the fundamental rule of free association; mild if brief).

5. The extratherapeutic contact between patient and therapist (a break in the frame that is not a gross behavioral resistance, but an inadvertent alteration in the usual ground rules and boundaries of the treatment experience and relationship; the treatment experience is to take place within the confines of the therapist's office and consultation room; strong).

6. The patient's abdominal cramps, diarrhea, and backache (physical symptoms with likely emotional underpinnings; moderate).

7. The feeling of unreality (a symptom in the form of derealization; moderate to strong).

8. The patient's anxiety dream (symptomatic; moderate).

9. The proposal that the therapist fill out the insurance form (a gross behavioral resistance, in that to do so modifies the total privacy and confidentiality of the ideal treatment situation and relationship and the responsibility of the patient to pay the entire fee; strong).

10. The upsetting visit to the patient's mother (a possible interpersonal crisis; weak).

The strongest symptomatic indicators appear to be the patient's physical symptoms and derealization; the most powerful resistances and alterations in the ground rules involve conducting therapy in the clinic setting, nonpayment of the fee, the outside contact with the therapist, and the proposal that the therapist complete the insurance form. Overall, these indicators combine to create a very high level of therapeutic need. There is a powerful warrant for intervention in this material.

When flooded with so many indicators, the therapist will selectively interpret and rectify those that are most powerful and best illuminated by the communicative material. He or she would maintain the frame and not generate other areas of ground-rule disturbance until the related indicators were subsequently clarified in later sessions.

As we familiarize ourselves with the manifestations of each category of indicators, it should be recognized that direct questions addressed to the therapist, calling for noninterpretive responses, are, as a rule, expressions of resistance; they are therefore notable therapeutic contexts. In addition, material that manifestly portrays patient-indicators may simultaneously represent, directly or indirectly, an adaptive context. (In this case, for example, if the therapist had seen the patient on the street, the description of that event in the patient's material would constitute both an indicator and an adaptive context. The very fact that the therapist was there to be seen by the patient constitutes an adaptive context.) The same material may also contain encoded, derivative implications. (For example, seeing the therapist on the street may in derivative form allude to the patient's sense of being exposed to others outside of treatment should the therapist complete the insurance form.) We will consider this type of multiple function in the last section of the book.

As a therapist collects indicators and puts them on mental file for later interpretation and framework-management response, he or she should also be asking the questions: *What intervention have I made that could prompt this particular symptom or resistance? Am I already hearing encoded derivatives that point to particular adaptive contexts and which can, in turn, help to explain these indicators?*

Thus, in addition to simply recognizing the presence of an indicator, it is well to begin to search for the unconscious factors that account for its existence. In principle, as noted before, those indicators that involve gross behavioral resistances and breaks in the frame tend to be produced by either an entirely secure set of ground rules (the ideal therapeutic situation) or, more typically, by acute and major deviations by the therapist (deviant-frame psychotherapy). Frame indicators should accordingly lead to a search for frame-related adaptive contexts. In addition, clinical studies have shown that tendencies toward somatization are a common symptomatic response to a poor hold as manifested by ground-rule alterations.

In this instance, the dream is an indicator because it had nightmarish qualities. Although it is clearly lacking in manifest allusions to an adaptive context (there is no direct mention of the therapist or his efforts in the dream), it is likely to contain encoded perceptions of the therapist in light of preceding intervention contexts. For the moment, it is of interest here only because it is a symptomatic indicator.

Exercise 3.3

The next vignette involves a depressed woman of 54 who was in psychotherapy with a woman therapist. The patient was being seen in the therapist's private office in twice-weekly psychotherapy. She began a recent hour as follows:

> *Patient:*   I had a rough week with my father. He seems to be senile and to need a full-time nurse. He thought I was trying to poison him, but I kept reassuring him his food was all right and managed to get him to eat. Despite the pressures, I slept well for the first time in months. I dreamt there was a fire in my apartment but I managed to get out. It was icy and the scene was a mess. One of the firemen looked like my brother.

What indicators, if any, can be identified in this excerpt? Again, classify them as to whether they represent symptoms or resistances, and state their strength.

_____

_____

_____

_____

_____

_____

Answer

In substance, this particular excerpt is without significant indicators. There may be an interpersonal problem between the patient and her father, but there is no sign of symptom or madness as far as the patient is concerned. It is, of course, possible that the patient's allusion to her father's illness could be an encoded or derivative representation of some emotional disturbance within herself. Without clear evidence that this is indeed the case, however, the therapist has little cause to intervene up to this point in the session. The dream, although described as "a mess," did not evoke anxiety. There is also no sign of gross behavioral resistance or framework alterations.

To the contrary, the patient here alludes to sleeping well for the first time in months. A reference to clinical improvement is *not* a therapeutic context or an indicator as defined here in terms of patient-madness. Instead, it is a sign of enhanced functioning that should, in its own right, be understood in light of prevailing adaptive contexts and encoded perceptions of the therapist. Typically, in a soundly managed treatment experience, this type of allusion appears after a validated interpretation or framework-management response by the therapist.

On the other hand, sometimes a patient will, in fact, derive a sense of well-being from an erroneous intervention or mismanagement of the frame. A non-valid intervention may offer a patient a manic or other type of defense, or some uninsightful form of symptom alleviation. In this way, just as certain resistances may be adaptive in light of the therapist's erroneous interventions, certain types of patient-improvement may stem from therapist-errors. There can be no substitute for an analysis of symptomatic remission or improvement in light of activated intervention contexts and the patient's derivative material.

Exercise 3.4

The patient is a married man in psychotherapy being seen by a male therapist on a twice-weekly basis. His reasons for seeking treatment were potency problems and depression. The therapist shares his waiting room with two other therapists, and the patient was referred to him by another of his patients.

The patient had cancelled the prior session because of a last-minute business engagement. Later in that same week, he had called the therapist because he had had an anxiety attack after a quarrel with his wife, and the two spoke briefly. When the therapist came into the waiting room to greet the patient and escort him into his consultation room for his session, the patient introduced him to his wife. The session then ran as follows:

> *Patient:* My wife wants to talk to you. If you have the time, I'd like to have an extra 15 minutes added on at the end of the session. I was pretty nasty with her and she really didn't deserve it. We tried to make love and I was impotent. That's when I had the anxiety attack and called you. You seemed distant on the phone, like someone else was there. I saw Ann yesterday [the patient who made the referral of the patient to the therapist]; she didn't look very well. Therapy is getting expensive. Ann pays a lower fee than I do; I wonder if you would reduce your fee for me. Oh, I have your check. It's in my coat in the waiting room. I better get it before I forget to give it to you. [The patient leaves the session and returns with the check; he hands it to the therapist. The therapist looks at the face of the check and observes that the patient has failed to pay for one of his eight sessions in the previous month.]

Once again, identify each of the indicators in this vignette, including those reflected in the introduction to the session. Classify them, state their general intensity, and evaluate the overall level of therapeutic need.

_____
_____
_____
_____
_____
_____
_____
_____
_____
_____
_____
_____
_____
_____
_____
_____
_____
_____
_____
_____

Answer

The background indicators in this material are as follows:

1. The patient's participation in a patient-referral (a gross behavioral resistance—frame break that modifies the one-to-one relationship, the therapist's relative anonymity, and a sense of total confidentiality; very strong).

2. The cancelled hour (a gross behavioral resistance—frame break; strong).

3. The two telephone calls, the first to cancel the session and the second to report the anxiety attack (both gross behavioral resistances that modify the ground rule stating that the transactions of treatment will take place in the therapist's consultation room; the first call also alters the regular frequency of the sessions; strong).

Notice that most of these background indicators are also referred to directly in the patient's material. The manifest indicators in this material may be presented in order of appearance as follows:

4. The presence of the wife in the waiting room (a gross behavioral resistance—frame break, a modification of total privacy and the one-to-one relationship; strong.)

5. The request that the therapist see the wife in session (a gross behavioral resistance—frame break; strong).

6. The request to extend the session by 15 minutes (a gross behavioral resistance—proposed frame break that modifies the set length of sessions; strong).

7. The patient's inappropriate nastiness with his wife (a characterological symptom; moderate).

8. The patient's impotency (a symptom; strong).

9. The patient's anxiety attack (a symptom; strong).

10. The direct reference to one of the patient's telephone calls to the therapist, and the reference to the patient who was responsible for this patient's referral.

11. The request for a reduced fee (a gross behavioral resistance—frame break that would modify the ground rule of a single fee commensurate with the therapist's expertise; strong).

12. The patient's forgetting to bring the check into the session and to pay the therapist (a resistance—frame break; moderate).

13. The patient's leaving the session to get the check (a gross behavioral resistance—frame break that modifies the ground rule that the patient remain in the consultation room for the allotted time; moderately strong).

14. The error in the check (a resistance—frame break that alters the patient's responsibility to pay for all sessions; strong).

The net effect of these many powerful indicators is certainly a reflection of a very strong need within this patient for therapeutic intervention—both with respect to managing the ground rules and with respect to interpretation. This situation is not uncommon when the psychotherapy involves a basic unrectifiable deviation, such as a patient-referral (it can never be corrected). It is well to stress again that the patient's participation in this particular means of obtaining a therapist is an indicator. It modifies the one-to-one relationship between patient and therapist, and it modifies the therapist's anonymity: The patient has knowledge of another patient whom the therapist is treating. As demonstrated in this vignette, the total confidentiality of all sessions is often altered as well—witness the patient's knowledge of Ann's fee.

At the same time, the patient-referral is an adaptive context, because it reflects the therapist's decision (an intervention) to accept the patient from this particular source. Similarly, if the therapist were to agree to the patient's proposals to extend the hour and to reduce the fee, these patient-indicators would now involve adaptive contexts constituted by the therapist's responsive participation. Refusal of these requests is also an adaptive context.

Clearly, a therapist must be sensitive to every impingement a patient makes on the fundamental ground rules of psychotherapy. It is largely by this means that patients unconsciously express their need for intervention from the therapist. Similarly, it is in the therapist's creation and management of the psychotherapeutic frame that his or her most powerful communications and influence on the patient are exerted. This is not to minimize the additional importance of interpretive intervention. The purpose is to stress the importance of the ground rules and boundaries of psychotherapy as a means of affording the patient a secure and safe setting, a basis for fundamental trust of the therapist, a clear picture of the realities of the treatment situation, unambiguous interpersonal boundaries, and the best available hold and containment. The fundamental mode of relatedness that occurs in this setting is constituted by a healthy symbiosis, fostering open conscious and unconscious communication in the patient and the opportunity for sound interventional response by the therapist.

Exercise 3.5

The focus in our discussion of indicators so far has been on expressions of disturbance in the patient. We have seen that these expressions reflect the patient's inner and interpersonal emotional difficulties (madness) and his or her needs for intervention from the therapist. We have also established that once a patient is in psychotherapy, these therapeutic needs are stimulated mainly by the therapist's interventions; that is, the therapist contributes to the therapeutic needs of the patient, although, of course, critical intrapsychic factors in the patient come into play as well. Both are involved as the patient selectively perceives the adaptive context that has created a particular patient-indicator.

Within the therapeutic interaction or bipersonal field, the therapist, too, may experience strong therapeutic needs and communicate these pressures to the patient through his or her interventions. Every erroneous intervention, inappropriate silence, mistaken interpretation, noninterpretive comment, and mismanagement of (deviation in) the frame—is an expression of the countertransference of the therapist. These traumatic interventions may be termed *therapist-indicators*. They not only reflect the emotional problems (madness) of the therapist, but they also create therapeutic needs within the patient. Because every intervention will relate patient-indicators (therapeutic contexts) to therapist-indicators (adaptive contexts), it is usually not necessary to single out therapist-indicators as the target of specific interpretations. The focus in intervening must be on the disturbance with the patient as contributed to by the disturbance in the therapist (i.e., on the patient-indicators as created, in part, by the therapist-indicators). When a therapist intervenes validly and sanely, no immediate therapeutic need is created in the patient; rather, there is generally a diminution of symptoms and resistances—perhaps followed, in paradoxical fashion, by reactive regressions.

The erroneous interventions of the therapist, on the other hand, lead in many instances to gross behavioral resistances and symptoms in the patient. These then become the focus of interpretation in light of activated adaptation-evoking contexts and derivative material. In principle, as long as there is a patient-indicator in evidence, the interpretive understanding offered by the therapist should be designed to explain the unconscious factors in it. As noted, such an intervention will necessarily allude to the unconscious implications of traumatic intervention contexts (therapist-indicators), thereby automatically taking into account their role in the patient's symptoms.

There are certain situations, however, in which the therapist's erroneous interventions do not create a gross behavioral resistance or symptom in the patient in a particular session. In the presence of blatantly inappropriate interventions, signs of the patient's disturbance will tend to diminish. Also, certain pathological interventions from the therapist gratify the patient's own pathological needs, reinforcing pathological defenses to a point where there is, for the moment, no evident manifestation of the patient's problems. It is in sessions such as these that therapist-indicators must be recognized and subjected to both rectification (correction) and interpretation in light of the patient's derivative and selected perceptive responses.

In other words, there are sessions in which the therapist's overt disturbance, as reflected in erroneous interventions, is both the essential indicator for intervention and the main cause of covert disturbance in the patient. In this case, the major therapeutic need in the bipersonal field is centered in the therapist, but it is also experienced unconsciously by the patient. Under such conditions, the therapist-indicator becomes the focus for intervening. This work becomes the means by which the patient is afforded some measure of relief from the inner, though covered-over, disturbance precipitated by the therapist's inappropriate intervention.

The most powerful therapist-indicators involve deviations from the ideal ground rules of psychotherapy. Because of the high level of conscious and especially unconscious sensitivity in patients to the therapist's interventions and communications in this fundamental area, almost all such deviations evoke strong communicative responses even in the absence of overt symptoms and gross behavioral resistances. There is therefore a strong need for interpretation and rectification in such hours; as already indicated, this effort will center on the unconsciously perceived implications of the therapist's intervention and the patient's encoded correctives.

The following vignette is illustrative. It involves a young woman patient who sought therapy because of depression and problems in establishing a lasting relationship with a man. She was in once-weekly psychotherapy with a male therapist in a private office. The hour in question began as follows:

> *Patient:* When I got home, it was 15 minutes later than usual after my session. It suddenly dawned on me that the session had been extended, I guess by 15 minutes. It was a pleasant feeling. Maybe you were so absorbed in what I was saying, you forgot to watch the time. Anyhow, I was pleased to realize you really care about me. I slept well even though I had a scary dream. In the dream, a man was trying to corner me in the basement of my building. I think he wanted to rape me. I was able to shrug it off in the morning. It makes me think of a time that my brother and I had to sleep in the basement of my aunt's house when we visited her in Chicago. We had to share a bed. I was only seven, but it seemed strange. I remember wanting to go to the bathroom upstairs, but somebody had locked the door to the basement.

To continue the main exercise of this chapter, what—if any—patient-indicators are reflected in this material? Name and classify them, state their power, and state the overall power of the patient-indicators that have appeared to this point in the session.

_____

_____

_____

_____

_____

Answer

To this point, there are *no* patient-indicators in this material. A dream, as already noted, is not an indicator, nor is the emergence of an apparently meaningful early memory. The patient seems to be coping well.

Extending this particular listening exercise, and as a way of preparing for the following chapter, what is the main adaptive context (therapist-indicator) for this session? How is it represented (portrayed) in this material? Is the representation manifest or encoded? Can you go so far as to identify at least two displaced and encoded perceptions of the therapist in light of the intervention context? If so, what type of pathology or madness within the patient has shaped these perceptions?

_____

_____

_____

_____

_____

_____

_____

_____

_____

_____

_____

_____

_____

The adaptive context for this material is the therapist's extension of the patient's 50-minute hour by 15 additional minutes. There are a host of implications to this particular deviation. (See below as well.)

As a further extension of this exercise, name as many as possible of the general or universal meanings of an extension of this kind. (We will systematize this exercise later on.)

_____

_____

_____

_____

_____

_____

_____

_____

_____

_____

_____

_____

_____

_____

Answer

Among the main meanings of this modification of the set length of sessions, the following are especially prominent:

1. Entrapment.

2. Loss of contact with reality.

3. Forced seduction.

4. Aggressive control and manipulation.

5. Inability to separate.

6. Incestuous entanglement.

7. Overgratifying the patient.

8. A reaction formation against the wish to get rid of the patient.

In addition to these relatively common or universal meanings, there would be specific personal meanings for both patient and therapist to this particular deviation. There would also be meanings for each in terms of the history of the therapeutic interaction and especially the nature of the interaction at this particular point in time.

Returning now to the original questions raised, the patient has encoded her unconscious perceptions of the therapist through her dream and her memory of her brother. In the first instance, the therapist's failure to dismiss the patient at the appointed time is perceived as an entrapment and rape. In the second instance, both the incestuous qualities of this extension and the sense of entrapment (being locked in the basement) are conveyed. If we were to translate these two derivative communications into a single decoded and raw (anxiety-provoking) image, it might be stated as follows: *The therapist is attempting to corner and rape me, to have me sleep with him as I once slept with my brother. He had a need to lock me in his office together with him.*

In this instance, the allusion to sharing the bed with the brother does *not* represent a genetic experience that has led to a distorted image of the therapist—transference as it is generally defined in the classical psychoanalytic literature. Rather, it is a genetic connection aroused by the immediate intervention of the therapist; it indicates an earlier experience that is being repeated in some form in the present therapeutic interaction—a nontransference genetic factor. Such repetitions are extremely common in today's psychotherapy.

The intrapsychic fantasies and memories that shaped this patient's selected encoded perceptions of the implications of the therapist's deviation involve fantasy-memory systems of entrapment, rape, and incest. Despite all these stirrings, the modification in the frame has not as yet created a major symptom or resistance in the patient. Thus, there is no patient-indicator available for intervention. Nonetheless, the deviation, or therapist-indicator, is quite powerful, and the patient's associations show a need for intervention lest her inner disturbance intensify and lead to maladaptive symptomatic responses. Such an intervention would be organized around the patient's representation of the errant intervention context (the extension of the patient's hour) and would concentrate on the patient's encoded perceptions of the therapist in light of his mistake, including their genetic connections. In interpreting the patient's selected unconscious perceptions of this particular adaptive context, one would necessarily be illuminating the introjective aspects of the patient's original problems and their current repercussions, including her difficulties with men, in light of the recent stimulus.

If during this hour the patient had mentioned a specific incident in which she had behaved inappropriately or experienced frigidity with a man, this characterological or symptomatic problem could have been taken as the patient-indicator for interpretation. The patient's frigidity would have been understood in this particular manifestation as a response to the adaptive context of the therapist's extension of the hour and as an indication of the patient's selected encoded perceptions of the meanings of this particular deviation. Two possible unconscious meanings to the frigidity could have been developed: (1) that the frigidity occurred because men are unconsciously perceived as similar to the therapist—as entrapping, raping, and incestuous objects, or (2) that the frigidity was unconsciously intended as a model of rectification—an encoded and symptomatic message to the therapist that he should not be sexually stimulated in the presence of his patient. In either instance, the patient would have responded to a traumatic intervention from her therapist with an expression of her own madness.

Interpretation in light of the adaptive context establishes the most active and currently truthful unconscious meanings of the patient's symptom in its immediate manifestation. Clearly, this particular constellation of meanings will share much in common with the implications of the symptom as it has functioned at other times in the patient's life, and also with its sources and origins. Assuming the therapist's rectification of the frame and his commitment to henceforth maintain the proper length of the patient's sessions, the interpretive therapeutic work surrounding the symptoms at issue would illuminate their unconscious basis. This kind of therapeutic effort affords a patient effectively meaningful cognitive insight that can foster a health-promoting alteration of pathological introjects, the modification of pathological unconscious fantasy-memory systems, conflict resolution, and better adaptation.

SUMMARY

To integrate some salient points:

1. The therapist attends to both the patient's behaviors and free associations in a search for indicators.

2. The first class of indicators is symptomatic, ranging from psychosomatic and physical symptoms to characterological disorders and emotional disturbances, such as anxiety, depression, phobias, and the like. Whenever a symptom is reported in a particular session, it is labeled as the target for interpretation and framework-management response.

3. The second class of indicators comprises gross behavioral resistances. These include all efforts by the patient to alter the basic ground rules of psychotherapy. (Because of their importance, we may recall that the ground rules of therapy include a single set fee; a specified and consistent length, appointed time, and frequency of sessions; the fundamental rule of free association; the patient on the couch with the therapist sitting behind him or her out of sight; the therapist's relative anonymity and use of neutral interventions—silences, interpetation–reconstructions and framework-securing efforts; total privacy and a one-to-one relationship; and total confidentiality.)

4. Both symptoms and gross behavioral resistances are communicative responses and vehicles, but they are poor carriers of decodable meanings.

5. Resistance indicators are critical to the continuation of the therapeutic work. The therapist must have considerable sensitivity to impingements on the ground-rule boundary area of the therapeutic relationship.

6. In general, it is through attempts to modify the usual ground rules of psychotherapy (which ideally should be evoked by frame-securing adaptive contexts) that patients express their immediate needs for intervention. Such efforts are

identified in the patient's manifest associations and direct behaviors, and should be marked for subsequent intervention.

7. The use of currently evident indicators as targets for interpretation and framework-management responses makes psychotherapy an immediately meaningful and alive treatment experience. The target for intervention is active, compelling, and an actual, present-tense expression of the patient's madness. On this basis, every session that involves a meaningful indicator and similarly meaningful communicative material can be structured as a mini-analysis of cogent therapeutic work. It is the accumulation of such therapeutic moments that leads to symptom and characterological change based on genuine insight.

4
Identifying the Adaptive Contexts

The interventions of the therapist (adaptive contexts, intervention contexts, adaptation-evoking contexts—all synonyms) are the fulcrum of the listening process. These contexts are the stimuli for the patient's pathological expressions—symptoms and resistances (indicators). Thus, they also serve to organize the patient's manifest and latent, direct and encoded behaviors and associations. Because of this, adaptive contexts occupy much of the therapist's thinking in the course of a session. The therapist consistently alternates between loose, unformed, empathic, and intuitive listening and momentary efforts at formulation and shaping. A well-represented (portrayed) adaptive context is the single most important signal to a therapist that an intervention is likely to be both feasible and advisable. (All that is needed in addition are an indicator and several meaningful derivative perceptions.)

In exploring the patient's material for the representations and implications of intervention contexts, four major operations are utilized. Each must be carried out in order to minimize the possibility of overlooking either a critical adaptive context or one of its most important meanings. The four operations are:

1. *Name all known and still active adaptive contexts,* remaining open, however, to direct allusions concerning intervention contexts not yet recognized and to representations that are strongly suggested by the patient's derivative material.

   a. *Distinguish background contexts from contexts that are currently active.* Background contexts may have been important in the past or may be relatively fixed deviations that continue to be a factor in the present.

2. *Identify all direct and manifest representations, portrayals, or allusions to adaptation-evoking contexts.*

3. For adaptive contexts that are not directly alluded to, *identify those contexts which the patient portrays and represents in strong (close) derivative form.*

4. *Identify all possible meanings and implications of these known adaptive contexts.*

The therapist, in a sense, is listening in two different ways at the same time. In keeping with the recommendation of Bion (1967), the therapist should enter each session with half the mind free from memory, desire, and understanding, in order to allow the patient's manifest and derivative material to suggest unrecognized adaptive contexts, missed derivative meanings, and overlooked indicators. The therapist is listening receptively, as free from bias as possible, and open to new discovery.

The other half of the therapist's mind must have some sense of the recent sessions, the nature of his or her latest interventions, and the *flow* of the ongoing therapeutic and communicative interactions. Otherwise a therapist will have considerable difficulty in properly formulating the material at hand and in sorting out and interrelating the three basic elements of communication—indicators, adaptive contexts, and derivative complex. By keeping in mind something of the previous therapeutic work, in particular the most pertinent adaptive contexts, formulation and understanding are facilitated. The therapist should not allow this part of the mind, however, which begins with what is known, to interfere with his or her openness to that which is not yet recognized.

As the initial part of a session unfolds, the therapist should subjectively recall his or her most recent interventions and keep some sense of their implications in mind. These will help to guide the therapist in identifying manifest and derivative representations or portrayals of the contexts.

As a guide to those interventions most likely to be powerful adaptive contexts for the patient—and most evocative of symptomatic responses (indicators) and derivative reactions—adaptive contexts can be classified according to four basic types:

1. Silence.
   a. Valid silence.
   b. Erroneous silence (a missed intervention).

2. The management of the ground rules and boundaries of the treatment situation and relationship.
   a. Maintaining and securing the frame (valid interventions).
   b. Deviating from the ideal frame (deviant interventions).

3. Interpretation–reconstruction—interventions geared toward the discovery of activated unconscious meanings and functions.
   a. Valid interpretations (explaining the unconscious basis of an indicator in light of the most pertinent adaptive context and the patient's selected encoded perceptions. Encoded confirmation validates an accurate interpretation).
   b. Erroneous interpretations (the failure to obtain validating derivative confirmation).

4. Other verbal-affective efforts, those not geared toward understanding (invalid noninterpretive interventions).
   a. Support, manipulation, advice, and the like.
   b. Self-revelations and alterations in neutrality.
   c. Other.

Although the patient does respond to each and every valid and invalid intervention by the therapist, those interventions that involve the ground rules of psychotherapy are by far the most significant. This sector of interventions is at the heart of a healthy therapeutic symbiosis or is the major factor in a pathological mode of relatedness—pathological autism, pathological symbiosis, and/or parasiticism. The therapist should thus pay special attention to pressures from patients in this area, and should keep in mind every interventional response, whether to secure the frame or to modify it. Any deviant aspect of the basic conditions of treatment and any deviant intervention whatsoever constitutes a critical adaptation-evoking context for the patient. It follows, then, that when a patient needs an intervention from a therapist, the most common means of expressing this therapeutic wish is to create pressures to alter a particular aspect of the basic framework of psychotherapy.

In most clinical situations, there are several—often three or more—activated adaptive contexts to which a patient is in the process of responding. For this reason, it is important to decide, first, which interventional contexts are likely to have had the most powerful influence on the patient, and second, which adaptive contexts appear to best organize the patient's derivative material—that is, which context does the patient seem to be actually working over at the moment? In general, interventions in the area of the ground rules of treatment have the most powerful influence on the patient; then, in descending order of impact: invalid noninterpretive interventions, erroneous silence and erroneous interpretations, and valid silence and valid interpretations.

NAMING ADAPTIVE CONTEXTS: EXERCISES

We will begin our exercises related to the therapist's interventions by naming the adaptive contexts reflected in a series of vignettes, and assigning them a general level of strength as evocative therapist-efforts to which the patient is likely to respond more or less intensely.

Exercise 4.1

The patient is a black woman in her early fifties who is being seen in a clinic psychotherapy situation for episodes of depression. She sees her male therapist on a once-weekly basis, and she receives medication from a psychiatrist who works at the same facility. The patient pays the bookkeeper of the clinic a two-dollar fee before each session, and shows her receipt to the therapist before the hour begins. The sessions are 50 minutes long and set for Thursday mornings at 10:00. Because clinic policy dictates that the patient is not charged for any cancelled hour, the therapist has in the past offered make-up sessions for hours that the patient was unable to attend. At the time of the session on which we will eventually focus, the therapist was planning to take a two-week Christmas–New Year's vacation at the end of the month.

In the previous hour, the patient had complained of tiredness and somatic symptoms. She had stated that the therapist's pending vacation would be a pause and a relief and that she was pleased she hadn't missed a session in the last two months. Besides, she said, she had now made plans to go away during the same time that the therapist would be out of the clinic. The therapist intervened and suggested that the patient was trying to imply that his vacation would have no effect on her. When the patient denied that this was her meaning, the therapist pointed out that the patient had also stressed her own recent consistency in keeping their appointments. With resentment, the patient responded that the therapist seemed to jump to conclusions, much as the people did at her church. She herself preferred to keep her mouth shut. There was a period of silence before the session ended.

For the purpose of conducting a search for known adaptive contexts, we may divide this material into the introductory segment, which presented the background of the treatment situation, and the description of the preliminary hour. Name the adaptive contexts contained in both segments of the material. Specify the type of intervention involved (silence, ground-rule related, interpretive, or other verbal effort) and indicate the strength with which it is likely to serve as an evocative stimulus for the patient's communicative, symptomatic, and other reactions (strong, moderate, and weak).

_____

_____

_____

_____

_____

_____

_____

_____

_____

_____

_____

_____

_____

_____

_____

_____

_____

_____

_____

_____

_____

_____

_____

_____

_____

_____

_____

_____

_____

_____

Answer

The introductory material indicates some of the basic ground rules and conditions of this treatment experience. These serve as the framework for each session. In order to evaluate each particular hour, the main attributes of the overall framework must be known. Often, the ground rules are background adaptive contexts, to which the patient responds in immediate or foreground fashion from time to time, when a related issue arises. In order for the patient to have a sound psychotherapeutic experience, it would be necessary ultimately to rectify those deviant ground rules that are indeed rectifiable, while interpreting the implications of each deviant *and* secure aspect of the framework to which the patient actively responds at some juncture in the treatment experience. Such work is based, of course, on a recognition of each existing intervention context.

With respect to the introductory material, the following are the recognizable intervention contexts—both valid and invalid—in the order in which they are mentioned:

1. The existence of clinic psychotherapy (frame deviations implying, though not specifying, possible modifications in fee, anonymity of the therapist, the one-to-one relationship, privacy, and confidentiality; strong).

2. The prescription of medication from another therapist, a psychiatrist at the same facility (frame deviation, an alteration of the ideal principle that the therapist's interventions are confined to verbal-affective communications, as well as a violation of the one-to-one totally private relationship between patient and therapist; strong).

3. The payment made to the bookkeeper and the requirement that the patient show the therapist a receipt (ground-rule deviations, modifications of the absence of physical contact and its equivalent [the receipt], and alterations in the one-to-one relationship; strong).

4. The two-dollar fee (framework deviation, a known reduced or comparatively low fee; strong).

5. Once-weekly psychotherapy at a set time and for a set duration (these are reflections of ideal ground rules which, if maintained with utmost consistency, would constitute positive holding and intervening [though such maintenance was not in evidence here]; mild).

6. The absence of a fee for missed sessions (frame deviation in regard to the ground rule of a single fixed fee for all hours at which the therapist is present; strong).

7. The offer of make-up sessions when the patient misses an hour (frame deviation, an alteration in the ground rule of a fixed time for each session; strong).

8. The therapist's planned two-week vacation (a ground-rule intervention, a hurtful aspect of the ideal frame rather than a deviant break in the frame; moderate).

Virtually all basic deviations from the ideal set of ground rules and boundaries of psychotherapy are strong adaptation-evoking contexts for the patient. Here, they are identified as background adaptive contexts; any one of them may appear in a particular hour as a foreground or immediate (active) context as well.

It should be noted that the use of medication per se is an important deviant intervention because it is a departure from the exclusive use of verbal-affective interventions by the therapist as the means of therapeutic cure. Note, too, that a vacation planned and taken by a therapist is not a deviant intervention context, but a necessary though hurtful part of the ideal therapeutic frame. It is essential that a therapist be away from the patient and from work on occasion, perhaps four to eight weeks in a given year. In general, an intervention context involving the therapist's plans for a vacation will be less powerful than contexts involving framework-deviation interventions.

For the moment, then, the most powerful background adaptive contexts described here involve deviations in the ideal psychotherapeutic frame. Lesser contexts would include the consistency of the length and day of the patient's sessions—unless altered—and the therapist's pending vacation—aspects of the ideal ground-rule conditions.

Exercise 4.2

Let us turn now to the brief summary of the patient's prior session. In a standard approach to the evaluation of an hour, the therapist would begin with the patient-indicators evident in the session. As a first step, therefore, name all of the patient-indicators in this prior hour. Identify the type of indicator (symptom or resistance) and its strength. (Note should be made that the patient's chief complaint as indicated in the introductory material was the symptom of depression. This background indicator may or may not come to the fore in a particular session.)

_____

_____

_____

_____

_____

_____

_____

_____

_____

_____

_____

_____

_____

_____

Answer

In sequence, the major patient-indicators reported in the preliminary session are:

    1. Tiredness and somatic symptoms (symptoms; moderate to weak).

    2. The patient's denial of the therapist's intervention and her resentment that he seems to jump to conclusions (gross behavioral resistances that appear to be adaptive and essentially nonpathological; weak).

    3. The patient's silences (a gross behavioral resistance; moderate).

Notice that the patient's gross behavioral resistances—her denial of the therapist's intervention and her resentful accusation that he seems to jump to conclusions—do not seem inappropriate in light of the therapist's efforts. An intervention that relies on obvious inferences is often appropriately denied by the patient and seldom followed by derivative validation. Without engaging in a full analysis here of the phenomenon, we may take this particular response as a model, recognizing that at times, a patient's opposition to treatment and to the interventions of a therapist is highly adaptive and quite appropriate. Such patient-responses should be identified, first, as gross behavioral resistances, then subjected to analysis in terms of the prevailing adaptive contexts and available derivative material.

    Let us now identify the intervention contexts in this briefly summarized session (an exercise that should have been completed above). They are:

    1. The therapist's pending vacation (a reflection of the ground rule that permits the therapist to interrupt treatment on occasion; moderate).

2. The therapist's suggestion that the patient was trying to imply his vacation would not affect her (an interpretation as conventionally defined [an attempt to make something unconscious conscious for the patient]; moderate to weak).

3. Pointing out to the patient that she had stressed her own consistency with appointments (a confrontation; moderate).

It is also possible to consider the therapist's silence in the initial part of the hour as an intervention. But in general, it is only when silence extends over half or more of a session that it should be registered as an existing intervention. In all such instances, the silence should either be validated or recognized as erroneous, using the patient's derivative material as a guide.

Of course, all verbal interventions by the therapist are adaptive contexts. We have also identified the therapist's vacation as an adaptive context in this briefly summarized hour because the patient has alluded to it directly. Although this allusion represents, as we shall see, a simple example of a manifest representation of an adaptive context, one should recognize that the context itself exists for this hour whether or not the patient alludes to it.

Exercise 4.3

In entering the next hour with the patient, the therapist would be thinking over both the prior session and the basic conditions of the treatment. For example, if an adaptive context had recently been at issue—say, the patient had failed to pay her bill for several sessions (an indicator related to the context of the low fee)—this particular framework context would be experienced by the patient with some measure of intensity. But the therapist would remain alert as well to the possibility of other background contexts coming to the fore in this pending hour. In addition, the therapist would try to have an overall sense of his verbal-affective interventions in the prior hour, bearing in mind both their general nature (in this case, the therapist's having attempted to interpret aspects of the patient's reaction to his vacation) as well as the patient's direct and encoded responses (her lack of derivative validation, her direct criticism, and her self-referential model of rectification: the allusion to keeping her own mouth shut, which undoubtedly was an encoded directive to the therapist. The patient's final silence, in the form of a gross behavioral resistance, carried the same encoded message).

An excerpt from the initial segment of the following hour is:

Patient: I've been alone a lot at home. I need someone to talk to who really understands me. Did you get the card I sent you for Christmas?

Therapist: Yes, thank you.

Patient: I hope you liked it.

Therapist: Yes, it was very nice. It's on my mantlepiece at home.

Patient: By the way, when is my next med-clinic appointment? I lost the card.

Therapist: Monday morning at 11:00. You seem to have a need to ask many questions of me today.

Patient: My nephew drove me here. He got lost on the way. He is easily confused. The bookkeeper was snippy today. Did you complete my forms?

Therapist: Yes, they're complete now. You keep asking me for something. I wonder if you're not reacting to my coming vacation.

Patient: I don't think so. I'm all paid up, aren't I? The slate is clean. You can rest in peace. I clean someone's house now and then so I can keep coming here. This place needs a cleaning too.

For this part of the exercise, the reader should begin by simply listing here all those adaptive contexts from the previous session and the conditions of treatment that he or she can recall. Enter these below. (The contexts will not be listed again but may be reviewed from the previous discussion once they have been listed from memory.)

_____

_____

_____

_____

_____

_____

_____

_____

_____

_____

Next, before dealing with the adaptive context, identify and classify the patient-indicators in this hour.

_____

_____

_____

_____

_____

_____

_____

_____

Answer

Patient-indicators usually appear in the patient's manifest material and evident behaviors. In this session they are as follows:

1. The patient's having sent the therapist a Christmas card (a gross behavioral resistance—frame deviation, a modification of the ground rule that the patient's fee is the only direct satisfaction or contribution made to the therapist by the patient; strong).

2. The patient's asking the therapist a direct question about the card (a resistance—frame deviation, an alteration of the fundamental rule of free association; weak).

3. The additional question regarding the med-clinic appointment (see #2).

4. Losing the appointment card (a symptomatic act; weak).

5. The question regarding the therapist's completion of the forms (see #2).

In all, these indicators reflect only a moderate measure of therapeutic need; the strongest is the patient's decision to send the therapist a Christmas card. It is this break in the ideal frame that reflects the most powerful wish for intervention in the patient; the other indicators are all relatively weak.

Exercise 4.4

Let us turn next to the adaptive contexts in this material. As the reader may have noticed, some are reflected in the patient's manifest associations (direct representations of adaptive contexts), and others emerge in the therapist's comments and interventions. List all of these contexts in sequence, noting the source of each, and classifying them once again in terms of type—therapist-silence; managements or allusions to ground-rule issues; interpretations; and other verbal-affective interventions. Indicate too their power as evocative stimuli for the patient (strong, moderate, weak). Finally, state which of these adaptive contexts is most likely to be the most powerful stimulus for the balance of this session.

_____

_____

_____

_____

_____

_____

_____

_____

_____

_____

_____

_____

_____

_____

_____

_____

_____

_____

_____

Answer

In sequence, the following adaptive contexts appear in this material (unless otherwise stated, the source of the allusion to the intervention context is indicated by underscoring):

1. The therapist's acceptance of the Christmas card from the patient (suggested in the patient's associations and reflected manifestly in the therapist's response; ground-rule deviation, an alteration of the frame in respect to the satisfactions that accrue to the therapist which should be confined to his receipt of the fee and other intangibles; strong).

2. The therapist's comment ("Yes") which indicated that he had received the Christmas card (a ground-rule deviant intervention that is self-revealing and noninterpretive, modifying the therapist's relative anonymity and neutrality; strong).

3. The therapist's expression of gratitude ("Thank you") to the patient (a ground-rule deviation in the form of a nonneutral intervention; strong).

4. The therapist's comment that the card was very nice (a ground-rule deviation, a noninterpretive intervention that modifies the therapist's neutrality; strong).

5. The therapist's revelation that the card was on his mantlepiece at home (a ground-rule deviation and nonneutral intervention that modifies the therapist's neutrality and anonymity, revealing a private aspect of his life; strong).

6. The patient's question as to the time of her next med-clinic appointment (a ground-rule deviation that involves both medication and third parties to treatment, modifications of the verbal-affective communicative mode of cure and of the one-to-one relationship; strong).

7. The therapist's response that the appointment is Monday at 11:00 A.M. (participation in a ground-rule deviation with respect to the medicating physician and the

use of medication, as well as a noninterpretive intervention in the form of a direct answer to the patient's question; strong).

8. The therapist's comment that the patient seemed to have a need to ask questions of him today (a nonneutral intervention in the form of a confrontation; moderate).

9. The patient's allusion to the bookkeeper (a framework deviation that modifies the total privacy and one-to-one relationship of the ideal frame; strong).

10. The patient's allusion to the therapist's completing the form regarding her clinic care (a ground-rule deviation that modifies the one-to-one relationship, the total privacy and confidentiality of therapy, and the therapist's neutrality; strong).

11. The therapist's response that he had done so (participation in a ground-rule deviation—the characteristics are identified in #10—and a noninterpretive intervention that involves a self-revelation; strong).

12. The therapist's comment that the patient keeps asking him for something (a noninterpretive intervention in the form of a confrontation; moderate).

13. The therapist's proposal that the patient may be reacting to his coming vacation (an allusion to an alteration in the frame that is not pathologically deviant, as well as a premature general interpretation lacking a related derivative complex; moderate, mainly because the patient has not as yet represented the vacation in her associations).

14. The patient's allusion to her fee (a ground-rule deviation, given that the fee is considerably reduced; strong).

15. The patient's comment on the messiness of the therapist's office and clinic setting (a rather vague allusion to the general conditions and ground rules of the treatment; weak).

This exercise demonstrates the strikingly large number of adaptive contexts that can be active at any given moment in a clinic psychotherapy—and in a private treatment situation with multiple deviations as well. It also shows the extent to which an active therapist creates multiple adaptation-evoking contexts that will generate patient-responses. By and large, when there are more than three significant adaptive contexts in operation in a bipersonal field, the situation becomes somewhat chaotic; the patient's communicative responses are likely to be fragmented—there is far too much for him or her to deal with in any coalescible and sensible form. Consistent meaning will emerge only if there is an overridingly significant intervention context that the patient unconsciously selects for direct representation and derivative response. Otherwise, confusion and fragmentation reign.

Exercises of this kind, then, can serve as fair warning to a therapist to think through each and every intervention—silences as well as active efforts. It is well to recognize the enormously powerful and meaningful output (projections) contained in a sequence with interventions of this kind. Each comment is quite loaded with conscious and unconscious meaning. In fact, there is a quality of dumping or *projective identification* reflected in this level of activity, and the patient will be hard pressed to contain her therapist's pathological interactional projections and metabolize them into a meaningful response.

As for the question regarding the most powerful intervention context in this particular segment of material, the answer appears to be the therapist's acceptance of the Christmas card and his revelation of his decision to place it on his mantlepiece at home. This is, for the moment, the most immediate, active, and powerful adaptation-evoking context with which the patient will have to deal. Second in power would be the background adaptive contexts, here brought to the foreground by the patient, concerning the medication and third party to treatment. The therapist's completion of forms regarding the patient would also be an especially strong context in this particular session.

Several side issues deserve brief comment. First, it is best upon receiving a Christmas card or other item in the mail from a patient to not open the card, letter, or package, and to return it to the patient in the next session. Analytic exploration can then follow. In a situation where a patient is known to be suicidal or homocidal, it may prove necessary to read a letter, though this too should be returned to the patient in the next hour. This type of rectification would spare the therapist the need to answer questions regarding the state of the card, because in principle, the therapist should not answer queries from the patient unless absolutely necessary and only after full associative exploration. Thus, the patient's question regarding her next appointment for medication should obtain an initial response from the therapist to the effect that the patient should continue to say whatever comes to her mind. After the associations have unfolded, and if the patient has not as yet recalled the time of her appointment—often, the repression is lifted through such exploration—it would then be necessary for the therapist to provide this information to the patient as long as he believed the medication was vital to the patient's mental health. The patient's question regarding her medical forms deserves a comparable response in order to afford the patient an opportunity to free associate and to reveal related intervention contexts and unconscious perceptions and meanings. Often, a question regarding an adaptive context that is brought up on a manifest level serves in some fashion to represent in encoded form a different and more disturbing context. For example, it may well be that in this instance, the allusion to the medical forms refers not only to the forms themselves but to the Christmas card as well—the first direct and manifest, the second in encoded form, derivative and latent.

Finally, patients should not be permitted to help out—cleaning or otherwise—at clinics. No arbitrary injunction would be necessary because this very answer would be contained in the patient's subsequent derivative associations. This material would then form the basis for intervening.

CONCLUDING COMMENTS

The exercise of naming all known adaptive contexts as one listens to the patient's material at the beginning of each hour is a critical means by which a therapist gets a sense of those issues that are most likely to be mobilizing the patient's adaptive, communicative, and other responses. The following principles apply to this effort:

1. Enter each hour with half the mind open to the leads generated by the patient's material. With the other half, attempt to recall all known intervention contexts.

2. In naming each adaptive context, separate out those that have been active in the most recent session or two (including any activity by the therapist between sessions) from those that exist as background contexts.

3. In addition, classify all recognized intervention contexts as to their nature (silence, frame-related, interpretive, and noninterpretive), affording special emphasis to frame-related deviations and immediate efforts to secure an aspect of the ground rules.

4. In naming all known prior intervention contexts, gradually begin to sense and identify their implications—an exercise to which we will turn in Chapter 7.

5
Adaptive Contexts: Manifest Representations

As a session begins, the therapist endeavors to remember those intervention contexts that were active in the previous hour. This includes, as we have seen, his or her most immediate interventions as well as any frame issues that have been brought up either by the patient or by the therapist in the session.

While the therapist is considering these aspects of the interaction, the patient is, of course, beginning to free associate. The therapist therefore begins to sort out in the patient's material allusions to indicators, direct representations of adaptive contexts, and derivative themes.

As we have already seen, indicators tend to appear early in the hour. With the adaptive context and derivative complex, there are two patterns: (1) One or more adaptive contexts are represented *manifestly* early in the session, and the remaining listening effort concentrates on decoding the derivative complex in light of these intervention contexts. (2) The patient's initial material is largely derivative in form, with an occasional encoded representation of an adaptive context, but no manifest portrayal. In this second type of session, the therapist allows the derivative complex to suggest the activated adaptive contexts to which the patient has not yet alluded directly. More often than not, the patient will refer to these intervention contexts manifestly toward the middle or latter part of the session. If the therapist's consideration of the derivative complex has been sensitive, he or she will recognize this manifest representation. Often, this is the point of intervention in such an hour.

The focus here for the moment is on the specific task of identifying manifest allusions to adaptive contexts in the patient's associations. As discussed, this is perhaps the most important communicative requisite for a valid intervention. A direct reference to an intervention context enables the therapist to convincingly demonstrate to the patient that his or her indirect associations (derivatives with latent meaning) have in fact been stimulated by the therapist's interventions and center around the selectively and unconsciously perceived implications of those interventions. Because all human adaptation and communication takes place in this way, such an intervention most faithfully represents the conscious and unconscious realities of the therapeutic interaction. It also represents the most cogent unconscious meanings of the patient's material as they illuminate his or her madness (indicators). When a manifestly represented adaptive context appears in passing early in the session, the therapist will nearly always be able to intervene interpretively or with framework-management responses as the session unfolds.

The initial task of the therapist, therefore, is communicative, rather than concerned with dynamics, genetics, narcissism, or other similar implications of the patient's material. Before anything else, the therapist must be concerned with the clarity of the portrayal, the recognizability of the adaptive context in the patient's representations. Many different kinds of issues are brought into play within the therapeutic interaction, dynamic and otherwise; only those that are clearly represented or characterized in the patient's material can be subjected to intervention. The search for manifest representations of adaptive contexts is thus a prime therapeutic task.

MANIFEST REPRESENTATION
OF ADAPTIVE CONTEXTS: EXERCISES

Exercise 5.1

The patient is a young man being seen by a male therapist in once-weekly psychotherapy because of episodes of acute anxiety and difficulties in holding a job and relating to women. The patient is being seen in a clinic at a relatively low fee, which he pays to a secretary. He is aware of the existence of clinic records. The session we will consider took place immediately after the therapist's vacation. At the recommendation of the clinic director, the patient had been tested psychologically while the therapist was away.

The session begins as follows:

Patient: I've been wondering about the results of the testing.

Therapist: I have not as yet talked to the psychologist who did the tests.

Patient: I've been thinking about going back to school. I should pay for it myself. I don't know if I should date now. I did see someone during your vacation and had a good time. Her aunt showed me bizarre pictures. The only problem is that she is Oriental. What would people think? Sometimes she's rather smart. I think I messed up the intelligence test. I feel unattractive, used, and manipulated. I experience people intruding into my space. You were right in advising me to get a job and support myself. My mother's therapist [someone in the same clinic; the mother had referred her son to the clinic] forgot her session last week. When I worked as a nurse's aide, we were not supposed to date the patients or take gifts from them. I was tempted to break the rule, but I never did.

First, identify and classify any indicators (therapeutic contexts) that have emerged in this material. Next, state all of the known adaptive contexts, classifying them as to type and strength. Finally, identify all adaptive contexts that are manifestly represented in the patient's material, again classifying each context as to type and strength.

Answer

There are no clear or strong indicators in this material. There are, however, several possible manifest or implied (latent) therapeutic contexts. They are, in order of sequence:

1. The allusion to the bizarre pictures shown to the patient by his date's aunt (a possible encoded or latent indicator reflecting through displacement something bizarre in the patient; weak).

2. The attraction to an Oriental woman (a possible interpersonal dysfunction that would require considerable exploration before being identified as a clear indicator; weak).

3. The patient's concern as to what people will think about his involvement with an Oriental woman (a possible interpersonal dysfunction that would also require considerable exploration before being identified as a clear indicator; weak).

4. "Messing up" the intelligence test (a possible symptomatic response; weak).

5. The patient's feeling that he is "unattractive, used, and manipulated" (symptoms; weak to moderate because of their lack of specificity).

6. The patient's experience of people "intruding into his space" (a possible interpersonal dysfunction; weak because of its lack of definition).

7. The patient's allusion to his not having a job (a possible symptomatic disturbance also requiring additional material before being identified as a meaningful therapeutic context; weak).

In substance, then, there is no clear and powerful patient-indicator in this session. As we shall see, it is the kind of hour in which *therapist-indicators* constitute the most compelling need for intervention within the patient.

As the next step in this listening exercise, we should identify all of the known intervention contexts. These are reflected, of course, in the introduction to the session. They include the following adaptive contexts:

1. The clinic site for the psychotherapy (implies a variety of frame deviations related to the fee, privacy and confidentiality, the one-to-one relationship, and the like; strong).

2. The relatively low fee (frame deviation; strong).

3. The secretary to whom the fee is paid (frame deviation, a modification of the one-to-one relationship; strong).

4. The existence of clinic records (frame deviation, a modification of total confidentiality and the necessary fleeting and unrecorded qualities of the ideal therapeutic interaction; strong).

5. The therapist's vacation (the application of an appropriate but hurtful ground rule of psychotherapy; moderate to weak).

6. The recommendation by the clinic director that the patient receive psychological testing (a frame deviation that alters the one-to-one relationship, total privacy, and total confidentiality; strong).

7. The psychological testing (a frame deviation that modifies the fundamental rule of free association as the relatively exclusive mode of communication by the patient, as well as altering the one-to-one relationship, the confidentiality of treatment, and the therapist's neutrality [psychological test information biases the therapist]; strong).

We turn now to the adaptive contexts manifestly alluded to or represented in the patient's associations in the hour at hand. In sequence, they are:

1. The psychological testing (a frame deviation; strong).

2. The therapist's vacation (a traumatic aspect of the secure frame; moderate to weak).

3. The therapist's advice to the patient to get a job and support himself (a noninterpretive intervention; moderate).

4. The therapist's acceptance of the patient into psychotherapy despite the presence of the patient's mother in the clinic (frame deviation, a modification of total privacy; strong).

The therapist's acceptance of the patient when he had been referred to the clinic by his mother is an intervention context that is not mentioned directly in the material under consideration. But it is a relatively strong intervention context. It constitutes a frame deviation and a form of patient-referral—tantamount to the same therapist's accepting both mother and son into therapy. The result is an alteration of the one-to-one relationship, the total privacy of treatment, and the relative anonymity of the therapist.

Although this specific adaptive context is not alluded to in its entirety, the part that is touched upon in the patient's manifest associations is a sufficiently direct representation to facilitate an intervention built around the fact of his mother's presence at the clinic. This kind of partial representation is not uncommon and will usually support an interpretation and/or a framework-rectifying intervention. Here, the patient's manifest allusion to his mother's treatment at the clinic implies both her presence at the treatment site and the patient-referral. Notice, however, that although it would be possible for the therapist to readily intervene with respect to *the mother's presence at the clinic*, an effort to organize the material around *the patient-referral* aspect of this context would require additional and specific bridging images to facilitate intervening.

In any given session, a patient may fail to represent either the background or basic-condition adaptive contexts, or may manifestly represent one or more of these interventions. Further, the patient may or may not allude directly to the interventions made by the therapist in the prior hour. In this session, the allusion to the therapist's advice to the patient that he should get a job touches upon an intervention that was in fact made in the prior hour. Similarly, the circumstances of the therapist's vacation and the psychological testing immediately preceded this particular session.

The most powerful intervention contexts represented in the session at hand are most likely the psychological testing, the mother's presence at the clinic, and the mother's referral of her son to therapy. The low fee and the presence of the secretary would appear to be next in importance. In making this type of rating of evocative power, remember that ground-rule deviations virtually always take precedence over other types of interventions, and those that are most immediate and deviant are especially important.

This thought process helps the therapist to anticipate the locus of the patient's derivative responses, and it focuses the listening–formulating process on the unconscious implications of those intervention contexts to which the patient is most likely responding. In complex therapeutic interactions in which there are several important and active adaptation-evoking contexts for the patient, this type of general appraisal is essential lest the therapist become utterly confused. While this evaluation is being made, the therapist should also be attending to the patient's derivative material, attempting to discover which particular intervention context best organizes the encoded implications of the patient's associations. A therapist develops clear hypotheses, but simultaneously remains open to their refutation and to new leads evident in the patient's associations.

For those readers who are already sensing encoded and disguised meaning in the patient's associations, it may be noted that the concern expressed toward the end of this excerpt about ground-rule infringements provides an encoded validation of the importance of the framework of this therapy for this particular patient. Other derivative implications of these associations will not be pursued here for the moment.

Exercise 5.2

The patient is a young man being seen by a female therapist in once-weekly psychotherapy. He had been referred to her by a male therapist, a Mr. Jackson, who was seeing both him and his wife individually at a clinic. He had also been involved in group therapy with the same therapist at the clinic along with his wife and other friends. He was referred to his present therapist when his individual treatment deteriorated, and he initially saw her at the clinic as well, where he was paying a low fee. The male therapist continued to see the patient's wife for individual treatment. Eventually, the female therapist transferred the patient to her private office and raised his fee to her usual one. Aside from this change, the ground rules during his sessions with her were secured.

Two weeks prior to the hour we are about to consider, the patient had cancelled his session in order to go on vacation. In accordance with the prevailing ground rules, he was responsible for the fee for that hour. While away, he met someone who knew the therapist, and this individual told the patient about the therapist's husband and child.

During the session a week prior to the current one, despite a direct representation of the break in the therapist's anonymity and clear derivative material, the therapist had been entirely silent. On the way to the session to be partially excerpted, she and the patient met unexpectedly on the street. They had greeted each other and walked together for about one block before they came to the therapist's office. Upon reaching the door, the therapist put her key in the lock, but was unable to turn it. She turned to the patient and asked him, "How good are you with keys?" As she was attempting to pull the key out in order to hand it to the patient, the lock turned and the two went into her waiting room. Here is the beginning of the session that followed:

> *Patient:* I hope you won't be silent again today. When I was away with my wife, I couldn't get close to her because there were too many people around. I withdraw because she comes on too strong. She acknowledged that she's pressing too hard these days. When I was in treatment with Mr. Jackson [the male therapist who treated both the patient and his wife], he told us that we ought to get divorced, but now I don't think he's right. I think he had a thing for my wife. Seeing you on the street was strange. I was surprised when you talked to me. When I was on vacation, Arlene [a friend and a member of the same former therapy group] tried to seduce me by stroking my arm. I knew it wasn't right and that she shouldn't have done it, but I didn't do much about it.

First, identify any indicators evident in this material. Be sure to classify them as to type and strength. Next, name all known adaptive contexts in evidence before the session in the therapist's consultation room. In doing so, classify the type of intervention context and its strength. Following this, specify those adaptive contexts that are manifestly represented in the patient's material, once again indicating their type and evocative power. Finally, suggest which adaptive context appears to be most powerful for this session, and if possible, suggest whether the patient's derivatives seem to be organized around that particular context. Do this exercise slowly, rereading the material if necessary. (Ideally, however, one should read the material once and proceed to evaluate it from there.)

_____

_____

_____

_____

_____

_____

_____

_____

_____

_____

_____

_____

Answer

Turning first to the patient-indicators, they are:

1. The patient's vacation two weeks prior to the session (a gross behavioral resistance; strong)

2. The patient's inability to get close to his wife (an interpersonal disturbance; moderate).

3. The patient's acceptance of a seductive overture by a woman other than his wife (an interpersonal disturbance with a strong interactional foundation; moderate).

4. The patient's accidental meeting with the therapist before the session began (an inadvertent participation by the therapist in an alteration of the ideal frame; strong).

In the immediate session, then, there are only moderate patient-indicators. Once again, the therapist-indicators, as constituted by a highly traumatic intervention context, appears to be for the moment the most powerful cause of a need within the patient for intervention (see following).

There are of course many major background adaptive contexts in this particular excerpt:

1. The sessions in the prior clinic, some of which were conducted by the present therapist (multiple frame deviations; strong).

2. The specified low fee in the clinic (frame deviation; strong).

3. The use of group therapy (a deviation from the ideal frame from the one-to-one relationship, and from total privacy and confidentiality; strong).

4. The presence of personal friends and the patient's wife in the group (a framework deviation that violates the confidentiality, privacy, and one-to-one relationship of the ideal frame, as well as the therapist's anonymity and the patient's own need for similar therapeutic anonymity; strong).

5. The fact that the same therapist saw both the patient and his wife (a frame deviation that modifies the one-to-one relationship, privacy, and the need for anonymity and a relatively exclusive personal relationship with the therapist; strong).

6. The referral to the present therapist (a frame *rectification* in that it provided the patient with his own therapist and corrected an existing deviation in the prior therapy; moderate).

The reader may be questioning this list, given that all of the intervention contexts indicated took place *before* the shift from the clinic to the therapist's private office. But even though the present therapist was not directly involved in some of these deviations, her presence as a therapist in the clinic will result in the patient's unconsciously perceiving her as partly responsible for their existence and implications. It is important under such circumstances that the therapist recognize her responsibility for these contexts and not assume that the patient's references to them concern other clinic personnel—such as the male therapist.

Of particular note beyond these major breaks in the frame (of which the therapy group and sharing the same therapist with the wife are perhaps the most powerful) is the intervention made by the male therapist: his having referred this patient to the present therapist. The present therapist's participation in this corrective—a rectification of the frame, an important class of intervention—is highly positive and constructive; efforts of this kind lead to unconscious positive introjects of the therapist and to highly constructive therapeutic work.

Shifting now to information regarding the hour under study, we may identify the following additional intervention contexts involving the therapist's private office:

1. The ongoing relatively secure or ideal frame, including the therapist's request for her regular fee (further framework rectification efforts; strong).

2. The therapist's maintenance of the patient's responsibility for the fee for his missed session (maintaining the secure or ideal frame; strong).

3. The personal information that this patient had learned about the therapist (a ground-rule deviation that modifies the therapist's anonymity; strong).

4. The therapist's silence in the previous hour (in this instance constituting an erroneous silence or missed intervention; moderate to strong).

5. The meeting in the street (an alteration in the ideal frame—the interaction between the patient and therapist should take place only in the therapist's waiting room and especially in the therapist's consultation room; moderate).

6. The therapist's query of the patient at the door (a modification of the ground rule of therapeutic neutrality and of the rule regarding the locale of the therapist-patient interaction; strong).

All of these intervention contexts existed prior to the patient's associations in the hour at hand. It is quite surprising to realize, upon study, how many intervention contexts may be generated before a first consultation and sometimes between sessions. These contexts usually involve frame deviations and are therefore quite important. Often, they will not be manifestly represented in the material from the patient in the hour that follows, though, as a rule, there will be some measure of derivative representation (see Chapter 6).

The institution of a secure frame for this private psychotherapy rectified many of the deviations of the prior treatment in the clinic setting. Framework-rectification intervention is an important therapeutic effort that puts to right a deviant adaptive context. Similarly, the therapist's adherence to the ground rule of the patient's responsibility for missed sessions is a framework-maintenance intervention. This is another critical therapeutic effort, which is made in response to a patient's pressures to deviate or to the patient's actual unilateral alterations in the ideal frame.

As for the modification in the therapist's relative anonymity, even though the therapist herself was not the source of the personal information obtained by the patient, the revelations constitute an important intervention context that will require interpretive response. Clearly, this is an unrectifiable framework deviation, an alteration in the ideal frame that cannot be undone or corrected. Thus, the therapist can only interpret and make certain that she will not in any fashion add to the break in anonymity. Nevertheless, under such conditions, highly effective therapeutic work can be carried out. The patient will express selective encoded perceptions in light of the knowledge about the therapist that has been revealed. Quite unfortunately, in the previous hour, despite the presence of strong derivatives in response to this particular intervention context, the therapist had shied away from the patient's material and maintained an erroneous silence.

An accidental meeting in the street, although it alters the ideal frame, can also be subjected to interpretive response based on the patient's derivative material. The therapist must be comfortable with such incidents, though in this case, the therapist would have been well advised to simply greet the patient and not engage in any conversation as they walked together on the street. Further, the therapist's question of the patient at the door and her appeal to him for help in opening up her office (in creating the therapeutic setting) are major deviations that violate important canons of the psychotherapeutic relationship, including the therapist's basic responsibility to establish and create the fixed setting of the treatment experience. Such comments are typically countertransference-based (mad) and powerfully evocative of derivative perceptions and other (often adverse) reactions in patients.

Turning now to the session that has been summarized in part, the following are the adaptation-evoking contexts that are represented manifestly in the patient's material:

1. The therapist's silence in the previous hour (silence as an erroneous intervention; moderate to strong).

2. The previous therapist and treatment experience, in which the therapist played a peripheral role (implies breaks in the frame and nonneutral interventions; strong).

3. The therapist's inadvertent meeting with the patient on the street (a frame deviation which modifies the ideal ground rule specifying the locus of interaction between the patient and therapist as the therapist's office; strong).

4. The therapist's comment to the patient at the door (frame deviation that modifies the locus of the therapeutic interaction, the therapist's neutrality, and her responsibility to establish the therapeutic setting before the beginning of the patient's hour; strong).

For this hour, it seems clear that the most powerful intervention context is the therapist's question regarding help with the key. The reader who wishes to anticipate later work with the derivative complex, and especially with encoded perceptions, may wish to identify some prominent selected perceptions of the therapist registered unconsciously by the patient in light of this intervention. Certainly, the most evident encoded representations involve the patient's wife "coming on too strong," the male therapist's having a thing for (i.e., wanting to seduce) the patient's wife, and the seductive overture by Arlene, the former group member from the clinic. These encoded images clearly and validly portray the high seductive aspects of the therapist's deviant intervention, and they reflect both the provocative qualities of the stimulus and the patient's own unconscious sexual fantasies, memories, and needs.

Of note here, too, is the allusion to a nonneutral intervention by a previous therapist—the suggestion that the patient and his wife get a divorce. It is to be stressed that such allusions to interventions made by other therapists almost always represent in encoded or derivative form an intervention made by the present therapist—a topic to which we will turn in the following chapter. The therapist should not simply accept this manifest material as such and begin to wonder about the problems of the other therapist; instead, all such allusions should be examined as likely encoded representations of a deviant intervention by the present therapist.

We have studied two sessions with a multiplicity of background and immediately active intervention contexts. Except for private practice—secure-frame psychotherapy—it is not uncommon to experience the type of clinical situations illustrated. But they are not limited to clinic settings; they also occur in the private practice of therapists who handle the ground rules of psychotherapy rather loosely. In order to avoid sessions of this kind, the therapist must identify a relative hierarchy of adaptation-evoking contexts, concentrating on those interventions most likely to organize the patient's derivative material. As already noted, the most powerful ground-rule deviations will usually stand in such a hierarchy, whereas erroneous attempts at interpretation will stand toward the bottom.

Unquestionably, a great deal of patience and practice is required to suitably assign each segment of associations from the patient to one of the three major categories of meaning and function: indicators, adaptive contexts, and derivative complex. But this sorting-out process is the only means by which a therapist can truly comprehend and formulate the massive amount of material from any given patient in a particular hour. On the other hand, the cognitive process by which we (1) identify manifest allusions to patient-indicators, (2) name existing background and active adaptive contexts, and (3) identify manifest representations of these contexts in the patient's material is relatively easy to master, if cumbersome to put into practice. The search for derivative representations and encoded perceptions in the patient's material is somewhat more complicated and involves intuitive capacities.

6
Adaptive Contexts:
Derivative Representations

When an adaptive context is directly mentioned in the patient's associations, the therapist can generally assume that on an unconscious level, the patient wishes to express himself or herself in meaningful fashion. There are many sessions, however, in which direct allusions to intervention contexts do *not* appear. In these hours, it is incumbent upon the therapist to carefully go over in his or her mind all known intervention contexts, and to actively search for derivative or encoded representations—portrayals—of these contexts in the patient's material. If the material should also contain a meaningful derivative complex and indicators—a need for intervention—the therapist would begin the intervention with the encoded representation of the relevant adaptation-evoking context.

COMMUNICATIVE RESISTANCE

A patient's failure to directly represent an activated adaptive context that is being worked over unconsciously by way of derivative expressions is a sign of *communicative resistance*. This kind of resistance is usually an interactional product to which the therapist has contributed significantly. Typically, the patient has unconsciously perceived an error on the part of the therapist and is fearful of directly representing the intervention context that is stimulating his or her adaptive and maladaptive responses. This defensive need is designed (1) to spare the therapist a direct and painful confrontation with a blatant expression of his or her own madness, and (2) to protect the patient from his or her anxiety in response to the threatening unconscious perceptions of the therapist. Through displacement and symbolization, the patient creates a *compromised communication* that satisfies both the need for expression and the need for defense. In intervening, the therapist must accept and respect this need for defense, calling the patient's attention to the derivative representation, rather than jumping what has been termed the *denial barrier* and alluding directly to the unmentioned adaptive context. This principle is followed mainly because patients will tend to deny the importance of a context that they have not yet represented manifestly themselves, particularly if the therapist attempts deliberately to force that context into the patient's awareness.

To be useful, a derivative representation of an adaptive context must be a close derivative and easily decoded. Thus, it must share with the actual prior intervention of the therapist one or more strong and common themes. Although a therapist should be attending to any derivative portrayal of an intervention context, those that are thinly disguised are most useful for formulating and intervening.

Here again, one is always placing communicative considerations above all else when formulating. If the therapist is aware of an important deviant adaptive context, for example, he or she should be listening for an allusion to it in the patient's associations and determining either the extent of a direct reference or the recognizability of a disguised representation. The initial emphasis must be on portrayal and representation rather than on meaning. The portrayal itself will *include* meaning and implication. The first issue, therefore, involves the extent to which the portrayal—an encoded description of the context—can be readily recognized by both participants to treatment.

To illustrate this point before turning to specific clinical material, let us suppose that a therapist has inadvertently extended a session by 15 minutes. If a patient talks in the following session about a long trip home, the derivative representation is moderate to weak. If he tells a story about having visited his parents' house, there is no representation of the intervention context at all. On the other hand, were the patient to allude to his having been forced to sit in his boss's office for an extra hour after a difficult conference, the therapist would have a fairly close encoded representation of the intervention context, as he would, if the patient were to mention—as in a previous illustration—a dream about being locked in a bedroom where something seductive or threatening is going on. Even closer would be an allusion to a neighbor who had cornered the patient after everyone else had left her party and kept him there for an extra 15 minutes. A derivative that would be moderately distant from the adaptive context and yet move toward the themes involved might entail a comment by the patient that the therapist's office seemed stuffy and close that day.

Perhaps the most important means by which the therapist recognizes an encoded portrayal of an intervention context is the prior assessment of the major unconscious implications of that context. The better these implications are known and understood, the more readily the therapist will be able to pick up a disguised allusion to them.

Because an encoded representation of an intervention context implies an interactional need for defense, it follows that the patient will often resort to this type of portrayal in response to highly traumatic and threatening interventions by the therapist. This particular defense is facilitated when the intervention has taken place in a prior session or between sessions. Patients find it more difficult to utilize this type of repression and encoding when the traumatic intervention is immediate to the hour at hand. Thus, a therapist may expect a patient to portray an intervention context in derivative form when he or she has modified the frame in a prior session, especially when the deviation is on some level pathologically gratifying to the patient. As illustrated by the vignette described at the end of the previous chapter, deviations that take place just before sessions may also be indirectly represented. Of course, there are also exceptions to this trend.

In general, interventions that are portrayed in derivative rather than direct fashion include reductions in the patient's fee, excusing the patient for responsibility for missed sessions, certain gratifying self-revelations, the use of non-neutral interventions, and pathologically gratifying breaks in confidentiality, such as completing an insurance form. But virtually any adaptation-evoking context may be represented indirectly in a particular hour, depending on the balance between the patient's need to communicate meaningfully in order to adaptively obtain a much-needed interpretation or rectification from the therapist and the patient's wish to maintain pathological gratification and communicative defenses.

DERIVATIVE ADAPTIVE CONTEXTS: EXERCISES

Exercise 6.1a

The patient is a male adolescent in twice-weekly psychotherapy with a male therapist. In the previous session, the therapist had rectified the ground rule regarding the patient's responsibility for missed sessions. Until that point in the treatment, it was the therapist's policy to not charge for sessions that a patient cancelled with at least 24 hours' notice. After several absences for which the patient was not charged, the material in his sessions permitted an interpretation of his unconscious perceptions of the therapist based on this deviant ground rule. The images had centered on an incident in which the patient had permitted himself to be fondled by an older man instead of pulling away from this obviously homosexual and disturbed individual. There were also associations to a customer whom his father had quite inappropriately allowed to escape payment for goods received. At a point where the patient stressed the inappropriateness of his father's attitude in the last situation and also alluded directly to an hour for which he had not been charged, the therapist was able to both rectify this ground rule (establishing full responsibility for all sessions) and to interpret the patient's selected encoded perceptions (which concentrated on the therapist's latent homosexuality and masochism—the unconscious wishes to overgratify and to be exploited).

Once this ground rule had been rectified, the framework of this psychotherapy was almost entirely secure—the only flaw being that because the patient was still in high school and had only a part-time job, his father was paying three-quarters of the fee for treatment.

The session that followed the rectification began with a rather extended description of an examination the patient was about to take in school and his concerns as to whether he would pass or fail. His associations then shifted as follows:

> *Patient:*   My father's an odd guy. When I was a kid, I would take money from his wallet. I was sure he knew what I was doing and looked away. I thought of it because just two weeks ago I lifted a 20-dollar bill. I realize now that it's wrong and crazy. Hell, I'm earning money of my own now. I should only have what I can afford to pay for with my own bucks. Another thing I hate about him is the way he snoops around the house. It's a lot more peaceful when he isn't home.

We will begin our listening exercise again by identifying the indicators both in the introduction to this hour and in the session itself: Specify the type of indicator and its power. Next, name all known intervention contexts that exist prior to this session. Classify them as to type and strength. For the session itself, state first whether there are any adaptive contexts to which the patient is alluding manifestly. If they are present, name and classify them. Next, attempt to identify any existing intervention contexts that are portrayed in disguised and encoded form in this material. For the moment, make no attempt to propose a meaning, but concentrate instead on representation and portrayal. Review the known intervention contexts, focus on those that are most recent, and attempt to identify close or good encoded representations of at least three contexts:

_____

_____

_____

_____

_____

_____

_____

_____

_____

_____

_____

_____

_____

_____

_____

_____

_____

_____

_____
_____
_____
_____
_____
_____
_____
_____
_____
_____

Answer

The following indicators are in evidence in this material:

1. The patient's request for treatment even though he is unable to pay the entire fee (a necessary gross behavioral resistance—frame deviation that is both an indicator and a major adaptive context once the therapist accepts the patient into therapy; strong).

2. The patient's stealing from his father when he was younger (a symptomatic act and interpersonal difficulty; moderate to strong).

3. The patient's recent act of stealing $20 from his father's wallet (see #2).

Notice that an indicator may involve an old symptom that is referred to in a particular hour. When this type of therapeutic context emerges in a patient's associations, it is likely that it can be given unconscious meaning and understood in terms of a currently active intervention context and derivative complex (mainly encoded perceptions of the therapist). An earlier interpersonal or symptomatic disturbance is generally reported in a particular hour when an activated intervention context has prompted an adaptive or communicative response in the patient that in some way unconsciously relates to the past event. In this case, the material introduces an additional factor—the recent repetition of the symptom, which constitutes a second indicator, similarly stimulated in important ways by current intervention contexts within the therapeutic interaction. This material demonstrates the manner in which the therapist's interventions and the ongoing treatment interaction contribute to a symptom and/or interpersonal disturbance within a patient. It is evident here that the patient's stealing has something to do with the therapist's ground rule regarding responsibility for sessions. We will give further consideration to this interplay toward the end of this discussion.

Also present in this material is a symptomatic improvement—the patient's determination to stop stealing from his father. Although in a strict sense, this is not a reflection of pathology and a patient-indicator, it does represent an advancement in functioning (the determination itself is promising; of course, enforcing it over the ensuing months would be more definitive) and should be treated as a therapeutic context. When positive changes in symptoms, attitudes, and behavior occur, it is essential that a therapist analyze the situation in order to determine the intervention contexts that help to account for the positive and constructive change and to identify the encoded derivatives that explain the unconscious basis for improvement. It is only when positive symptomatic change follows a rectification of the frame or a validated interpretation that we may conclude that the enhancement of the patient's functioning is based on underlying constructive unconscious alterations. Because symptom alleviation may be based on any number of factors, many of them quite pathological, an analysis of this kind is the only means by which a therapist can be assured of the presence of true adaptive insight and genuine growth.

There is support in this material for the position that the patient's change in attitude is indeed constructive and based on insight into unconscious factors and on the establishment of a sound holding relationship. This emerges when the patient proposes that he should have only what he can afford on his own. We have here a model of rectification that pertains, as we will see, to the remaining deviation—the fact that the father pays for two-thirds of the treatment. Because this model is disguised and encoded—outside of the direct awareness of the patient—it is a sign of a genuine change in attitude in the patient. As a rule, patients tend to express highly valid and genuine insights and meanings on the unconscious or encoded level of expression.

Turning now to the background intervention contexts, the following may be identified:

1. The initial deviant ground rule that the patient was not responsible for sessions cancelled with 24 hours notice (a ground-rule alteration of the patient's full responsibility for each hour that the therapist attends; strong).

2. The shift to the patient's full responsibility for all sessions (a rectification of a deviant frame; strong).

3. The therapist's intervention concerning the patient's selected unconscious perceptions of the implications communicated by the original deviant adaptive context (a true interpretive intervention—which received additional derivative validation not recorded here; moderate to strong).

4. The payment of two-thirds of the therapist's fee by the patient's father (a deviant intervention context that modifies the tenet of the patient's sole and full responsibility for all sessions; moderate).

The deviant acceptance of part of the fee from the patient's father is rated moderate because of several qualifying considerations. First, we may recall that this young man had a job that would cover the cost of one session per week. Thus, as the patient himself hinted at or proposed in derivative form through his comment that he should have only what he could afford, it appears that the ideal frame for his psychotherapy would entail the use of a single weekly session that he could afford, rather than a twice-weekly treatment for which the father assumed partial responsibility. Were the patient unable to work because of school pressures and economic circumstances, it would of course be necessary for the father to pay for his treatment, and there would be little consequence as to whether the patient had two sessions a week rather than one. This kind of third-party payment would in any case be different from payment by an insurance company, because no information whatsoever should be released to the parent about the treatment. Under such conditions, the deviant context would have only a moderate influence on the treatment situation; the realities of this necessity would minimize its pathogenic influence on the patient. The context would, however, serve from time to time as an active stimulus for the patient's direct and derivative responses—perhaps at time of payment (which should be made with the patient's own check). In most instances, this material would be interpretable and would lend itself to working through. Nevertheless, the therapist would recognize the deviation as unrectifiable (uncorrectable), and it would have a small but lasting influence on the course and outcome of the treatment process.

Similarly, patients who must of necessity be seen in low-fee clinics do suffer to some degree because of the deviations involved. They show a certain measure of unmodifiable communicative resistances. Again, the necessity of the deviant conditions lends both conscious and unconscious perspective on them, so their influence is somewhat modified. In private practice, however, the use of an absolutely unnecessary deviation will *lack* such conditional justification; under such circumstances, a deviant context will have compelling consequences, and relatively fixed ones, unless subjected to rectification—to the greatest extent feasible—and interpretation as well.

If the subject of this exercise were in once-weekly psychotherapy and fully responsible on his own for his sessions, we would have an example of an ideal frame. Under these conditions, the critical intervention contexts would involve the dangerous qualities of the highly reliable and necessary optimal ground rules. Depending on the patient's sensitivities and pathology, he would feel especially endangered by one or more of these basic propositions. Additional critical intervention contexts would arise when the patient attempted to have the therapist modify a ground rule (such as requesting a change in hour or the forgiveness of a fee under special circumstances). Were the therapist to respond by maintaining the frame, that intervention would become the critical adaptive context for the patient's subsequent material.

In general, initial clinical studies indicate that among the most critical ground rules in secure-frame psychotherapy are those rules surrounding full responsibility for sessions with respect to time, place, and fee and those related to placement on the couch, total privacy, and confidentiality. These elements are essential to the basic trust and hold that a therapist should ideally offer to a patient, but each will create a measure of danger for the patient as well. For example, the elements of full responsibility for the sessions create claustrophobic and paranoid anxieties because of the dangers involved in the sense of entrapment conveyed by these particular ground rules.

In the situation that actually exists in this treatment, it is likely that the patient will react to the relatively secure frame from time to time by either attacking (trying to change) or becoming disturbed by one of the basic components of this ground-rule constellation. Nonetheless, the presence of the father as a third-party payer will remain one of the most prominent frame-related adaptive contexts with which the patient will be concerned. Work with issues related to this particular ground rule would prove extremely meaningful and helpful for the patient. The eventual rectification of the existing deviation would be especially salutory. Not only would the patient experience positive introjects of the therapist in the course of this rectification, but highly meaningful interpretive work would undoubtedly prove feasible around the patient's selected unconscious perceptions of the therapist in light of his participation in this deviation.

Turning now to the session itself, the following adaptive contexts are represented in derivative form:

1. The deviant ground rule specifying that the patient be forgiven the fee for a session if he gives 24 hours' notice. The encoded representation lies in the patient's manifest description of how his father let his son steal from him, take money from his wallet—choosing to look away rather than recognize that the theft was going on. The themes shared by the manifest and latent content involve money, deprivation (of the parent and therefore of the therapist), and denial (the father's looking away connects to the therapist's failure to realize the disruptive qualities of the deviant adaptive context). Because of the central shared theme of inappropriately (and dishonestly) depriving of money someone who permits the theft to occur, we would consider this particular representational portrayal to be relatively strong and clear (a close derivative representation). Of course, the patient's report that he had recently stolen $20 from his father is another encoded representation of the initial ground rule regarding exceptions to the patient's financial responsibility for his hours.

2. The second encoded representation portrays the therapist's rectification—his introduction of the full-responsibility tenet. This rectification is portrayed in derivative fashion by two communications from the patient: (1) that he had decided to stop stealing from his father, and (2) that he should have only what he could afford to pay for on his own. The decision to stop stealing is a close derivative representation of the rectification measure. Because the shared themes of taking money inappropriately from someone else and stopping this practice are prominent elements of the rectification, this portrayal is an exceedingly good derivative representation of the corrective intervention context.

The second portrayal of this context involves the themes of responsibility and money (it also includes a number of other themes that are unrelated to the rectifying intervention context). The only clear theme shared by this segment of the manifest material and the rectification that it represents through displacement and symbolization is that of money. Because of this, it is a remote or weak derivative representation, one that would not readily facilitate intervention.

Finally, as has already been mentioned, this same derivative element (segment of associations) simultaneously through condensation contains within it a model of rectification. It suggests a way to secure the frame with respect to the deviant ground rule of permitting a third party to pay for part of this psychotherapy. This is an excellent example of an associational element serving two major communicative functions. It is a reminder that rich imagery should be examined for all three communicative components—indicators, representations of adaptive contexts, and derivative, perceptive, and other meanings.

3. The third adaptive context portrayed in encoded fashion in this material involves the therapist's acceptance of two-thirds of the patient's fee from his father. This is also represented through condensation in the patient's allusion that he should have only as much as he can afford and in his comment about his father's prying when in the house with the patient. Here, the first portrayal contains in its manifest elements several themes that it shares with the latent intervention context it portrays—being unable to afford something, money, and taking full responsibility for what one has. This is a moderately strong and clear derivative representation that simultaneously, as noted, contains an unconsciously proposed model of rectification—a correction of the deviant arrangement.

In similar fashion, the allusion to a sense of disturbance and prying when the patient's father is with him in their house portrays in somewhat more remote fashion the adaptive context of the father's financial responsibility for a major portion of this patient's treatment. Here the theme shared by the manifest and latent content (the surface associations and the represented intervention context that is latent in them) are those of father's presence in an enclosed space and the sense of intrusion or prying. Here, too, there is a model of rectification: The patient alludes to the situation being far more peaceful when the father is not in the house.

Exercise 6.1b

Most critical to the identification of encoded portrayals of an adaptive context is an understanding of the implications involved. For this reason, and in anticipation of the exercises in the next chapter, we may attempt here to identify the implied meanings contained in these encoded representations. Essential to this effort is the identification of the themes that link manifest and latent contents, the surface associations, and the underlying and selectively represented intervention contexts. The reader should carry out this exercise for each of the three intervention contexts that we have identified as represented in encoded fashion in this material: (1) the deviant ground rules, (2) the corrected ground rules, and (3) the acceptance of part of the fee from the father.

_____

_____

_____

_____

_____

_____

_____

_____

_____

_____

_____

_____

_____
_____
_____
_____
_____
_____
_____
_____
_____
_____
_____
_____
_____
_____
_____
_____
_____
_____
_____
_____
_____
_____
_____
_____

Answer

Whereas conscious communications are not infrequently distorted and unreliable, unconscious expressions—those that are automatically communicated
outside of awareness and in disguised and encoded form—tend to be surprisingly perceptive and valid. It is possible to develop an unconscious misprecep-
tion, but these are quite rare.

Despite the fact that the patient's pathology is the single most important
determinant of his or her unconscious selection of a perceived meaning of an
adaptive context, these indirectly communicated implications prove to be quite
reliable and sensitive. It is largely because of this finding that the patient's

derivative communications may be used as one of the most important resources available to the therapist in the treatment interaction. A therapist should take quite seriously each encoded representation and disguised meaning assigned to a particular intervention context, and should accept it as meaningful and valid until absolutely proven otherwise. Often, careful self-analysis and silent exploration of the implications of an intervention context will demonstrate the validity of what the patient has selectively perceived and then communicated in encoded form.

In the present vignette, the first representations involve the therapist's ground rule that permitted the patient to cancel certain sessions without paying a fee. The first encoded representation and perception (in this instance both apply—portrayal and expression of meaning) is the patient's statement that his father let him steal from him. In searching for decoded meaning, we are attempting to undo the unconscious mechanisms of disguise—mainly displacement and symbolization (a representation of one meaning by another). We already know that the displacement is virtually always from the therapist onto someone else. Thus, a meaningful derivative alludes to someone other than the therapist and portrays his or her image through this other person or event. It follows that the decoding of derivative meaning therefore comes down to one critical and already identified exercise: identifying the particular theme that links the manifest with the latent content (note again that the latter always involves an intervention by the therapist). Because most images have a multiplicity of meaning at a variety of levels, it is a matter of clinical sensitivity and skill to be able to select the most cogent *linking themes* in each segment of associations. Of course, the more familiar a therapist is with the implications of an intervention context, the easier this task is made. The adaptive context remains the most important guide to the selection of bridging themes (it is, after all, the context itself that has stimulated the disguise pertinent to these bridges).

In the first segment of this particular patient's associations, we can identify three themes that link the manifest communication to the intervention context with which it deals: (1) The theme of a parental or authority figure links the therapist to the patient's father (doing so with the implication that the therapist is in some way behaving in a manner that is *similar to* the patient's father—i.e., this is an encoded *nontransference* communication; it records a valid perception). (2) The theme of stealing links the conscious image of a theft to the unconscious implication that the therapist has been stolen from, deprived of money that is his due. (In this instance, the dishonest quality may be an exaggeration of a valid perception; such exaggerations, which follow initial unconsciously registered valid selective encoded perceptions, do fall into the realm of transference.) (3) The theme of someone who is permitting the stealing to occur is one of sanction, reflecting the fact that the therapist has established a ground rule enabling the patient to deprive him of money which is his due. (This, too, is a selective encoded perception that has considerable validity and so falls mainly into the realm of nontransference.)

The themes of taking money from his father's wallet and of the father looking away basically reinforce the formulations already made. This applies as well to the $20 that the patient had taken from his father recently. For the purposes of the present exercise, we will not develop further formulations in this area.

The second adaptive context is that of the therapist's rectification of the deviant ground rule. Here, the main representation involves the patient's decision to stop stealing from his father. The theme that links the manifest with the latent content is that of stopping a practice of thievery. (Remember that latent content virtually always alludes to an intervention of the therapist; it is this particular type of danger situation or communication-perception that the patient encodes and to which he or she assigns disguised meaning.) Here, the first link lies in the word "stopping," which bridges the surface reference (stopping thievery in the patient's relationship with his father) to the latent level (involving a model of rectification for the therapist in the psychotherapeutic relationship). The latent or basic raw image involves the cessation of a dishonest practice. To state this as a translation from the manifest to latent content, the patient is encoding his perception that the therapist had stopped allowing him to steal from him.

The second link lies in the word "thievery," manifestly described in the relationship with the father and latently in the one with the therapist. Although the theme of stealing is readily recognized, the main problem in listening would lie in identifying just how this word relates to the interventions of the therapist. One would begin decoding by testing the image as a possible encoded perception of the therapist: How is the therapist perceived to be stealing from the patient? What would lead the patient to perceive the therapist as a thief? Then one might try the idea that the therapist is somehow perceived as the *object* of a theft, which he is permitting (as the young man's father permitted his stealing from his wallet). What intervention context could be creating that impression? This question would be clarified and shaped by additional derivatives that point toward the same intervention context. If the therapist had done the preliminary work of thinking out the implications of his interventions, he would eventually hypothesize that the patient was encoding perceptions about the therapist's policy of nonpayment for missed sessions.

This second adaptive context is more remotely represented in the patient's comment about properly having only what he can afford with his own money. Here the shared theme that links the surface and the depths is one of taking responsibility rather than being inappropriately supported by others. Although this is a rather heavily encoded derivative, it does have a measure of meaning.

Through condensation, this same communication also represents the deviant intervention context that still exists in this psychotherapy—the therapist's acceptance of three-quarters of the patient's fee from the patient's father. (It is important to stress that the problem for the patient is an *adaptive* one. It is the therapist's participation in the situation as it evokes responses in the patient, that we are interested in.) The theme that links the surface with the depths is being able to afford something and paying for it with money. In the main, this particular communication is the patient's *reaction* to his unconscious perceptions of the implications of the fee arrangement. This reaction takes the form of a disguised model of rectification. The unconscious or raw (decoded) message is to the effect that the patient should have only those sessions that he can afford with his own resources.

The manifest associations regarding the father's prying and the sense of disturbance when he is present in the house contains themes that link the surface of these associations with derivative perceptions of the implications of the father's participation in the payment of the fee as accepted by the therapist. The shared themes are prying and the father's presence in a contained space. The stress is on the disturbance caused by the father's presence in the house, but the material lacks the important theme of the father being in a space where he does not belong. This theme did indeed appear later in the session when the patient spoke of resenting his father's barging into his bedroom even though the door was closed.

At times, then, it takes several manifest sequences to fully portray the patient's full range of encoded perceptions of a particular intervention context. The most common means by which this is done involves the patient's *shift from one narrative or image to another*—now a dream, next a movie, next an incident from the previous week, next a memory, and the like. When a patient unconsciously wishes to convey meaning, each of these storied segments will reveal another encoded dimension of the perceived implications of an adaptive context. It is for this reason, then, that the therapist's *silence* is the most important means by which he or she can facilitate a full range of communicative expression from the patient.

Sometimes, when a therapist has completed an evaluation of the implications of a given intervention context, the patient will represent in encoded fashion meanings that had been overlooked or do not seem to fit. A patient's encoded material does correspond more often than not to the implications that the therapist has been able to consciously identify. But when derivative implications do not seem to match up with those adaptive contexts that a therapist has already recognized, it is extremely important to allow the derivatives to shape the search for one or more missing intervention contexts.

Exercise 6.2a

This patient is a young married woman who had been hospitalized for a severe depressive episode. She has one child. She was seen in psychotherapy on a three times weekly basis in the office of her male therapist, which was located on the in-patient service ward. Ancillary personnel such as nurses and occupational therapists were also in contact with the patient. Early in the week of the session to be described, the patient had been tested psychologically.

The hour in question took place one evening after the patient had been in the hospital for about a month. Earlier that afternoon, the patient's husband had spoken to the therapist in the hall, requesting that his wife be permitted to leave the ward on a pass. The therapist had consented to this request. Sometime later, the therapist passed the cooking area on the ward and found the patient showing other staff members a cake that she had just baked. When the patient sliced up the cake, she offered a piece to the therapist, who willingly accepted her offer and, with some pleasure, ate the cake in her presence. The therapist was then 15 minutes late for her session, having been involved in an emergency situation on another ward.

> *Patient:*   I'm glad you came. I'm tired of listening to that other patient; it's not good listening to others. My husband is too intrusive on the ward; I don't want him to visit me more than once a week. He doesn't let me think for myself. My problem is that I let him push me around. Alice is out on pass and I miss her. When I was first married, I baked cakes and cookies and things. I enjoyed preparing food for my husband, but then all I got back was being treated like a doormat. He was so greedy that he would eat the children's cookies and leave nothing for them. Then he would disappear somewhere and not come home for two nights.

Once again, begin by identifying and classifying all of the indicators in this material. Next, state the known intervention contexts as they existed prior to this session. Classify each context and suggest its strength. Then examine the material for encoded representations of those contexts that are most immediate and pertinent. With each encoded portrayal discovered in the material, indicate whether it is a close and relatively clear representation, or one that is distant and heavily disguised. Select those intervention contexts that you believe to be most powerful and those derivative representations that appear to be most clear, and identify any theme that connects the manifest associations to the latent, raw image of the intervention context. Assign the most essential meanings to these themes as they illustrate the patient's selected unconscious perceptions of the therapist in light of his interventions. Because of the complexity of this particular exercise, it is strongly recommended that the reader proceed step by step. If any of these assignments prove difficult, the text to follow should be consulted for clarification. Once a particular step has been understood, the reader should return to the present exercise and carry it out to completion.

_____

_____

_____

_____

_____

_____

_____

_____

_____

_____

_____

_____

_____

_____

_____

_____

_____

_____

_____

_____

_____

_____

_____

_____

_____

_____

_____

_____

_____

_____

_____

_____

Answer

The indicators in this session include the following:

1. The patient's severe depression (a symptom; strong).

2. The husband's request for a pass for his wife (an impingement on the ground rules of therapy; strong).

3. The patient's offer of a piece of cake to the therapist (a gross behavioral resistance-frame deviation; strong).

4. The indications of problems between the patient and her husband (a symptomatic interpersonal problem; moderate to weak).

The husband's request for a pass for his wife is included as a patient-indicator because the patient may have been involved in this procedure and, if not, because it nonetheless represents a therapeutic need within the patient herself. Beyond this particular issue, the indicators are straightforward.

Turning next to the known intervention contexts, the following appear in the material prior to the hour:

1. The patient's hospitalization, the location of the therapist's office on the ward, and the ancillary personnel (modifications in the ideal frame—deviations in the ideal locale of therapy, the therapist's anonymity, the one-to-one relationship, total privacy, total confidentiality, and the like; strong).

2. The psychological tests and tester (a deviation in the ground rules and a modification of the one-to-one relationship and total confidentiality; strong).

3. The therapist's conversation in the hall with the patient's husband, resulting in the therapist's providing the patient with a pass (a framework deviation that modifies the one-to-one relationship, total privacy, total confidentiality, the therapist's neutrality, and the locale of sessions; strong).

4. The therapist's acceptance of a piece of cake from the patient (a modification of the ground rules involving the principle that the main satisfaction provided the therapist by the patient is the fee; no other direct gratifications are to be obtained from the patient; strong).

5. The therapist's 15-minute lateness for the session (a frame deviation and modification of the therapist's responsibility to be present for each session at the appointed time; strong).

Once again, we are faced with a treatment situation that encompasses several powerful framework-deviation intervention contexts, each with a rather extensive constellation of meanings—though there is considerable overlap between the implications of one deviant adaptive context and another. Blatant breaks of the frame of this kind tend to evoke intense adaptive and communicative responses from patients. They therefore lead to meaningful treatment sessions—but only if the material is properly understood and interpreted, and if the efforts directed toward insight are supplemented with the rectification of those deviations that are possible to correct. Again, both interpretation and rectification are essential; neither sustains the patient without the other.

Hospitalization is a sometimes necessary modification in the ideal frame constituted by private-office psychotherapy. As with a clinic setting, its necessity creates a perspective that renders the deviations involved tolerable and interpretable for the patient. Nevertheless, the deviant conditions that exist in an inpatient setting can and should be minimized in order to provide a patient with the best possible holding environment under the conditions.

The deviant aspects of psychological testing have been overlooked in the psychotherapeutic literature. In private practice, given that the substance of treatment involves the ongoing therapeutic interaction between patient and therapist, there is virtually no justification for it. A well-trained and sensitive therapist should have all of the information he or she needs regarding the patient's diagnosis, dynamics, treatability, and such from the immediate psychotherapeutic experience.

There is a greater measure of uncertainty regarding the utility of psychological testing with a patient who is hospitalized. At times, there may be legal and other procedural needs for these tests, though here, too, they should not be necessary for the therapist who is treating the patient—the diagnosis, prognosis, treatment plan, and so forth should unfold from the therapeutic experience. The potential hazards of this type of deviation should be recognized, however, and at the very least, the use of psychological testing should be restricted to situations where it is of absolute necessity. In particular, it must be borne in mind as a deviant adaptation-evoking context in which the therapist is perceived to have participated.

Well-meaning intentions notwithstanding, there is no place in sound psychotherapy for accepting cake from a patient. This behavior reflects powerful countertransference-based needs in the therapist, which will be selectively but intensely perceived by the patient unconsciously. Such behaviors often shift the mode of cure from insight and holding to action and discharge. A polite refusal is the appropriate intervention under these circumstances; of course, this, too, then becomes an adaptive context—though in the direction of securing rather than breaking the frame.

The therapist should take seriously his or her responsibility to begin each session at the appointed time. Of course, an emergency may arise that delays the start of a particular hour. When this is the case, the therapist should apologize to the patient and then suggest that the session be extended an amount of time equal to the time of the delay. If the patient is unable to stay, or if the schedule of the therapist does not permit this modification (it is quite destructive to disrupt the frame of still another patient), the therapist should propose to make up the time as part of a future hour and do so as quickly as possible. If such an extension proves unfeasible, the fee for the session at hand should be reduced in proportion to the amount of time lost.[1]

Among these contexts, the most powerful are likely to be the sanctioned intrusion of the psychological tests and tester, the conversation with the husband that culminated in writing a pass for the patient, and the therapist's acceptance of the cake (the 15-minute lateness is no small matter, but it was caused by an emergency and would have a less destructive impact than these other deviations). With this in mind, we may now review the session in order to identify which of these contexts is represented in derivative form, the manner in which the representation is portrayed, and the meanings involved—the selected and encoded unconscious perceptions of the therapist in light of the represented interventions. For this exercise, it would be best to consider each association in sequence in order to determine whether it functioned in this manner. If the reader did not approach this part of the assignment given earlier in these terms, he or she might do so in the space already provided before reading on.

The patient's first comment was that she was glad her therapist had come to the session. This particular association is not a derivative; it contains an implication rather than a symbolized meaning. The difference between a true encoded communication and a manifest association that contains an implication is a crucial one. A derivative is a manifest image that contains a theme tying it to a latent image or meaning. An encoded derivative has been created by displacement and symbolization and requires the specific undoing of a disguise in order to discover the raw image from which it has been derived.

---

[1] Recent clarification suggests that the ideal (least deviant) frame management response under these circumstances is to end the session at the regularly scheduled time and to reduce the patient's fee accordingly.

A manifest association that contains an implication has no connection to latent images or meaning. It does not require decoding. It requires only inference making based on its evident manifest content. For example, the statement, "I am glad you came," does contain an implication: It implies that the therapist was late; it may imply that the patient was worried the therapist would not show up for the session at all. It suggests in and of itself that the patient felt relieved when the therapist appeared.

These implications can be pulled directly from the manifest content. They are not *symbolized* by the expression "I'm glad you came." They are *indicated* by it; they are part of what the statement is intended to express consciously. The patient may be unaware of some of the implications the statement may have for herself or the therapist; but they are readily available to her if she chooses to examine the remark. They represent potentially conscious meanings—denotative meanings. Encoded messages, on the other hand, are always unconscious for the patient who expresses them. They are not directly available for examination and immediate understanding unless the patient actually engages in the decoding process.

Furthermore, and this is the most crucial point, the unconscious foundation of madness is not inferential. Madness is based on unconscious perceptions, fantasies, and memories, whose raw images are communicated through *image derivatives*, encoded communications that contain disguised expressions of these unconscious elements. Manifest associations and the implications they contain are not derivatives at all. One might call them a form of communication by inference, or communication by implication.

It should be stated that the process of generating inferences is far easier than the process of decoding. This is especially true for the psychotherapist. The problem lies not only in the complexity of decoding, but also in the fact that the decoding process yields many raw images of the therapist, and these images often embody his or her own madness. Psychotherapists will therefore direct powerful defenses against this type of operation. This is why virtually all of present-day psychotherapy and psychoanalysis is carried out in terms of manifest associations and their evident inferences, rather than through any notable use of the decoding process and an attempt to arrive at unconscious meaning. But the rewards of using the communicative approach are considerable for both patient and therapist, however painful the truths that are discovered in this way—about each party.

Moving on to the next sequence of associations, the allusion to the patient's being tired of listening to another patient appears to represent the adaptive context of the therapist's contact with the patient's husband. It is a derivative portrayal that also serves as a model of rectification. Thus, the raw and dangerous encoded message appears to be that the therapist has inappropriately been listening to someone other than the patient, and that he should grow tired of such practices (and in all likelihood, desist).

In attending to this particular derivative, the therapist might also consider an adaptive context that has not as yet been mentioned (and regarding which we lack sufficient data). The theme of failing to listen should always be evaluated for its use as a derivative that reflects an unconscious perception of the therapist's failure to hear and understand the patient. This failing could have taken the form of an erroneous silence in the prior hour (a missed intervention) or the use of a nonadaptive-context intervention that had failed to truly reflect insight into the patient's material. Because we do not know the therapist's most recent interventions, it is impossible to determine the validity of this hypothesis. It is offered mainly as a model of how listening to manifest material and tapping their possible derivative meanings can lead to the recognition of a previously overlooked intervention context.

Next, the patient states that it is not good to listen to others. Here we have a further representation of the therapist's conversation with the patient's husband in the hallway. This is a moderately disguised representation. The theme of listening to others and the advice not to do so contains a perception of the therapist that is represented through displacement through an allusion to the patient herself. The association also contains a model of rectification through which the patient once more, and this time rather clearly, though on an encoded level, advises the therapist not to pay attention to others—in raw terms, not to listen to her husband. In all, these images expand and validate a number of earlier silent hypotheses and formulations, and provide further clear representations of intervention contexts reflected in the patient's initial associations.

To break down this example in the interest of clarity, the advice that it is not good to listen to others can be seen as a reaction to the patient's perception of the therapist in light of his conversation with her husband. This reaction takes the form of a corrective on the therapist's behavior. Encoded in this association is the raw (disguised) message: *You should not have listened to my husband.* The image of listening as it applies to the husband also touches upon giving the patient a pass on the basis of the discussion with the husband—again, something that the patient has perceived and now advises the therapist not to do.

Next, there is the image of the husband as an intruder, which represents the adaptive context of the *therapist's* acceptance of the husband as an intruder into the patient's treatment and therapeutic space. (Remember that we are concerned here with the interventions of the therapist, and not with indicators or the derivative complex.) The same image undoubtedly represents, however, through condensation, the therapist's acceptance of the piece of cake from the patient—an intrusive contact that extended beyond the usual treatment setting. This derivative portrayal, then, serves as a rather clear and close disguised expression of the adaptive context related to the therapist's conversation with the husband; it is a far more remote representation of the cake-eating context. For both situations, however, the key theme that ties manifest to latent images is that of intrusiveness.

The patient's wish that the husband visit her only once a week is another moderately disguised representation of the contact between the therapist and the husband. Its main function again appears to be that of proposing a corrective model: The husband should not be permitted to intrude into her relationship with the therapist as much as he does.

Having focused on but two of these intervention contexts, let us now add the means by which the associations to this point reflect still a third intervention context—the therapist's recommendation to the patient that she undergo psychological tests. This particular context is represented in distant form almost immediately in the patient's allusion to her attempt to listen to another patient. It is then extended in the patient's comment that it is not good to listen to others. Here, the connecting link between manifest and latent content is the presence of others. Contained in this association is a further model of or directive toward rectification: *You (the therapist) should not have proposed the psychological tests, nor should you have need to hear the report from the psychologist who did the testing.*

Next, of course, the husband-as-intruder is a disguised portrayal of the tester-as-intruder (the psychologist was a man). The wish that the husband would visit less often is a further directive toward rectification—the psychologist should be given less of an opportunity to see the patient.

In addition, the allusion to the other patient, the listening to others, and the intrusive husband are all very broad and general representations of the basic deviations of this particular hospital treatment setting and therapeutic experience. By and large, we will not attempt to trace out the representations of these background adaptive contexts, but will continue to focus on the major specific adaptive contexts that stimulated the material in this hour—the psychological tests, the therapist's contact with the patient's husband, the therapist's acceptance of the piece of cake, and his 15-minute lateness to the session.

The patient's comment that her husband does not let her think for herself portrays in encoded form the psychological testing, the meeting with the husband in the hall, and possibly the acceptance of the piece of cake. In regard to the first context, there is an encoded representation of one of the functions of the testing, and we may be dealing more with derivative meaning than portrayal in this instance. Nevertheless, the crucial theme that links the manifest content to the latent intervention context is the therapist's need to have the psychologist do his thinking for him. Here, then, is a dramatic encoded perception of considerable sensitivity.

The same principle applies to the connection between this derivative and the therapist's contact with the husband. There is a small measure of portrayal and a large measure of unconsciously perceived meaning here. The raw image latent to this manifest derivative is that the therapist is incapable of thinking for himself because he permitted the husband to influence his decision regarding a pass for the patient. Similarly, this derivative seems to convey one of the meanings of the therapist's acceptance of the piece of cake—that the therapist needed the patient to function for him in some fashion—more than any *portrayal* of that particular incident. Overall, then, this particular association belongs more to the derivative complex than it does to representations of intervention contexts. It was possible, however, to arrive at this decision only after analyzing its connection to each of the adaptive contexts at hand.

The next image—that the patient let her husband push her around—has a similar quality. It is perhaps most clearly a representation of the therapist's contact with the husband in the hall, and his agreeing to the pass for the patient based on the husband's request. There is, then, a small measure of portrayal here, but the larger measure of meaning falls into the realm of derivative perception. In this regard, the underlying raw image is that the therapist allowed the husband to push him around. The patient is therefore implying on an unconscious level that she and the therapist are much alike in submitting to the power of her husband. To the extent that this is true, the therapist will be unable to help this patient to better deal with her husband in their daily interaction.

The allusion to Alice, another patient who was out on pass, represents an aspect of the contact between the therapist and the patient's husband. Through the manifest theme of the pass, there is a clear and strong link to the key topic of that hallway conversation. The allusion to Alice is therefore a good derivative representation of that particular adaptive context and could be used in intervening to the patient. This would be done by referring to the theme of passes rather than specifically suggesting that the patient was upset that the therapist had given her a pass based on the conversation from the husband.

Next, there is the allusion to baking things for her husband—a strong derivative representation of the therapist's acceptance of the cake. The unconscious perception encoded in this particular derivative is that the therapist, in accepting the cake, was unconsciously functioning as husband to the patient.

Next, being treated like a doormat may be a rather distant representation of the therapist's decision to send the patient for psychological tests, and more closely (though still quite remote), of the therapist's 15-minute lateness. This lateness is more clearly represented in the allusion to the husband's staying away from the patient and his house for two nights at a time. Here, the manifest element is absence for two nights (the symbol), and the latent raw image portrayed derivatively in the material is the therapist's 15-minute lateness (the symbolized).

Finally, the allusion to the husband's greed in taking his children's cake and cookies contains a further strong (close) representation of the therapist's acceptance of the piece of cake—along with a well-represented image of the therapist as greedy and selfish. This is a valid perception of the therapist in light of his behavior.

In the actual clinical session, the therapist should keep in mind all known intervention contexts and their implications, attempting to identify the most cogent meanings of these contexts and attempting to discover those that are most clearly represented in the early part of the session. Each image from the patient should then be evaluated as a possible encoded representation of one of these active contexts (much as each image is evaluated as a means of conveying indicators and derivative meaning). If the therapist determines that a particular context is receiving repeated encoded representation, he or she will quite likely discover that the patient's derivative material also organizes meaningfully around the same intervention context. Not infrequently, an intervention context that has been represented through several derivative portrayals will eventually find manifest expression in the patient's associations. This greatly facilitates the intervening process.

Once more, it is to be stressed that the therapist must subjectively determine the adaptive context (or two) appearing to be the strongest potential stimulus for the patient's communicative responses. At the same time, it is necessary to determine the context(s) that the patient appears to be working over for the moment—that is, those contexts that are most clearly portrayed and best organize the encoded assocations and perceptions. As long as the patient is responding on a derivative level to a strong intervention context, the therapist should intervene once the context itself is represented manifestly. If, on the other hand, the patient has defensively avoided a powerful context and instead has represented and responded through derivatives to a relatively minor intervention context, it is well for the therapist to remain silent until the more chaotic issues are represented in the patient's material.

For example, if the patient under consideration had mentioned a hurtful comment made by a nurse on the ward, and then associated in derivative form to the therapist's having permitted the nurse to intrude into the therapeutic space, it would have been unwise to intervene in terms of this particular adaptation-evoking context alone. The therapist could include it in an intervention if it were possible to link it to other more powerful contexts. It is important, however, that the therapist not make use of this type of minor stimulus as a way of avoiding far more powerful issues.

Exercise 6.2b

Unfortunately, the therapist in this particular case failed to interpret and rectify the deviant intervention contexts and derivative associations contained in the hour whose beginning has just been described. The patient then began the next session as follows:

> *Patient:* I had a dream the other night, right after the last session. I was watching this man with a gun threatening to shoot a doctor. The doctor seemed frightened of him and picked up a telephone to call for help. The man pulled out the telephone wire so the doctor couldn't reach anyone. A baby was sitting there eating a piece of cake.

In terms of the formal listening exercise to be carried out here, consider only representations of intervention contexts. Keep in mind those adaptive contexts that were activated prior to the previous session, as well as any identifiable adaptive contexts within that particular session. With these contexts in mind, take each element of the dream and determine whether it represents or portrays an intervention context. State the context and the clarity of the portrayal.

_____

_____

_____

_____

_____

_____

_____

_____

_____

_____

_____

_____

_____

_____

_____

_____

_____

_____

Answer

In terms of portrayal, the allusion to the man with the gun threatening to shoot the doctor would appear to portray in moderately disguised form the contact between the therapist and the patient's husband, including the therapist's decision to give the patient a pass at the request of her spouse. The attempt by the doctor to pick up the telephone and call for help best represents, once again in moderately disguised form, the therapist's request that the patient be tested psychologically. At this level, the man represents the patient, and the theme that connects the manifest with the latent level of communication has to do with fear of another person and a call for help.

The disconnection of the telephone is a rather disguised representation of the therapist's failure to intervene, portrayed in terms of the patient's perception that the therapist had not heard her cry for help—her derivative associations. Finally, of course, the baby eating a piece of cake represents the intervention context of the therapist's acceptance of the patient's baked product.

We can see, then, that dreams are stimulated by day residues, and that the day residues which prompt dreams in psychotherapy are constituted most importantly by the therapist's interventions. Only rarely does a dream contain a manifest representation of an adaptive context. This dream comes close in the image of the baby eating a piece of cake. Had the patient simply dreamt of the therapist eating a piece of cake, the portrayal would have been direct.

In general, however, dreams tend to convey *encoded* representations of intervention contexts, and particularly encoded *responses* to these intervention contexts. These responses, as always, are basically disguised and selected unconscious perceptions of the therapist, guided by the patient's madness and the nature of the intervention at hand.

Because dreams are almost always communicated by way of narratives and images, they have the potential to carry considerable meaning in light of intervention contexts. This is true of most detailed narratives, such as the description of a movie, a recent incident, an early memory, and the like. Narratives and images, as opposed to intellectualizations and speculations, are in a sense the language of the unconscious part of the mind—the best vehicles for encoded expression. The dream should by no means become the center of the hour in which it appears, however. The communicative therapist does not ask for associations to dream images. Instead, he or she accepts the dream as one of many responses to prevailing intervention contexts, and permits the patient to develop his or her own associations as well as to shift to other themes and contents. Of course, associations to dreams may be especially meaningful in that they elaborate upon an unconscious perception of the therapist in light of an intervention context. Still, understood as an encoded communication, the dream narrative is often extremely revealing in and of itself. In principle, it is always best to allow the patient to shift about, freely selecting his or her own vehicles for communicative expression, rather than constricting his or her communicative range through questions and highly selective responses to associations already available.

SOME CONCLUDING PRECEPTS

When an adaptive context is not represented manifestly, it is incumbent upon the therapist to identify its best encoded representation. Should the therapist decide to intervene, this portrayal will serve as the main illustration supporting a playback of other derivatives organized around this particular intervention context. If the representation is relatively clear and strong, the patient is likely to consciously recognize the relevant intervention context simply on the basis of a playback of the associations that portray it. If the representation of an intervention context is distant and well disguised, it is best that the therapist not intervene, but wait for clearer communicative expression.

As we have seen, embedded in each portrayal or representation of an intervention context is a selected encoded perception of the therapist in light of his or her intervention. Often the portrayal involves encoded perceptions of considerable importance. Still, before intervening, it is critical to have available in the patient's material additional encoded perceptions pertinent to the particular adaptive contexts.

The identification of manifest and encoded representations of adaptive contexts is perhaps the most important aspect of the listening–formulating process as it influences the decision of whether to intervene. Direct, and well-represented indirect, portrayals of intervention contexts greatly facilitate active efforts by the therapist. Their absence often renders it virtually impossible for the moment either to comment or to rectify the frame.

Therapists should, however, learn to respect a patient's need to communicate or to disguise and obliterate (defend), patiently awaiting those sessions in which clear portrayals and derivative responses appear in the patient's material. It is only in the presence of very powerful indicators that a therapist should be inclined to intervene in the face of a high level of communicative resistances—a poorly represented adaptive context and a weak derivative complex.

The listening–formulating process that a therapist must use in order to determine the true implications of the patient's material can be carried out with full respect for the patient's therapeutic needs. Once integrated into the therapist's style of working with a patient, it can be used with ease and facilitate empathy, especially in regard to the patient's unconscious concerns and communications. It is essential, however, to allow the patient to lead the way, and to permit him or her to work at his or her own pace. It is essential to create a therapeutic space and attitude that enables the patient to communicate meaningfully when ready, to destroy meaning when need be, and to place into the therapist whenever he or she wishes to do so (however unconsciously) all of the elements needed for an intervention. Psychotherapy sessions should be first and foremost the patient's creations. So should the therapist's interventions. These are the precepts of sound therapeutic efforts.

7
Adaptive Contexts: Known Implications

We have seen that there is a gradual transition between what are understood as encoded representations of adaptive contexts and the unconsciously perceived meanings of these interventional stimuli. Soon, we will consider the derivative complex and its central element: the selected encoded perceptions of the therapist in light of his or her interventions. As a bridge to this final component of the listening–formulating process, we will now study the effort by the therapist who has recognized a particular activated intervention context to consciously identify as many of its implications as possible.

IMPLICATIONS OF INTERVENTIONS

As we know, there are four classes of intervention: (1) silence, (2) ground rules, (3) interpretations, and (4) noninterpretive interventions. It therefore behooves the therapist to consider the implications of each intervention made in any of these categories. Most often, the critical intervention will involve the ground rules and frame of treatment; because of this, the therapist must understand the vast implications—the nature and function—of the framework of treatment. The present chapter can offer only a highly selected overview and a sequence of brief exercises designed to prepare the therapist for independent listening and assessment.

For every single intervention context there appears to be four levels of implication and meaning. It is important in formulating the meanings of an intervention context to take each into account as much as possible. They may be described as follows:

1. *Universal meanings.* In this sphere the therapist identifies an implication of an intervention that would exist for virtually every patient and therapist. For example, a decrease in fee has seductive or feeding implications; cutting off a session has exploitative and deprivational attributes. A severe confrontation is hostile. Feeding the patient is overly gratifying and an attempt to fuse. It is possible, indeed, to develop a

catalog of these universal implications, a list that should enlarge as our understanding of the broad implications of interventions expands.

2. *Personal meanings for the patient.* Each patient brings with him or her a personal history, including genetics, dynamics, narcissistic qualities, and the like. Here, what is unique for a particular patient comes into play. Especially important in this constellation is the nature of the patient's madness (psychopathology), including its current inner meanings and prior history. It is this latter constellation that is the most critical determinant of the patient's personal and highly selected perceptions of the universal meanings to an intervention context. Furthermore, it is these personal experiences and current internal factors that give definitive and particular meaning to an intervention by a therapist for a specific patient. Thus, the personal factor within the patient accounts for both selected perceptions and personal interpretations of an intervention context.

3. *Meanings in light of the present therapeutic interaction.* Each intervention is part of a *flow,* an unfolding and spiraling conscious and especially unconscious communicative interaction between a particular patient and a particular therapist. Thus, each effort by a therapist has a special coloring in light of the moment in therapy at which it is offered. This moment itself has a prehistory and anticipates the future unfolding. At times, this factor significantly influences the patient's selected perceptions of the meanings of the therapist's efforts.

To briefly illustrate, let us suppose that a therapist has recently secured the ground rule regarding responsibility for sessions—shifting, based on the derivatives from the patient, from allowing cancellation with 24 hours' notice to full responsibility for all hours. Suppose, then, that the therapist is 15 minutes late for the next session. Based on this particular sequence or flow, the patient will experience the therapist's framework break as a contradiction of his or her recent efforts to secure the frame. The two contradictory messages are of a kind that tend to drive patients crazy, and such craziness will indeed be subjectively or otherwise experienced. There will be an image of uncertainty communicated by the therapist, and the patient will view him or her as basically inconsistent, unable to hold the frame, and fearful of the secure therapeutic environment.

Suppose, instead, the therapist had recently given the patient a make-up session because of a cancellation due to illness. In the next session, the therapist is 15 minutes late. Here, in terms of the flow, there is a consistent rather than inconsistent pattern—the therapist repeatedly deviates. There are no contradictory messages, no perceived quality of uncertainty about the therapist or even a split image of the therapist. Instead, there is one basically consistent image of a therapist who unconsciously needs to deviate, to modify the frame, and to pathologically gratify either himself or the patient. Of course, there would be some measure of contradiction in that the first deviation gratifies the patient, whereas the second creates frustration and pain. Nevertheless the deviant attitude toward the ground rules is consistent.

4. *Personal meanings for the therapist.* Every intervention made by a therapist is embedded in the personal history and current mental world of the therapist. It therefore has a specific meaning for each particular therapist, for the particular moment in his or her professional and personal life, as well as for his or her side of the relationship with the patient at hand. This dimension will be known only minimally to the patient, based on unconscious readings of peripheral implications communicated by other dimensions of the relationship as well as by the immediate adaptive contexts. This, of course, assumes a relative attitude of nonrevelation by the therapist; should there be personal leakage, this particular factor could be quite significant as a deter-

minant of the patient's encoded responses to a particular adaptation-evoking context. In all, in a well-managed psychotherapy, this last factor would be least influential in determining the patient's responses to interventions. Under extraordinary circumstances of extensive self-revelation, however, it can prove to be most critical.

For each intervention made by a therapist, there is need to quickly catalog the possible implications in each of these four spheres. The therapist's subjective knowledge serves as an important means of comprehending the patient's derivative material, while in turn, the patient's derivative material directs the therapist to the unconscious implications of his or her own efforts. There may be a measure of subjective or initial validation if an implication of an intervention that has been consciously formulated by the therapist is confirmed by a derivative image from the patient. This stands among the most important forms taken by what is called *silent validation*—efforts to confirm one's initial formulations in the course of a given hour. In principle, interventions are offered to the patient only if there is silent validation in the form of enlarging communicative support from the patient, directly and through derivatives, of the formulations under consideration by the therapist.

In exercise form, we will now attempt to identify the universal implications of each type of intervention available to the therapist. It will be possible here to identify only the most common interventions and their most salient meanings and functions. But, in general, the types of meanings to be identified on this level are recognized without undue effort. It is hoped, in fact, that the reader will be able to extend the list offered in this workbook. It is really the other categories of meaning, each of them rather personal and specific, that require a more intense search for definitive meaning. The first level of meaning requires common sense and seeing the self-evident attributes of an intervention. The others demand attention to the patient's free associations for critical clues and information.

For those therapists who wish to be systematic about taking into account the major attributes of an intervention context, there is a basic resource similar to the three basic components of the listening process. Like them, a schema of the main dimensions of the therapeutic experience and communication may feel cumbersome at first; but eventually it will become a natural part of the therapist's thinking process. We are repeatedly caught between the Scylla of loose and nonspecific formulations and the Charybdis of overly systematized categorizations. The following guide can resolve that problem: It is designed to be integrated with the thinking of the therapist in a way that is facilitating and inclusive without being unduly restrictive.

THE SEVEN DIMENSIONS OF THE THERAPEUTIC INTERACTION

To this point, clinical communicative studies have revealed seven dimensions to the therapeutic interaction (indeed, to all human interplay). Five of these categories have been presented in some detail in an earlier work (Langs 1982a)—(1) the state of the frame, (2) the mode of relatedness, (3) the mode of cure, (4) issues of communication, and (5) dynamics and genetics. Two additional categories are added in the present work: (6) issues of self and identity and (7) the realm of sanity and madness. Whereas previously, these dimensions of the therapeutic experience were identified as categories of observation or information, it has of late become clear that they are actually basic dimensions of human interaction and expression. This implies, first, that any complete statement of the therapeutic experience at a given interlude should take into account factors in each of these realms; and second, that both the therapist's interventions and the patient's communicative responses touch upon each of these dimensions of experience in various proportions.

It has been shown empirically that a patient's manifest and derivative associations will shift from one category of experience to another in a given session and over the span of an entire treatment experience. In each instance the patient is first and foremost representing his or her perceptions of the *actualities* (manifest and latent) of the therapeutic situation and of the interventions of the therapist. As in all of life, issues of reality take precedence over those pertaining to fantasy, and in the main, fantasies themselves are reactions to realities (inner and outer) that must be taken into account.

In response to the patient's material, a therapist's intervention will quite naturally fall into the particular categories of adaptation and experience that the patient is working over. This will occur because the therapist makes use of the patient's images as they touch upon these categories of experience. Also, the category of experience that is being worked over and analyzed by both participants to treatment is determined largely by the attributes of the therapist's interventions as they impinge upon these seven dimensions of interaction and on the patient's own inner madness. A fundamental premise of this conception is that no single area of human experience is sufficient to fully explain a patient's (and therapist's) madness. A full comprehension in depth must ultimately take into account all seven of these interrelated areas.

This particular schema serves the therapist in the evaluation of the implications of intervention contexts as well as in the evaluation of the patient's encoded responses and other reactions. It is therefore essential to introduce these elements as a framework for the understanding to be developed in the balance of this book (see Appendix B).

Structure

In outline form, the following indicates the structure of the seven dimensions of the therapeutic interaction:

I. *The Ground Rules of Psychotherapy*

The therapist's management of the frame is, as repeatedly suggested, the most fundamental component of the therapeutic interaction. It is a major determinant of all other dimensions of the therapeutic experience. There is a basic distinction between the ideal, or secure, frame and the deviant frame, each providing the patient with a constellation of protective functions and danger situations. Adherence to the basic ground rules in their entirety creates an unconscious image of the therapist as trustworthy, sane, stable, capable of creating clear interpersonal boundaries and of managing his or her own inner mental world and madness, and as offering a clear sense of reality and an ideal sense of hold and containment. In addition to these critical positive features, the secure frame creates as its primary danger the dread of a claustrum (claustrophobia)—fears of entrapment, abandonment, and annihilation within the closed space. *Death anxiety* in particular is aroused. Another danger arises when a therapist who secures the ideal frame fails to interpret material properly (meaningful relatedness is based on the establishment of a meaning link between patient and therapist). In the presence of a therapist capable of valid interpretive response, other dangers arise, such as those related to envy and the power of others. Here, in general, the adaptive context involves the therapist's maintenance of the framework in the face of the patient's attempts to alter the conditions of treatment.

The secure frame, then, mobilizes basic phobic-paranoid-schizoid anxieties in the psychotherapy and psychoanalytic patient (and therapist)—danger situations comparable to Melanie Klein's basic initial infantile issues and position. In addition, there is within such a frame a sense of separation and loss that corresponds to Klein's depressive position—a danger that arises because of the relative absence of pathological gratification and inappropriate relatedness within a secure frame.

In all, the secure frame offers basic trust and basic holding, while creating the paranoid-phobic-separation anxieties of the claustrum. In contrast, the deviant frame consistently generates an image of the therapist as untrustworthy, mad, unable to manage his or her own inner mental world, unpredictable, pathologically gratifying, relating in pathological fashion to the patient, uncertain of interpersonal boundaries and external reality, and incapable of establishing a secure hold and sense of containment. In addition to these basic dangers, however, each deviant-frame intervention offers the patient a pathological mode of relatedness, pathological defenses (especially defenses that are counterphobic or antiphobic and manic—escape from the claustrum and forms of fusion and merger), and a basically pathological mode of cure. Of special interest is the additional finding that every deviation by a therapist is experienced unconsciously by patients as a form of perverse gratification for the therapist. In essence, then, the deviant frame creates an inherently dangerous image of the therapist, while offering the patient pathological modes of defense, gratification, and relatedness. In all, each of the two basic modes of therapy—secure-frame therapy and deviant-frame therapy—gives something to the patient while creating danger situations and potential anxiety.

The basic elements of the secure frame, as stated before, include:

1. A single unchanging locale, set fee, set length of sessions, set frequency and time of hours.

2. The patient on the couch with the therapist seated behind him or her, out of sight.

3. The fundamental rule of free association for the patient and evenly hovering attention for the therapist.

4. The relative anonymity of the therapist.

5. The neutrality of the therapist (interventions restricted to silence, positive managements of the frame, and interpretation–reconstruction).

6. The one-to-one relationship with total privacy.

7. Total confidentiality.

In addition to these explicit ground rules, there are those that are implicit, such as the absence of physical contact (except for a handshake at the beginning and end of treatment), confinement of the meetings of the patient and therapist to the therapist's office, and similar amenities.

These ground rules create a therapeutically necessary claustrum that mobilizes the patient's madness. Perhaps the most basic of them is the ground rule of full responsibility for sessions and the requisite that the patient appear at a particular time each week for a specific hour. The sense of confinement generated by these aspects of the frame is supplemented by the use of the couch, the total privacy and confidentiality of the treatment experience, and an absence of contact between the patient and therapist outside of the session.

A therapist establishes by way of this particular constellation of ground rules an image for the patient of a trustworthy and sane individual who is nonetheless dangerous. Initially, the patient responds with precisely this type of unconscious perception when a frame is secured, though the dangerous aspects are frequently exaggerated and sometimes distorted. It is then and only then that a transference component is introduced into the therapeutic experience. As noted before, valid and selected unconscious perceptions consistently emerge first, and whatever distortions appear do so secondarily (for further details see Langs, 1979, 1982a).

II. *The Mode of Relatedness*

The following are the modes of relatedness that may be established between a patient and therapist:

A. *A Healthy Symbiosis.*   For the therapist, this can be developed only by securing the ideal frame and adopting an interpretive approach. For the patient, it involves acceptance of the frame in some broad fashion and a capacity both to communicate meaningfully to the therapist and to respond meaningfully to his or her interventions.

B. *Pathological Symbiosis.*   Here, the therapist deviates and/or intervenes noninterpretively in a fashion that provides the patient with considerable pathological gratification. In similar fashion, the patient accepts such inappropriate gratifications and often attempts to offer pathological satisfactions to the therapist in return.

C. *Healthy Autism.*   For the patient, this implies the absence of an activated and disturbing intervention context. This is a fallow period, during which the patient does not communicate meaningfully (because there is no basic need to do so). For the therapist, this mode of relatedness is constituted by silence in the absence of a clear need for intervention (i.e., the material lacks a pathological indicator, a clearly represented adaptive context, and meaningful coalescing derivative perceptions).

D. *Pathological Autism.*   For the patient, this implies failure to communicate meaningfully in the presence of an activated intervention context. For the therapist, this mode of relatedness occurs when the patient offers material that is communicatively meaningful, but the therapist fails to intervene. This mode is also reflected in an intervention that fails to identity the true meaning of the patient's material—one that is derived more from the therapist's needs and fantasies than from the implications of the patient's association.

E. *Parasitic.*   This mode of relatedness involves the direct exploitation of one participant to treatment by the other. It is constituted by personal and exploitative deviations and verbal interventions. It is always pathological.

In addition to this classification based on maturational modes of relatedness, it is possible to identify three interpersonal or relationship links between patients and therapists (Bion, 1962):

1. *The Meaning Link.*   Here, the patient communicates meaningfully when confronted with an activated intervention context, and the therapist is capable of valid silence or active intervention in keeping with the communicative properties of the patient's behaviors and associations. This is the only means through which a patient feels truly related to and understood by the therapist.

2. *The Hate Link.*   This occurs in the presence of destructive behaviors (expressions of pathological aggressive instinctual drives) of the patient that are directly hurtful to the therapist, and interventions from the therapist that are exploitative and hurtful of the patient. Under such circumstances, the patient feels abandoned by the therapist and used as an object (thing) rather than as part of a meaningful human mode of interaction.

3. *The Love Link.*   Here, the patient or therapist inappropriately and pathologically offers a variety of gratifications, loving and merging in type, infused with pathological instinctual drives. The patient feels essentially abandoned by the therapist and seduced and exploited.

III. *Mode of Cure*

The continuum here has, at one end, cure through genuine insight, and at the other, cure through action-discharge and merger. The former implies cure through basic holding and containment, supplemented by interpretations that explain indicators in light of adaptive contents and derivative complex responses. No other form of (ostensible) interpretive intervention creates genuine insight; other so-called interpretations are actually (functionally) verbal efforts at action-discharge and merger. The latter implies the use by the therapist of various forms of active behaviors and/or verbal-affective interventions that do not meet the definition of interpretation–reconstruction and management of the frame toward its securement. Under such conditions, words are used for evacuation, discharge, and merger, rather than true understanding.

IV. *Issues of Communication*

Basic here is whether the patient, faced with an activated intervention context, is communicating meaningfully or destroying meaning. Similarly, at one extreme, the therapist is capable of a sound interpretation as defined above, while at the other, fails to do so. In the former instance, the therapist is expressing true meaning and truth, whereas in the latter circumstance, he or she is creating fictions and lie formations that do not hold up as truly insightful. Other communicative issues include the therapist's adherence to the level of communicative expression and defense reflected in the patient's material, the question of whether the patient and therapist are communicating within the same general category of experience, efforts by patient and/or therapist to disturb the communicative interplay within the therapeutic dyad, and endeavors by either participant to treatment to enhance communicative contact.

V. *Dynamics and Genetics*

This dimension includes all of the aspects of psychosexual and aggressive development, intrapsychic conflict, matters of instinctual drive expression and defense, historical factors, and all of the other components of the classical psychoanalytic drive, conflict, and ego, superego, and id developmental theory and observations.

VI. *The Realm of Self and Identity*

Included here are all issues related to self and identity. This includes the search for mirroring and idealization, the establishment of goals and ideals, issues of aspiration, concerns about exhibitionism, the regulation of tension states and self-esteem, the establishment of object constancy and a firm personal identity, the development of a cohesive sense of self, and all the other dimensions of narcissistic and identity pursuits, conflicts, and achievements.

Perhaps the most overlooked component of this particular aspect of the therapeutic interaction is the influence of the therapist's interventions on the patient's communications and experiences in this sphere. In principle, it is only the well-functioning therapist, capable of securing the framework of treatment and responding to the patient's material with sound interpretations, who presents himself or herself on an unconscious level as having a clear and mature identity and a strong sense of self. All deviant interventions and erroneous verbal-affective comments from the therapist are unconsciously perceived by the patient as reflecting identity and narcissistic disturbances. Often, these errors involve the pathological use of the patient as a selfobject and failures in empathy (especially a lack of attunement to the patient's unconscious communications). Thus, in the narcissistically disturbed patient, unconscious perceptions of flaws in the therapist's identity and narcissistic equilibrium are an important selected and perceptive means through which their own pathology in this sphere is mobilized and worked over. There has been a basic failure to consider this dimension of the therapeutic experience in interactional terms.

VII. *The Realm of Sanity and Madness*

Madness has emerged as the most meaningful term for the basic psychopathology in the patient and therapist. In general, the therapist's madness is expressed through deviations in the frame and erroneous verbal-affective interventions. Under these circumstances, his or her madness occupies the therapeutic space and becomes the primary unconscious concern of the patient. As a result, the direct and derivative responses of the patient deal primarily with the madness of the therapist as perceived in terms of the patient's own madness—and healthy capacities as well. It is only when the therapist has secured the frame and proven capable of sound interpretive interventions that he or she is viewed unconsciously by the patient as sane. Under these conditions, it is the patient's madness that is primary to his or her own communicative responses. As such, they are mobilized by the therapist's securing of the frame and the unconsciously perceived dangers experienced selectively by the patient. In general (and up to a point), as the therapist's madness finds increasingly intense expressions, the patient's expressed madness tends to wane.

Madness has its own vicissitudes, contagion, rules of expression, and such. It is therefore a separate and critical dimension of the treatment experience, quite different from unconscious dynamics and genetics.

These, then, are the dimensions of the therapeutic interaction. In attempting to evaluate a communication from either the therapist or the patient, it is well to identify where these expressions fall in terms of this particular schema. In this fashion, it is possible to locate the central area of concern and issue for either participant to treatment and to eventually focus one's listening and intervening in the proper sphere. In preparation for our study of the implications of the therapist's interventions, we will now engage in a brief series of exercises. We will identify the dimensions of human experience most central to a therapist's intervention or to an associational sequence from the patient.

DIMENSIONS OF EXPERIENCE: EXERCISES

Exercise 7.1

The patient is a married woman with a son and daughter both under the age of ten. She entered psychotherapy because of a sense of depression and futility. She was referred to her male therapist (who works in a private office with a shared waiting room) by her cousin, who was herself a patient of the therapist. This cousin terminated her treatment soon after the patient under consideration began. Sessions are twice weekly, and the fee is presently paid by the patient's husband, a manufacturer who has yet to investigate the insurance coverage available to him to determine whether the patient is eligible for some return of fee for psychotherapy.

Most striking about this psychotherapy has been the therapist's failure to intervene in terms of activated adaptive contexts and the patient's derivative responses. In early sessions, there were many allusions to intruders into the treatment setting and even a direct mention of the cousin who was the therapist's patient; no interpretation was made of the unconscious meanings of this material, however, nor was rectification considered. It was characteristic of the therapist to either be inappropriately silent (and to miss critical interventions) or to respond to the patient's material on a manifest-content level, directly confronting her with her sense of depression and hopelessness. An intervention of this latter type had been made prior to the session from which the following excerpt was taken. The material alluded to here was reported very near the beginning of the hour:

> *Patient:*   I don't know who I am, what I'm supposed to do with my life. I ran the dance for the church and it was a success. They filled me with praise, but it feels empty. It's not who I am. Even in bed with my husband, something is not right. I keep thinking the children can hear us; they're always there. Sometimes they come into our bedroom unannounced. I'll never be able to work again. Everything I say is ridiculous. I go off in a dozen different directions, and none of them give me satisfaction. I'm missing something for sure.

In the space provided below, the reader is advised to first consider this excerpted material for indicators, known adaptive contexts, and direct and derivative representations of intervention contexts. Then focus on the following task: Take each sequence of associations and identify the main dimension of human experience with which it is concerned. Briefly state the intervention context within the therapeutic interaction that has stimulated the particular segment of material—whether direct or derivative. Concentrate on the interplay between the adaptive context and the sphere of the patient's response. Attempt to formulate as well the nature of the madness within the patient that helps to account for the selective perceptions of the therapist conveyed in this material. (Remember that such perceptions simultaneously work over a view of the therapist along with the patient's own self-perceptions and view of the interaction with the therapist.) In essence, then, for each dimension identified, state a specific stimulus or adaptive context and the patient's contribution in terms of her own psychopathology.

_____

_____

_____

_____

_____

_____

_____

_____

Answer

Turning first to the basic tripartite listening–intervening schema, the following indicators are alluded to in the material (the first four are to be found in the introduction to the excerpt, and the balance are reflected in sequence in the patient's associations):

1. The patient's sense of depression and futility—the reason she entered psychotherapy (symptomatic; moderate).

2. Accepting a referral to a therapist from her cousin, a patient-referral (a gross behavioral resistance—frame deviation, one that modifies the total privacy and one-to-one relationship between patient and therapist; strong).

3. Arranging for the patient's husband to pay the fee (a gross behavioral resistance—frame break, modifying the patient's full responsibility for the fee; moderate).

4. The desire by the patient to use her husband's insurance coverage (a gross behavioral resistance—frame deviation that introduces third parties and therapist-revelations into the therapy; strong).

5. The patient's uncertainty as to who she is (symptomatic; moderate).

6. The patient's experience of emptiness in response to praise (symptomatic; moderate).

7. The patient's experience that "something is not right" in bed with her husband (symptomatic; moderate).

8. The patient's feeling she will never be able to work again (symptomatic; moderate).

9. The patient's feeling that everything she says is "ridiculous" (symptomatic; moderate).

10. The patient "going off in a dozen different directions," none of them giving her satisfaction, and her feeling that she is "missing something for sure" (symptomatic; moderate).

The known intervention contexts are all presented in the introduction. In sequence they include:

1. The therapist's use of a shared waiting room (frame deviation, a modification in the ground rule of total privacy and total confidentiality; moderate).

2. The therapist's acceptance of a patient-referral (frame deviation, an alteration in total privacy, total confidentiality, and in the relative anonymity of the therapist—each patient knows that the therapist is seeing the other; strong).

3. The therapist's acceptance of a fee paid by the patient's husband (frame deviation, an alteration in the ideal ground rule of the patient's full responsibility for her own fee; moderate to mild).

4. The possibility that the therapist might complete an insurance form and accept payment from an insurance company (frame deviation, an alteration in the total privacy and confidentiality of treatment, and of the therapist's relative anonymity [the revelations of his diagnosis and other views of the patient]; strong).

5. The therapist's failure to intervene in terms of adaptive contexts and his use of inappropriate silence (missed interventions), manifest-content interventions, and confrontations (the use of noninterpretive interventions and missed interventions; strong).

6. The therapist's failure to rectify the deviant frame (an interventional failure; strong).

In the excerpt from the session at hand, there are no direct representations of adaptive contexts. There are, however, several derivative (encoded) representations of such contexts. In sequence, they are as follows:

1. The patient stating she does not know what she is supposed to do with her life: a derivative representation of the therapist's lack of understanding as to what he is supposed to do in psychotherapy.

2. The children coming in unannounced into the patient's bedroom: a derivative representation of the patient-referral.

3. The patient's comment that everything she says is ridiculous, that she goes off in a dozen different directions, and that none of them give her satisfaction: representations of the therapist's erroneous interventions.

4. The patient's comment that she is "missing something for sure": an encoded representation of the patient's unconscious realization that the therapist has failed to intervene when material has been available for interpretation and rectification.

In this manner, we have identified some of the main components of this material in terms of its nature and function. Because we have not as yet studied the derivative complex, it is not possible for us to complete the task of assigning segments of this material to each of the three dimensions of the basic tripartite listening–intervening schema—indicators, adaptive contexts, and derivative complex. Nonetheless, this exercise provides a solid grounding for our understanding of this material, and it enables us to now turn to each segment in sequence in order to identify the dimensions of the therapeutic interaction with which it deals.

Thus, the opening segment of associations clearly involves issues of identity and narcissism. There is a manifest statement regarding a lack of clear identity and one that implies the absence of a cohesive sense of self. There is the uncertainty regarding life goals and feelings of emptiness. Involved here, then, are moderate indicators that suggest an identity and narcissistic disturbance.

Because of the confusion in the existing literature on both of these topics, it is to be stressed that the communicative approach has demonstrated that statements of this kind are on the surface manifest allusions to psychopathology—in essence, they are indicators or therapeutic contexts. Although at times they may also embody a direct or encoded representation of an adaptive context, more frequently they serve a derivative function. Their first communicative assignment, however, should be as indicators—surface manifestations of psychopathology that do not reveal their own unconscious basis.

The unconscious meanings of such indicators can be determined only by identifying the stimulating intervention context and the patient's derivative perceptions and other reactions. Failure to understand this has led to much manifest-content listening and intervening. Adherence to the principle that every communication from the patient has functional meaning as an adaptive response to an intervention from the therapist permits a consistent approach to formulation that takes into account both the surface and the depths—and especially the unconscious dimension of psychopathology and madness.

What then is the main adaptive context for this first segment of material that touches upon issues of identity and narcissism? The answer lies in two of the known adaptive contexts reported in this material (there may, of course, be additional adaptation-evoking stimuli not reported in this brief summary). Both the patient-referral and intervention failures of the therapist project an image of himself as someone with an uncertain identity and no cohesive sense of self supported by clear therapeutic goals. It is because of the pathological identity and narcissistic implications of these two intervention contexts that the patient has unconsciously and selectively perceived her therapist in these terms—all the while guided by her own narcissistic and identity disturbance.

To clarify, a therapist who accepts a patient-referral has identity problems, in that he is not able to establish a clear commitment to one patient that excludes others to whom the patient is related or with whom the patient is a personal friend. The therapist who cannot maintain a clear line of identity for the patient in some way reveals an identity disturbance of his or her own.

In similar fashion, patients consistently unconsciously perceive a therapist who is incapable of a valid adaptive context-based intervention as failing to achieve a clear identity as a psychotherapist. Such themes are quite common under those conditions.

Both of these therapist-problems generate unconsciously perceived images of disturbance in the narcissistic sphere as well. The therapist who accepts a patient-referral is revealing a pathological need for self-enhancement and self-gain; the therapist who fails to intervene properly conveys a lack of self-esteem and a failure to meet ego-ideal requirements. All of the material in psychotherapy and psychoanalytic sessions bearing on identity and narcissistic disturbances is stimulated either by failings in the therapist of this kind or by paradoxical reactions to sound interpretive and framework-management responses. In each instance, however, the latter interventions first generate associations that reflect the resolutions of identity disturbances and the achievement of a cohesive sense of self—responses based on constructive introjective identifications with the well-functioning therapist.

It is to be stressed that listening in terms of the dimensions of human experience *supplements* the fundamental listening task through which the therapist must assign each segment of associations to the categories of indicator, adaptive context, and derivative complex. Whereas this basic task is fundamental to understanding human communication, the assignment of the dimensionality provides the specific content and issues that the patient is working over communicatively at the moment.

The assignment of category and dimensionality, then, are two distinctive aspects of the listening–formulating process, and the category assignment task is most basic. When one has analyzed the implications of communications in light of their appropriate dimension of human experience, the information is always funneled into the basic tripartite classification. As psychoanalytic clinicians and theoreticians help to broaden our comprehension of human experience and the therapeutic interaction, the seven categories that I have introduced may well be further elaborated and even supplemented through the recognition of new dimensions of interaction. Even so, such developments will only provide added depth for what will remain the fundamental task: the identification of an indicator that may be explained unconsciously in terms of an adaptive context and derivative responses. Thus, it is entirely insufficient to confine one's listening to one or more dimensions of experience without carrying out the more fundamental task of category assignment.

In undertaking an analysis of the dimensions of the therapeutic interaction, it is necessary for the therapist to alter his or her usual set or approach to the patient's material. For too long now, therapists and analysts have adhered to the view that when a patient refers to himself or herself, the associational material similarly alludes to the patient. In contrast, when the material refers manifestly to the therapist or to an obvious displacement figure, the associations are considered to touch upon images of the therapist.

The communicative approach has shown that this attitude cannot be maintained. Instead, it should be recognized that each and every association from the patient alludes first to the therapist and second, though simultaneously, to the patient—that is, to both participants to treatment along what has been termed the me/not-me interface. It is therefore extremely important to realize that much manifest material regarding the patient alludes primarily on a derivative level to the therapist. In fact, self-references of this kind on the part of the patient stand among the most meaningful communicative vehicles for encoded perceptions of the therapist. This appears to be so because the patient is in this way able to express and yet conceal threatening raw perceptions of the therapist, which must be well disguised. What better person to allude to in disguising allusions to the therapist? This camouflage has proven so successful that it has interfered with the comprehension of the patient's material by most psychotherapists.

It follows, then, that in assigning implications of a patient's associations to a particular dimension of the therapeutic interaction, *this assignment should first be made to the therapist in terms of the actual implications of his or her interventions.* Patients do indeed work over these actualities in terms of their true underlying meanings long before they have the time and space for engaging in fantasy activity. Even then, such expressions are responses to the actual perceptions of the therapist and his or her interventions. Following the assignment to the therapist, it is necessary, of course, to make a similar and *second assignment to the patient in terms of unconscious self-perceptions.* Finally, it is important to remember that the particular dimension within which a patient perceives an intervention context of the therapist is *simultaneously determined by the nature of that intervention and the nature of the patient's psychopathology or madness* (this latter is the main guide for the patient's encoded perceptions of the therapist).

The next segment of material centers around the patient's sexual relationship with her husband, her concern that her children can hear them having relations, and the fact that the children sometimes enter their bedroom unannounced. The sexual problem with the husband is, as noted, a moderate symptomatic indicator. The material falls into the realm of dynamics; genetics, although not stated, are implied. (In later sessions, early memories of primal scene experiences did emerge in this patient's material.) Although not as yet defined, there is evidence of interpersonal and intrapsychic conflicts, concerns about being overheard during intercourse, and images of intruders—all components of primal scene issues and oedipal sexual conflicts. Further material would be needed to substantiate and expand these initial impressions. Nonetheless, the dynamic quality of this segment of material is quite evident. What then is the intervention context that has stimulated these associations?

The shared waiting room is undoubtedly contributing to these images of third-party intruders, but the patient-referral is the main stimulus for the patient's associations. The segment contains a rather disguised portrayal (intruders into the parental bedroom) of that adaptive context—the therapist's acceptance of the present patient into the therapeutic space of her cousin, a space that should have remained private and uninvaded. These associations also reveal an unconsciously perceived *meaning* of that intervention context: It constitutes the therapist's acceptance of an intruder into a private therapeutic space and his acceptance of someone who is in a sense listening in on what should be a confidential psychotherapeutic session.

Notice that we are again treating the patient's encoded material, first, as a representation of implications conveyed by the therapist's actual interventions and, second, in terms of the patient's fantasies, wishes, and self-allusions. The patient's sexual intrapsychic conflicts and earlier primal scene experiences have led her to unconsciously perceive the oedipal, sexual, and primal scene implications of the patient–referral. These are universal meanings that all patients involved in a similar intervention context touch upon to some extent.

The genuine implications conveyed by the real stimulus are perceived by patients in terms of their own experiences, memories, and conflicts.

In short, when we have identified a dimension of human experience being worked over by the patient in the therapeutic interaction, the material should be subjected to exploration for indicators, adaptive contexts, and derivative complex. In this way, we automatically and properly funnel our understanding of a particular experiential dimension into the fundamental listening–intervening schema.

Another dimension touched upon in this segment of material is the dimension of ground-rule and framework issues. This aspect of the therapeutic interaction is represented in the patient's allusion to her children entering her bedroom unannounced—a clear encoded reference to a framework violation. The main adaptive context for this representation remains the patient-referral. The break of the frame at home portrays in derivative form the break of the frame in the psychotherapy. Similarly, the leakage of sound from the bedroom portrays the deviant leakage that exists because of the referral situation. The shared waiting room may also be partially responsible for these images.

We see, then, that a given segment of material may touch upon two or more major dimensions of human experience. *Each* dimension, however, must be traced to a specific adaptive context and then understood for indicator and derivative implications. Given the powerful dangers associated with this aspect of human functioning, interaction, and communication, it is especially important to allow patients sufficient range of associations to communicate instinctual drive—dynamic and genetic—material. All too often a therapist will confine his or her understanding and interventions to the object-relationship or narcissistic sphere, failing to permit the emergence of far more chaotic and threatening instinctual drive-related material. Eventually, a patient's associations should touch upon each of the seven dimensions of human experience. A notable lack of communicative expression in any single area generally indicates interactional resistances stimulated by the interventions of the therapist and the defensive needs of the patient.

The final segment of the material, which refers to the patient's inability to work, her ridiculous comments, the scattering of her efforts, and so forth, touches again upon issues of narcissism and identity, prompted by the therapist's failed interventions. The material contains well-represented, though encoded, portrayals of the therapist's errors, such that the raw selected unconscious image could be stated as follows: *The therapist is unable to work, everything he says is ridiculous, he goes off on one tangent after another, none of it is satisfying to him or to me, and he is missing something for sure.* Each of these is a valid unconscious perception of the therapist's efforts in the prior and recent sessions. Notice again that the therapist's failure to offer valid interventions is selectively and unconsciously perceived by the patient in terms of her own difficulties in these areas. She sees the therapist's errors as a reflection of his narcissistic and identity problems. These implications are indeed conveyed by the therapist's behavior; but the patient's material reveals an attempt to work them over on the basis of their meaning for her personally.

An additional level of meaning is suggested by this material. In the patient's view, the narcissistic and identity disturbance is in some way related to primal scene issues and sexual interpersonal and intrapsychic conflicts and genetics (for both participants to therapy). Indeed, instinctual-drive conflicts do contribute to narcissistic and identity pathology, just as disturbances in the narcissistic sphere and in the realm of identity contribute to intrapsychic conflicts. One should always attempt as comprehensive a formulation of a given therapeutic interlude and specific patient-indicator as is feasible from the total material available.

Exercise 7.2

The patient is a young attorney being seen by a male therapist because of difficulties in establishing long-term relationships with women and a tendency to lose his temper when provoked. The therapist conducts the sessions in his private office and has established a secure-frame treatment setting. Just prior to the session under consideration, the therapist discovered to his chagrin that he had deposited a check from the patient which contained an overpayment—the young man had paid for five weekly sessions when there had been only four. The therapist decided to allow the material from the patient to unfold before intervening. He wondered if the patient would be aware of the error.

The hour in question began as follows:

> *Patient:* I really got upset with my boss yesterday. It's not like him, but he exploited me. He made me work all weekend on a case and he didn't give me the bonus I usually get for that kind of work. Sometimes he uses people; he becomes a greedy bastard. I told him how I felt. He apologized and said he would make it up to me. After all, he's usually pretty straight, someone I can rely on. He gives more than he takes, which is more than I can say for a lot of people. Now that I think of it, he's a lot like my father: pretty nice and caring most of the time, but when something sets him off, he loses perspective and exploits everyone in sight. Sometimes he gets quite crazy: He acts violently and blindly, though afterward, he's filled with regret.

First, name and classify the indicators in this excerpt, both in the introductory material and in the session itself. Next, name all known adaptive contexts, and using the excerpt alone, identify the best direct and derivative representations of each context.

When this has been completed, turn to the dimensions of human experience reflected in this material. For each segment, identify the dimensions of the therapeutic interaction involved and state the specific intervention contexts that have determined the manifest and latent content. Be certain to add whatever is known of the patient's pathology that has led to the selective perceptions of the therapist represented in each dimension.

_____

_____

_____

_____

_____

_____

_____

_____

_____

_____

_____

_____

_____

_____

_____

Answer

The first three indicators are alluded to in the introductory material, and a fourth is offered in the session. They are as follows:

1. The patient's difficulties in establishing long-term relationships with women (an interpersonal dysfunction; strong).

2. The patient's tendency to lose his temper when provoked (an interpersonal symptom; strong).

3. The patient's overpayment to the therapist (a gross behavioral resistance—frame devitation, a fee alteration; strong).

4. The patient's problem and feeling of upset with his boss (an interpersonal disturbance; moderate to weak [in light of the justification for the patient's upset]).

The following are the adaptive contexts in this material, both alluded to in the introduction:

1. The secure frame (the ideal frame; moderate to strong).

2. The therapist's acceptance of an overpayment from the patient (frame deviation in the area of the fee; strong).

There are no direct representations of either intervention context in the patient's material in the part of the hour under consideration. There are, however, several highly meaningful (close) derivative representations of each context. They are as follows:

1. The patient's allusion to the exploitation by his boss, including the boss's failure to give the patient a bonus for extra work—depriving the patient of money apparently his due; all of this is a representation of the therapist's acceptance of the overpayment.

2. The representation of the boss as "a greedy bastard," another derivative portrayal of the therapist's error in accepting the patient's excessive check.

3. The description of the boss as "pretty straight," reliable, and "nice and caring"—all representations of the therapist's capacity to offer the patient a generally secure frame.

4. Finally, there is another allusion to the boss as someone capable of exploitation—a further representation of the acceptance of the erroneous check.

We turn now to the dimensions of the therapeutic interaction. Responding in sequence, we may consider, first, the images related to the boss's (1) having exploited the patient, (2) having given him overtime work without extra pay, (3) generally misusing people, and (4) being "a greedy bastard." This sequence begins, then, with an image of the parasitic mode of relatedness—one that emphasizes exploitative qualities. The patient's reference to working over the weekend, beyond his usual hours, contains a ground-rule image.

Notice how quickly the patient has expressed himself in two spheres: mode of relatedness and framework. Patients readily find particular incidents in their lives as a way of representing in derivative and displaced form those unconscious perceptions of the therapist with which they are concerned. The therapist must be quite sensitive to the dimensional implications of life incidents that appear in the patient's material.

The allusion to not being paid for extra work is also a portrayal of the parasitic mode of relatedness, as are the references to the boss's misuse of people and his greed.

Another dimension portrayed here is the action-discharge mode of cure. The boss makes use of the patient in exploitative fashion in order to solve a problem of his own. All allusions to problem-solving based on inappropriate action, exploitation, and other negative qualities tend to represent the action-discharge mode of adaptation—and therefore of cure or symptom relief.

Other dimensions are more weakly portrayed: Images of greed and exploitation reflect unresolved dynamic conflicts with aggression and perhaps orality (greed). The material also carries a faint implication of irrationality or inconsistency: The boss failed to pay the patient on this occasion, although he had done so under similar conditions in the past. This suggestion of contradictory messages would represent a conflict in the dimension of madness.

Next, we should funnel all of these impressions into the tripartite listening–formulating schema. As proposed, there is a weak indicator here, in that the patient seems disturbed over what happened with his boss, although not irrationally or madly so. The adaptive context that has stimulated these communications is clearly the patient's conscious or unconscious realization that the therapist had accepted an overpayment for the previous month. (Later in the session, the therapist intervened by playing back the patient's derivative representations of this particular intervention context and interpreted his unconscious perceptions of the therapist as selectively stimulated by this errant intervention. The patient said that he had not clearly recognized the error, but all week had had a sense that something was wrong with his fee, because he had been uncharacteristically preoccupied with money and the cost of treatment.)

This context is not, of course, directly portrayed here, though it does receive relatively strong derivative representation. As noted, such representation involves mainly the images of the exploitative boss and an action of his through which the patient was inappropriately deprived of money. These images communicate valid encoded perceptions of the therapist's exploitative act, his infraction of the ground rules (the boss's keeping the patient overtime represents in weak form the therapist's acceptance of the extra fee), his misuse of the patient, and his greed. Nevertheless, the perceptions were selected in terms of the patient's own problems with aggression and greed, much of it related to intense latent homosexual conflicts. (Later in the hour, through allusions to a movie, the theme of homosexual prostitution appeared.) As stated earlier, it is important to allow the instinctual-drive component of a patient's unconscious responses—especially those elements that are sexual and latently homosexual—to emerge in derivative form so they may be included in the therapist's intervention. Again: Every major deviation by a therapist is perceived validly by the patient as containing a perverse quality.

In the next segment of the session, the patient describes feeling good, telling the boss how he felt, and obtaining an apology and a promise to correct the wrong. Here, there is representation of a solid sense of identity and self-esteem, a portrayal of open communication, and a shift from the parasitic to the healthy symbiotic mode of relatedness. Actually, the relationship between the patient and his boss may well be *commensal* (having equal satisfactions on both sides, as opposed to a healthy symbiosis, where both partners are satisfied, but one obtains more gratification than the other). In psychotherapy, because the therapeutic needs of the patient are primary and overriding, the ideal mode of relatedness is a healthy symbiosis. So even when a commensal relationship is represented in the patient's associations, it generally implies an unconscious perception of a healthy symbiosis within the treatment experience.

Again, implicit to this discussion is the communicative finding that patients first and foremost represent in encoded fashion the actualities (manifest and latent) of the therapeutic interaction. Only rarely do they portray unconscious fantasies and wishes as a primary communication, though these do emerge as *reactions* to initial perceptions of the true nature of the transactions between the patient and therapist.

The adaptive context for this segment of material appears to be (1) the therapist's ability to establish a secure-frame psychotherapy for this patient and (2) his previously valid interpretations and framework-management responses. Under such conditions, the patient unconsciously perceives the therapist as having a stable identity and as being available for all types of communicative material.

The boss's apology may represent a previous situation in which the therapist had erred and then corrected his ways, shifting from an invalid to a valid intervention. The best representation of these collective prior adaptive contexts appears in the next sequence of material, where the patient describes his boss as someone who is usually good to him, who can be relied on, and who gives more than he takes. Here, in regard to the dimensions of interactional experience, the patient is describing a sense of trust that he has with someone who maintains a secure framework for psychotherapy (the framework qualities are implied here because they contrast with the prior incident). This material also alludes to the usual healthy symbiosis that has existed between this patient and therapist. The frame-securing, interpretive psychotherapist does indeed give more than he takes (although he also receives). Another implication in this segment of the associations is that the patient's sound functioning is a response to the therapist's establishment of a secure frame and interpretive approach. This presumption would be formulated as a silent hypothesis (i.e., formulated internally and not told to the patient), requiring validation in the patient's subsequent associations.

An important dimension is reflected in the patient's representation of a problem that was evidently solved in a constructive manner. The patient's frank discussion with his boss and the boss's positive response represents the insightful mode of cure in psychotherapy. The adaptive context once again appears to be the therapist's ability to secure the frame and, in general, to respond with sound interpretations to the patient's associations.

Finally, the patient draws an analogy between his father and his boss. This, of course, introduces a genetic element into the relationship with the boss—and by extension, into the relationship with the therapist. The unconscious perception is a response to both major adaptive contexts: the background of a secure frame and interpretive approach, and the foreground of the immediate deviation. The patient implies that the therapist is in some fashion repeating in the present situation an aspect of the patient's earlier relationship with his father. Such genetic experiences, especially as they pertain to the patient's pathology, significantly determine the implications that are perceived unconsciously by a patient with respect to a particular deviant intervention context.

As indicated earlier, the last segment of this material also contains an allusion to madness. For the therapist to cash a check made out for the wrong amount does indeed represent a neurotic (though probably not psychotic) momentary and explicable break with reality. The patient will experience this type of break in the frame as a danger situation because he will be uncertain as to how far the deviations will extend. In addition, the therapist is conveying contradictory messages: On the one hand, he is using a secure frame, on the other, he is momentarily deviating. There is a shift with each deviation toward expressions of therapist-madness along with the patient's consequent responsive unconscious perceptions. Aptly, the patient characterizes this particular madness as violent and blind action. He anticipates, however, that the therapist will quickly recover and rectify the situation. This anticipation (an anticipatory perception?) is undoubtedly based on earlier interventions of the therapist. The clearest model of rectification in the material is the boss's decision to pay the patient for his weekend work after all.

This final segment also suggests dynamic issues related to aggression and possibly latent homosexuality. The patient describes his father's response to having engaged in crazy behavior as one of regret. This suggests a superego reaction that could touch upon issues of narcissism as well as intrapsychic or structural (id, ego, and superego) conflict. Those dimensions which would take on most meaning would depend on the patient's subsequent associations. For the moment, the patient in this particular vignette has stressed mode of relatedness, frame issues, positive communication, genetics (and to a lesser extent, dynamics), and madness.

Again, this overall schema is simply a pragmatic tool. The sensitive therapist need not be overly concerned at this point with *identifying* the specific dimension that is currently being experienced and worked over by the patient. A good interpretation will naturally take the proper dimension into account. For example, an interpretation of the patient's unconscious perception of the therapist's deposit of the check as exploitative would automatically take into account a perceived pathological mode of relatedness—even if the therapist has not registered this dimension as an identifiable area of human experience. Certainly direct recognition is preferable, but the listener should not feel anxious about knowing the name of a dimension, as though that knowledge were the main point. Close adherence to the imagery of the patient will generally lead to interventions carried out within the proper framework or dimensions of the patient's communications. The advantage of direct recognition of the experiential dimension of the material is that it facilitates the therapist's comprehension of the broader implications of that material and often helps to guide the search for the specific adaptive context that has served as the stimulus.

THE FOUR CLASSES OF INTERVENTION AND THEIR IMPLICATIONS IN EACH DIMENSION OF EXPERIENCE

It is not possible to consider every type of intervention that may occur in the course of a psychotherapeutic experience. The goal here is to accustom the reader to subjectively evaluating his or her own efforts—the adaptive contexts that stimulate the patient's material. The following are model exercises that should be answered in terms of the seven categories that constitute the dimension schema, with the addition, if necessary, of other possible implications not already identified.

Silence: Exercise 7.3

We will begin these efforts by considering appropriate and inappropriate extended silence by the therapist. Appropriate silence is used in the absence of interpretable material (a lack of a clearly represented adaptive context and derivative complex). Inappropriate silence is tantamount to a missed intervention; it occurs despite the presence of an important indicator, a sufficiently well-represented adaptive context, and clearly conveyed unconscious perceptions.

The reader should envision a therapeutic situation in which he or she has not intervened for the major portion of an hour, perhaps for one or more previous sessions. As therapist, one is monitoring the patient's material for *encoded* perceptions of that silence, attempting to gauge its validity. Although manifest complaints about the silence may well occur in the patient's material (rarely, however, when the silence is appropriate), the therapist's evaluation of the nature and function of his or her extended silence must include an understanding of the patient's *derivative* commentary.

This level of listening is supplemented by a reevaluation of the material in the current hour for indicators, represented adaptive contexts, and meaningful derivatives. Alternating with this task will be a subjective review of the implications of the silence, structured in terms of whether the therapist feels for the moment that it is valid or erroneous.

What then are the implications of appropriate and inappropriate silence? List the answer for each of these forms of silence in terms of the seven dimensions of the therapeutic interaction, adding additional qualities if necessary.

_____

_____

_____

_____

_____

_____

_____

_____

_____

_____

_____

_____

_____

_____

_____

_____

_____

_____

_____

_____

_____

Answer

Appropriate silence has the following universal characteristics:

1. Frame: Secure, sound holding and containment.

2. Mode of relatedness: Healthy autism—distance that is for the moment appropriate.

3. Mode of cure: Cure through insight—awaiting meaningful material.

4. Communication: Accepting the patient's need for noncommunication and attempting to understand its basis.

5. Dynamics and genetics: Dynamically healthy deprivation with genetic meanings for both patient and therapist. Genetics tie to good parental care.

6. Self and identity: Strong and cohesive for the therapist.

7. Sanity and madness: The therapist is sane and able to manage his or her own inner mental world.

8. Other: Overall, there is a sense of appropriate nonintrusiveness, a therapist capable of managing his or her own needs without forcing them pathologically upon the patient, and a sense of presence awaiting further developments.

In contrast, silence as a failure to intervene in the presence of meaningful material from the patient tends to have the following universal characteristics:

1. Frame: Poor holding and containing.

2. Mode of relatedness: Pathological autism.

3. Mode of cure: Silence as a negative form of action-discharge and pathological merger.

4. Communicative: A communicative failure on the part of the therapist who does not understand the meanings of the patient's communications.

5. Dynamics and genetics may involve the hostility of the therapist and pathological defenses against seductiveness. The genetic factor relates to poor parental care.

6. Self and identity: Conveys a confused and disturbed identity and pathological narcissism in the therapist.

7. Sanity and madness: Communicates therapist-madness and anxious flight from the patient.

8. Other: Overall, a missed intervention reflects an imposition by the therapist of his own defensive and resistant needs, a basic failure to understand, and withdrawal into a pathological autistic mode of relatedness.

In summary, a therapist evaluates his or her ongoing interventions (1) by having an immediate subjective awareness of their content, (2) by determining the universal and specific attributes of each intervention, and (3) by assessing the patient's manifest and especially derivative communications. A sound grasp of the universals helps the therapist to organize and understand the patient's derivative expressions, but the therapist should also remain open to meanings in the patient's material that have not yet been formulated.

Ground Rules—Frame Management:
Exercise 7.4

The relatively constant aspects of the ground rules of psychotherapy are called the *fixed frame*. The fixed frame includes the physical setting; the fee— including responsibility for all sessions; a set frequency that allows for the vacation policy of the therapist; and a fixed length of time for each session. In the area of the ground rules, the key factor is whether the frame is entirely secure or broken (deviant).

Once again, using the seven dimensions of the therapeutic interaction, list the universal qualities of the fixed frame and then list those qualities that apply to deviations from it—those infractions that either overgratify or overly frustrate, or even harm, the patient.

_____

_____

_____

_____

_____

_____

_____

_____

_____

_____

_____

_____

_____

_____

_____

_____

_____

_____

_____

_____
_____
_____
_____
_____
_____
_____
_____
_____
_____

Answer

Adherence to the fixed frame is always supported by the patient's derivative communications, even when it precipitates manifest opposition. These components of the ground rules are most responsible for the development of the claustrum that safely holds the patient secure, encouraging open communication regarding his or her madness, while at the same time creating intense claustrophobic (actually phobic-paranoid) anxieties. It is the claustrophobic danger situation as personally experienced by each patient that is the central source of danger and therapeutic movement within the secure-frame situation. Typically, such work unfolds as the patient from time to time develops these paranoid-claustrophobic anxieties and attempts to modify the fixed frame. The patient's derivative expressions guide the therapist's adherence to the frame, and the patient then responds to the frame-securing interventions.

To list now the main implications of the establishment and maintenance of the fixed frame:

1. Frame: All of the implications of maintaining the ideal ground rules—clear interpersonal boundaries, an unambiguous portrayal of reality, a sense of basic trust, a sense of a reliable, well-managing therapist, and a strong hold and sense of containment.

2. Mode of relatedness: An offer of a healthy therapeutic symbiosis to the patient and of a basic meaning link.

3. Mode of cure: The ideal setting for the insightful mode of cure, as well as cure through unconscious and inevitable positive introjects of the well-functioning therapist.

4. Communication: Conscious and unconscious communication is maximally open and meaningful.

5. Dynamics and genetics: The establishment of a claustrum with paranoid-claustrophobic anxieties and their genetic repercussions for the patient.

6. Self and identity: A basic sense of a stable and healthy identity and a cohesive sense of self for the therapist.

7. Sanity and madness: A sane therapist who holds the patient well; the patient then expresses his or her madness in response to the implications of the properly held, fixed frame.

Deviations of the fixed frame are distinguished in terms of those that are gratifying to the patient and those that are exploitative and hurtful. The general implications are as follows:

1. Frame: A basically deviant frame that implies blurred interpersonal boundaries, ambiguous and uncertain realities, basic mistrust, a sense of an unreliable, poorly managing therapist, and a poor hold and sense of containment.

2. Mode of relatedness: A pathological mode of relatedness that may be autistic, symbiotic, or parasitic.

3. Mode of cure: A shift to the action-discharge, merger mode of cure.

4. Communication: Meaningful interpretation concentrates exclusively around the deviation; other spheres of conscious and unconscious expression are restricted.

5. Dynamics and genetics depend upon the nature of the deviation. Each alteration in the fixed frame is also unconsciously perceived as a form of perverse sexual gratification and hostile assault. Dynamic issues of separation and merger are also mobilized. Much depends on the specific deviation invoked by the therapist.

6. Self and identity: Disturbances of identity and sense of self in the therapist.

7. Sanity and madness: Each deviation is an expression of therapist-madness to which the patient selectively responds.

The general pattern should be clear at this juncture. The secure frame provides a healthy mode of relatedness, promotes the insightful mode of cure, fosters open communication, and creates inevitable danger in terms of the specific implications of a given ground rule. A secure frame also generates an image of a strong identity and sense of self in the therapist, along with a perception of his or her sanity. In contrast, deviations lead to pathological shifts in each of these spheres.

Turning now in brief to the other main aspects of the frame: The use of the couch enhances the sense of the secure hold for the patient, along with enhancing claustrophobic anxieties. Issues of sexuality, passivity, helplessness, and paranoid anxieties are also prominent. The relative anonymity and neutrality of the therapist provide an appropriate interpersonal boundary; deviations in either area tend to produce merger, seduction, aggression, and overdependency.

The one-to-one relationship, total privacy, and total confidentiality tend also to reinforce the patient's basic sense of trust and safety, while enhancing paranoid-phobic anxieties and separation concerns. Deviations in this area tend to lead to feelings of betrayal, to primal scene and oedipal dynamics (through the creation of threesomes), and a sense of basic mistrust because of the intrusions of others into the therapeutic space.

A careful and detailed communicative study of each specific ground rule and the many possible deviations that may occur in its application by the therapist should reveal additional implications to the therapist's interventions in this very basic sphere of human relatedness. On the whole, psychotherapy is ground-rule issue therapy. The therapist's handling of these basic tenets constitutes the most fundamental adaptive contexts to which patients respond communicatively, behaviorally, and symptomatically. Thus, the therapist's management of the frame is the most basic stimulus for the vicissitudes of the patient's psychopathology and expressions of madness. As a result, much of the listening–formulating process concentrates on issues and communications in this sphere, as will most therapeutic interventions.

Interpretation–Reconstructions and Noninterpretive Interventions

All efforts at interpretation must follow the basic structure of utilizing an adaptive context and derivative complex to account for the unconscious meanings of an indicator or therapeutic context. Valid interventions imply a healthy symbiosis, the insightful mode of cure, communicative openness and understanding, dynamics related both to loving and to envy, and a strong sense of identity, self-cohesion, and sanity in the therapist. Interpretive errors will lead to pathological images in each of these spheres. In addition, the specific nature of the error—the material that the therapist has misunderstood, the additional material that the therapist has avoided, and the therapist's own selection of erroneous comment—will all play a specific role in generating a particular unconscious image of the therapist.

When an intervention does not obtain derivative validation in unique form, the therapist should examine the material from the patient that has prompted the erroneous comment or frame deviation. This material must be regarded as the adaptive context for the therapist, and much can be learned in the way of self-knowledge by comprehending the nature of that stimulus. Furthermore, each erroneous intervention contains the therapist's pathological unconscious communications, which are unconsciously perceived by the patient and will generate his or her direct and derivative responses. Thus, a nonvalidated intervention requires extensive exploration in order to determine the particulars of the erroneous adaptive context with which the patient has been confronted. To view such errors as simple empathic failures is entirely insufficient. They are fraught with content and meaning and must be understood with respect to each of the seven spheres of therapeutic interaction.

All noninterpretive interventions are inherently deviant and pathological, and the principles applied to interpretive errors extend even more strongly to these efforts. Noninterpretive interventions are more extreme forms of madness than interpretive errors, and they tend to evoke more powerful responses—

though not nearly as powerful as deviations in the basic ground rules. Because they virtually never obtain derivative validation, a therapist is well-advised to eliminate so-called supportive and other deviant responses from his or her lexicon of therapeutic endeavors. When interventions of this type are made, considerable self-analysis is required and a full exploration of the manifest and latent communications that the patient has experienced.

CONCLUDING COMMENTS

An attempt has been made in this chapter, to develop an important tool for the listening–formulating process. The introduction of the seven dimensions of the therapeutic interaction can serve as a guide not only to understanding the nature of the therapist's interventions and their most compelling implications, but also to identifying the intrapsychic and intrapersonal issues with which a patient is concerned in a given hour. Further, an understanding of the universal implications of sound and deviant interventions offers the therapist an important guide to both self-knowledge and the meanings of the patient's specific, selective derivative material.

As we have seen, the adaptive context plays a central role in the therapeutic interaction and in the listening–formulating process. For this reason, we have now identified four major tasks in dealing with these contexts: (1) identifying those that are known to exist as background and immediate contexts, (2) recognizing manifest representations, (3) attending to derivative portrayals, and (4) reviewing the known universal implications of each context. These endeavors may well be supplemented by an additional consideration of already known implications of particular contexts for a specific patient in light of a given therapeutic interaction. Ultimately, the goal is the definitive understanding of an individual patient's response. The understanding of universal implications is therefore only a first step in this direction, but it is an important and crucial step, and one that deserves repeated review and mastery.

8
Responses to Interventions: Encoded Perceptions

Only recently has it been possible to clearly sort out the variety of a patient's responses—direct, indirect, distorted, behavioral, and otherwise—to a therapist's interventions. Heretofore the communicative approach (Langs, 1978, 1982a) specified as the main consideration the identification of the derivative complex—ideally, a set of coalescing derivatives that illuminate the patient's unconscious registration of meanings communicated by the intervention context. The derivative complex was a potpourri of responses that had not been carefully teased out.

The present formulation makes a primary distinction between the patient's basic perceptions of an intervention context and the reactions generated by those perceptions. Each intervention of the therapist precipitates a variety of conscious thoughts and feelings on the part of the patient, as well as direct behaviors. But it is the patient's encoded unconscious perceptions of an intervention context that illuminate the patient's madness. As has been pointed out, the patient's pathology will determine his or her unconscious selection of implications from those that are conveyed by a therapeutic effort. Once these perceptions have been registered outside of awareness, they are processed very quickly and precipitate a series of similarly selected reactions to what has been perceived. These reactions depend not only on the nature of the patient's pathology, but also on the patient's capacity to adapt in a healthy manner to unconsciously perceived stimuli.

Reactions generated by encoded perceptions may take several forms: (1) free associations; (2) behaviors within and outside of the treatment situation; and (3) affective responses. Within the associational complex, along with encoded fantasies and memories, whose raw form is unconscious to the patient, there may be conscious memories, both recent and remote, as well as conscious fantasies and the recall of dreams.

As for the content of a patient's reactions to what has been perceived unconsciously, the following are most important:

1. Exaggerations of the initial perceptions, which grade into unconscious distortions—transference-based responses.

2. Symptoms and expressions of madness.

3. Sane or constructive reactions, including the offer of correctives and models of rectification to the therapist, as well as unconscious efforts to cure the errant therapist and to respond positively to his or her interventions no matter how destructive.

4. Primarily mad responses, which include efforts to harm the therapist.

In order to make clear the implications of the different elements of a patient's response to an intervention context, I will state directly some of what I have already foreshadowed: The patient's primary unconscious response to an intervention context is nontransferential. The patient is registering outside of awareness the various stimuli comprised by an intervention, along with their implications. These encoded perceptions are accurate and realistic, but they are, of course, shaped by the nature of the psychic instrument that is registering them. They will accordingly reflect the patient's psychopathology and earlier genetic experiences, because these have helped to determine the way in which a person takes in unconscious stimuli and gives them meaning. It is to be stressed, then, that nontransference reactions, like transference reactions, have their own genetic history.

Transference reactions come into play only after nontransference perceptions have been registered outside of awareness. Transference is a secondary response constituted by exaggerations or distortions of the patient's initial veridical perceptions of the intervention context. These distortions occur primarily on an unconscious level and take the form of unconscious fantasies and exaggerated or erroneous versions of valid perceptions. In other words, the realm of transference is established when the patient's pathology overrides the veridical qualities of his or her basic unconscious perceptions. Clinically, such responses occur mainly in the presence of a secure frame and the use of an interpretive approach.

The patient's pathology, then, influences both valid unconscious perceptions (nontransference) and distortions and exaggerations based on those valid perceptions (transference). Both realms have their genetic antecedents, which must be understood in light of earlier pathogenic and healthy life experiences of the patient. Interpretation in both realms clarifies the etiology and unconscious basis of a patient's madness.

The basic listening–formulating process as it applies to the patient's responses to intervention contexts is as follows: (1) The therapist identifies valid and selected encoded perceptions of implications communicated by the most recent and powerful adaptive contexts. (2) The therapist looks for indications of exaggerations and distortions based on these perceptions. (3) The therapist searches for evoked symptoms and resistances and responses that indicate efforts to harm the therapist. (4) The therapist seeks out highly constructive unconscious (and sometimes conscious) reactions that entail curative and corrective efforts. The therapist should master these categories of reaction so that he or she becomes sensitive to their emergence in the patient's material. Once familiar to the therapist, they are relatively easy to recognize.

ENCODED PERCEPTIONS: EXERCISES

Exercise 8.1

To begin with a brief and relatively simple vignette, we may consider the consultation session of a young man who had sought psychotherapy because of episodes of confusion and depression. He was being seen by a male therapist in a private office without contamination of the setting. Toward the end of this session, after the therapist had proposed the set of secure-frame ground rules, the following dialogue transpired:

> *Patient:* I have insurance at work. I assume you will complete the forms so I can afford your fee.
>
> *Therapist:* Bring them in and I will look them over.
>
> *Patient:* Fine. The only therapist I ever really got to know was this weird psychologist friend of mine. What bothered me was that he'd always talk about his patients at dinner parties, like he had nothing else to say. I thought it was kind of strange, making jokes about them, calling them fags and perverts to get a laugh. I sure hope that's not your style.

We will focus on the intervention described in this excerpt. To begin this exercise, the reader should identify its basic nature (including what it implies regarding the frame) and implications. Next, select at least two encoded perceptions of the therapist in light of the intervention context. What can be said of the underlying madness reflected in the patient's selection of meanings? To emphasize this aspect, compare the two main implications touched on by the patient with your own listing of the meanings of the adaptive context at hand. Remember to make use of the seven dimensions of human and therapeutic experience in developing your evaluation of this particular intervention. The reader who wishes, in addition, to anticipate future listening exercises, might identify at least one model of rectification in this material.

_____

_____

_____

_____

_____

_____

_____

_____

_____

_____

_____

_____

_____

_____

_____

_____

_____

_____

_____

_____

_____

_____

_____

_____

_____

_____

_____

_____

_____

_____

_____

_____

_____

_____

_____

_____

_____

_____

Answer

The main background adaptive context for this session is the effort by the therapist to offer the patient a secure-frame psychotherapy. These basic conditions, however, are then modified by the main intervention in the segment of material excerpted here. The therapist's proposal that the patient bring in the insurance form for his review is (1) a noninterpretive intervention in the form of a suggestion and (2) a comment implying that the therapist is prepared to complete this form should it meet certain unstated requirements. Thus, the suggestion is itself a deviation from the ideal conditions of treatment (which confine therapeutic exchanges to the free associations of the patient and the interpretive and framework-management interventions of the therapist). It implies further the potential completion of the form—a more dramatic alteration of the ideal frame. It is this latter implication that will be especially powerful as an adaptive context for the patient's reactions.

We will begin, then, with the universal implications of the completion of an insurance form (the anticipated adaptive context):

1. Frame: This frame deviation will generate a sense of basic mistrust and uncertainty in the patient's relationship with the therapist. There are alterations in total confidentiality and in the one-to-one relationship with total privacy (the insurance company and its personnel become parties to the treatment situation). There is also an alteration in the patient's full responsibility for the fee.

2. Mode of relatedness: The completion of an insurance form creates a pathological symbiosis and is usually viewed as parasitic for the therapist—exploitative and self-serving.

3. Mode of cure: Inherent in this intervention context is cure through action-discharge and merger.

4. Communication: This particular adaptation-evoking context will undermine the fundamental openness of the patient's direct and derivative communications. In addition, it will concentrate the patient's adaptive and derivative reactions on the implications of this particular deviant adaptive context.

5. Dynamics and genetics: Prominent among the genetics and dynamics inherent in the completion of the insurance form are its perverse and primal scene qualities and the elements of oral and anal greed. Despite the real justification for the use of insurance, the patient unconsciously perceives these pathological attributes in both the therapist and himself under these conditions. Involves, too, are conflicts in the exhibitionistic and voyeuristic spheres, and qualities of superego corruption. This is a universal reaction, notwithstanding the manifest legality of the situation.

6. Self and identity: In the areas of identity and narcissism, this intervention context implies a disturbance of identity in the therapist, because he is involving the insurance company in the treatment of the patient. This leads to images of disturbance in the narcissistic sphere and a lack of a cohesive sense of self.

7. Sanity and madness: As with virtually all deviations, the completion of an insurance form is seen as an expression of therapist-madness.

As represented in this segment of material, the patient has unconsciously selected certain implications of the insurance deviation as a vantage point from which to view the therapist. This selection was determined by reasons not evident in this particular session (which is fraught with genetic and dynamic implications). The patient's unconscious perceptions are as follows:

1. A view of the therapist as mad expressed by way of the allusion to the "weird psychologist" who makes strange jokes about his patients.

2. A view of the therapist as one who inappropriately exhibits his patients to others; these others, by implication, should not be involved in the treatment situation. This perception is represented in the allusion to the psychologist's discussion of his patients at dinner parties.

3. The parasitic qualities of completing an insurance form are unconsciously perceived and reflected in the allusion to the therapist's ridicule of his patients.

4. The perverse aspect of the therapist's intervention is unconsciously registered in the allusion to the psychologist's calling his patients "fags" and "perverts."

5. The psychologist's action-oriented misuse of his patients in conversations with others reflects the action-discharge mode of cure inherent in the completion of an insurance form.

6. Also implied by the psychologist's discussion of his patients at a social gathering is the therapist's deviation from the appropriate therapeutic frame.

7. A basic disturbance in communication may also be inferred from the patient's reference to the inappropriate qualities of the psychologist's communications about his patients.

The main selected unconscious perceptions of the implications latent in the therapist's anticipated deviation center around: the therapist's madness, his readiness to inappropriately expose his patients to others who do not belong in the treatment situation, his exploitativeness, and his desire for perverse gratification.

The reader may well be wondering why these perceived attributes are to be regarded as valid or even as exaggerated versions of real attributes. It must be recognized, however, that the criterion by which the patient unconsciously evaluates the interventions of the therapist is almost entirely his or her own therapeutic needs with respect to the therapist. The patient is not an *objective* psychic instrument; his or her perceptions are guided by tacit requirements for a secure hold and an authentic relationship based on both conscious and unconscious levels of communication. Whatever is consciously or unconsciously designed by the therapist to meet those requirements, the patient will perceive unconsciously in a favorable light. Whatever interferes with those needs will be viewed in a negative light. The patient's unconscious needs and premises are often different from those that are conscious.

As the following chapter makes clear, this particular criterion often makes difficult the task of distinguishing valid perceptions from those that contain exaggeration and distortion. In the long run, however, the patient's psychopathology is illuminated regardless of whether the material is primarily transference or nontransference-based. In marginal situations, the therapist simply intervenes in a manner that demonstrates the patient's selection of attributes as well as the nature of whatever has been perceived (the stimulus).

Finally, we may identify the model of rectification offered by this patient in encoded form. It is contained in the last statement of the excerpt. The patient expresses his hope that the therapist's style is not the same as the psychologist's. The corrective is stated as a wish rather than as a directive, and it is offered as a general statement rather than as a specific proposal. The patient is suggesting that the therapist should not in general be as loose as the psychologist. The patient does not go so far as to specify that the therapist not complete the insurance form, which, of course, would make concrete the similarity of the therapist's behavior to the psychologist's. This specification, however, is implied.

Much of the therapist's time in the fundamental listening–formulating process should be spent in the attempt to detect selectively communicated unconscious perceptions related to intervention contexts. Even when the therapist has recognized in the patient's associations an indicator and/or a manifest (or clear encoded) representation of an adaptive context, the search should be made for additional encoded perceptive meaning.

The key operation in this effort is the identification of the specific and general themes contained manifestly in each segment of material. When an intervention context is known, its recognized implications serve as a guide to selecting those manifest themes most likely to contain unconscious meaning; but if the adaptive context has not yet been established, the sequence of accumulated thematic meaning should direct the therapist to seek out a probable antecedent intervention that would account for the coalescing derivative material.

For example, in the preceding vignette, the initial segment of associations contains the themes of weirdness and an allusion to a psychologist. This should immediately alert the therapist that the material to follow may have something to do with a prior or anticipated intervention context perceived by the patient unconsciously as strange. The themes that come up next involve talking—particularly themes of talking about patients at dinner parties. The implication here should make the therapist wonder whether he had intervened in such a way as to publicly expose the patient under inappropriate circumstances. The allusion to strangeness and to making jokes implies exploitation and humiliation. The references to fags and perverts suggest a homosexual theme and perversity in general. Finally, the patient expresses a wish that there be a difference between the therapist and the psychologist described, which suggests that the intervention in question has not yet been made or should be corrected.

The therapist should not find difficult the task of connecting these manifest themes to the latent meanings of his potentially completing the insurance form. These allusions, after all, closely followed the patient's manifest reference to the form and the therapist's manifest agreement to look at it (for the purpose of filling it out). Notice again that one must undo the work of both displacement and symbolization in order to link the themes in the patient's material to the implications of the relevant adaptive context.

Exercise 8.2

The patient is a young married woman with two children. She had sought psychotherapy for severe depressive episodes. The treatment is with a male therapist, begun under rather deviant conditions with shared office space, two early sessions in a group, and the completion of insurance forms. Over many months, these deviations were rectified through the therapist's establishment of individual once-weekly psychotherapy, a shift to a private office, and within the past month, the elimination of insurance coverage at the behest of the patient's derivative communications. The session that will concern us began as follows:

> *Patient:* I never gave up on my husband. He's really cleaned up his act. For once, he took a stand with the children. He wouldn't let them run loose. He's even keeping them out of the bedroom now. I appreciated that. I can be close to him for once, alone with him more. I hope I don't mess it up or find out I'm sicker than I thought. It feels strange here without the insurance and all those third parties hanging around.

For this exercise, identify the major intervention contexts. Then, in sequence, identify each encoded perception of the therapist in light of the adaptive contexts involved. Select the themes in the patient's material that bridge from the manifest associations to these derivative images. Notice the allusion to a potential indicator toward the end of this session; attempt to formulate its basis in light of the intervention context and derivative complex. Concentrate for the most part, however, on identifying the patient's encoded perceptions of the therapist in light of his most recent intervention contexts.

_____

_____

_____

_____

_____

_____

_____

_____

_____

_____

_____

_____

_____

_____

_____

_____

_____

_____

_____

_____

_____

_____

_____

_____

_____

_____

_____

_____

_____

Answer

The major intervention context at this point in the patient's treatment is the therapist's decision to no longer complete the insurance forms. This decision was made, as noted, at the behest of the patient's derivative communications. The patient supported this decision consciously without reservation, and her initial derivative response showed both cognitive and interpersonal validation.

We have already reviewed the universal implications of completing an insurance form. The intervention context of its elimination will, of course, tend to have meanings directly opposed to those involving its completion. The reader may wish to identify them specifically by using the seven-part schema for the dimensions of the therapeutic interaction. Here, we will concentrate on the selected encoded perceptions that this rectification of the frame led this particular patient to convey.

In considering each of the encoded perceptions of the therapist in light of his intervention context as reflected in this material, we will identify both the perception itself and the manifest themes that connect to the latent or derivative images:

1. The first manifest theme involves the patient's comment that her husband has "cleaned up his act." The key theme is that of taking some type of corrective measure. The link, of course, is to the therapist's rectification of the frame. Unconsciously, the patient conveys through a simple displacement her image of the therapist as having cleaned up his act.

2. The next segment is about the husband's stand with the children—not letting them run loose. The main themes are those of firmness and setting limits, establishing controls for persons who are out of control. This, too, represents the therapist in light of his having rectified the frame. By no longer signing insurance forms, the therapist took a firm stand and helped the patient develop a sense of boundaries and controls. To this point, then, the patient is encoding some general unconscious perceptions of the therapist in terms of the broad implications of framework-rectification efforts.

3. The next image in the patient's narrative involves the husband's keeping the children out of the parental bedroom. Again, the theme is one of setting limits, but this allusion is specifically to entry into the parental bedroom and therefore suggests

primal scene issues. The patient is touching on another selected perception of the implications of the therapist's rectification efforts: the exclusion of inappropriate and unwelcome third parties into the treatment situation (represented by the parental bedroom).

4. The next allusions are to closeness (intimacy) and the opportunity to be alone with someone for whom the patient has strong feelings. Once again, these themes touch on some of the encoded perceptions of the therapist in light of his intervention and its consequences—an opportunity for genuine therapeutic intimacy and the chance to be alone with the therapist without the intrusion of third parties.

Notice that up to this point the images in the patient's material have been consonant with the implications of the rectifying intervention context identified. But the patient's subsequent allusion to messing things up and finding out that she is sicker than she thought introduces a negative theme that is more difficult to formulate as an encoded perception precipitated by a rectification. This segment of material reminds us that one must initially treat every derivative communicatom from the patient as a valid encoded perception of the therapist in light of a significant adaptive context. The temptation is to assume that this segment contains a distortion of sound perceptions, but the therapist must always assume first that the material is reflecting a primary nontransference response.

One would begin, therefore, by seeking a basis for the patient's view that the therapist's rectification had messed up their relationship, in some way reflected a deeper sickness in the therapist then previously perceived, or represented strange behavior on his part. As we know, these images are not in keeping with the validating perceptions prior to this material in the excerpt, nor are they consonant with the validation obtained in earlier sessions.

Two other likely possibilities are: (1) The images organize around a different and deviant intervention context. (Several sessions later, a minor context of this sort did emerge.) (2) The images allude to the patient rather than to the therapist. Communicative findings indicate that patients initially validate all rectifications of the basic frame both interpersonally and cognitively. Subsequently, however, they develop anxieties regarding the claustrum created by a secure frame. Typical among patients' concerns is their fear of the emergence of their own madness, now that the madness of the therapist has been eliminated. This formulation—that the image reflects anxiety over the security of the frame and the inability to take refuge in the madness of the therapist—is further supported by later images (not cited here) pertaining to the patient's dread of confinement and to rules that immobilize her to the point that she feels in danger of suffocating.

This exercise demonstrates that a therapist must be quite secure in his or her knowledge of the implications of an intervention before concluding that the patient's material reflects a distorted and erroneous perception or a reaction to a valid perception. Such formulations should in general be confined to silent hypotheses and subjected to subsequent validation through the coalescing of additional encoded images supporting the therapist's impressions of the material's function on an unconscious level. Again, it is best to accept all derivative communications as perceptive before deciding that another function is more critical. Recall that there was indeed a minor and hidden deviation to which the patient was also responding at the time of this session. That deviation had already been rectified even though the patient had never alluded to it; she was working over its prior existence in her material and correcting it unconsciously in her sessions.

Note that the sequence extracted here concludes with a direct allusion to the rectifying intervention context. It is this manifest portrayal that supports the hypothesis that these derivatives do indeed constitute encoded perceptions of the therapist in light of the elimination of the insurance forms. Notice, too, the ease with which these derivatives coalesce around various implications of the adaptive context. They first touch on the general securing of boundaries and limits, then move to the elimination of a specific dynamic and genetic meaning related to primal scene experience, and, finally, express secondary reactions to initial perceptions—the patient is anxious about the transactions that will emerge under secure-frame conditions. It is this type of *flow* and meaningful derivative sequence that lends important support to formulations of encoded perceptions.

In terms of the patient's pathology, the depression that led her to seek therapy was centered around her own impulsivity and unresolved primal scene memories and fantasies. The symptom had occurred after the patient's involvement in a brief affair. In this light, the therapist's rectification of the frame would serve as an important unconscious model and introject for the patient in revising her own acting-out. His intervention demonstrates his ability to control and manage a measure of pathology comparable to the pathology existing in the patient. That rectification would, of course, have to be supplemented by sound and validated interpretations so that the patient would understand the specific unconscious basis for her involvement in the affair and her control difficulties. Thus, therapeutically, the patient would need both the rectification of the frame (the sound model of the therapist as capable of managing his own impulses and pathological perception–fantasy–memory systems) and interpretation (insight through understanding the meanings and consequences of frame-rectification measures).

Exercise 8.3a

In examining the patient's material for encoded perceptions, the therapist is concerned with more than identifying disguised images and recognizing the interventions that prompted them. Meaningful communication is more than a number of scattered derivative perceptions. It is constituted by a sequence of perceptions that offer different vantage points on the same intervention. The conflicts surrounding the patient's experience of an adaptive context are partly the result of the same stimuli prompting contradictory forms of response; the patient's material reflects perceived cues for response that are being processed outside of awareness.

In the previous example, if the patient had simply provided a number of encoded images having to do with no longer being exposed inappropriately to others, we would have meaning, but no depth. The material would be restricted to a single theme and perspective. Although it might be possible to intervene on this basis, it is advisable to wait until the encoded perceptions are more varied and complex. A truly meaningful cluster of selected encoded perceptions in response to a single critical intervention context would include portrayals of at least two or more of the dimensions (implications) of a particular adaptive context. This is what I have been calling a *coalescing derivative complex*—a sequence of encoded images that shift about from one meaning to another and tend to include genetic implications as well.

When the therapist is scanning and evaluating the patient's material for representations of an activated adaptation-evoking context, he or she should have some sense of the seven dimensions of the therapeutic interaction and be attempting to identify the realm of experience specified by the patient's communications. As I suggested earlier, the ability to use the seven-part schema in this manner requires practice, and the beginning therapist should not be anxious about mastering the technique right away. But as the therapist "fine-tunes" his or her interventions, the categories become useful for making sure that the patient's material has touched on significantly different meanings and functions of the relevant intervention context. The derivative cluster should include meanings in several of the seven dimensions; in particular, the therapist should wait until dynamic and genetic implications emerge in the patient's material. Otherwise the derivative complex tends to be flat and highly intellectualized.

The following vignette illustrates this process of collecting different implications of an intervention context as represented in the patient's material. It concerns a female patient who was seeing a male therapist for severe depressive episodes. There had been three periods of treatment. The first two took place under rather deviant conditions. The last was a secure-frame approach, during which time the patient's symptoms had improved considerably, as had her general functioning and her sexual relationship with her husband.

Three days before the patient's next scheduled session, the therapist telephoned her to state that it was necessary for him to cancel the upcoming hour; he would see her the following week. Although the call had been made necessary by an urgent family situation, the therapist simply told the patient that something urgent had happened and he would not be able to keep their appointment. When the patient arrived for the next session, she began the hour as follows:

> *Patient:* I will be missing the next two sessions because of the holidays. I also will require back surgery in about a month and will have to be out for about three to four weeks. It's not fair: You can cancel a session and I have no choice, but if I cancel a session, I have to pay for the missed hour. I won't pay for those sessions when I'm out for the surgery. I'll terminate first. My husband uses me sexually. He gets off and there's nothing for me. It's time for me to speak up to him. I'm beginning to feel that treatment means too much to me. I don't like being boxed in. I never liked it as a child. Father left us stranded when I was just four years old. He disappeared. We thought he was dead, or that maybe he just went crazy. We never could rely on him. Because of him, I could never trust men.

The goal of this exercise is to identify the patient's selected encoded perceptions of the therapist in light of the prevailing adaptive context—the sudden cancellation of an hour. State as well the main universal implications of the key deviant intervention context in terms of the seven-part dimensional schema. Is there an additional background context to which the patient is responding in this session? If so, attempt to identify its nature. Next, specify the themes that bridge from the manifest content of these associations to latent perceptions of the therapist. Into which of the seven categories of the therapeutic interaction and experience does each of these themes and images fall? Does the cluster of derivatives identified constitute a multifaceted and therefore coalescing derivative complex? If not, how does it fall short? If possible, identify the source of anxiety (the danger situation) for the therapist, which has been unconsciously perceived by the patient. Finally, indicate whether there is evidence in this material of a model of rectification. Concentrate on identifying the implications of the key intervention context and identifying the patient's responsive encoded perceptions.

_____
_____
_____
_____
_____
_____
_____
_____
_____
_____
_____
_____
_____
_____
_____
_____
_____
_____
_____
_____
_____

_____

_____

_____

_____

_____

_____

_____

Answer

As noted, the main intervention context is the therapist's cancellation of the patient's hour by telephone. The major background adaptive context is the relatively secure therapeutic frame. To briefly identify the universal implications of the deviant intervention context, the following are the major ones:

1. Frame: A sudden break in the frame embodies all of the negative implications of an acute deviation—poor hold (being suddenly dropped), poor containment, mistrust, unpredictability, loss of reality certainty (there will be no session when there should be a session), and the like.

2. Mode of relatedness: A pathological autistic (sudden withdrawal and abandonment) and parasitic (exploitative) mode of relatedness.

3. Mode of cure: Action-discharge, evacuative mode.

4. Communication: Disruption to the point of its abrupt destruction.

5. Dynamics and genetics: Issues of sudden loss, separation anxiety, and abandonment with likely consequent death anxiety, rage and perhaps sexualized longings, and a stirring of similar earlier experiences in the life of the patient.

6. Self and identity: Uncertainty as to the identity of the therapist who is now unreliable and unpredictable, a sense of damaged narcissism on his part, and a sense of narcissistic mortification with likely consequent narcissistic rage in the patient. Self-regulation will be seen as impaired.

7. Sanity and madness: The cancellation will be seen as an expression of therapist-madness, a loss of control with dangerous and insane implications.

A communicative therapist would enter the session following the cancelled hour mindful of the implications generally perceived by patients in the prevailing intervention context. These meanings would guide and organize the patient's material and help the therapist to determine its manifest and latent common themes. The following appear to be the main communicative segments in this patient's associations, their key bridging themes, and the category of experience into which the images best fit:

1. The first segment of material is linked to the prevailing intervention context so linearly and so directly that it carries little or no encoded and unconscious meaning.

The patient alludes directly to the theme of cancelled sessions, which by implication—since it initially alludes to herself—would represent the intervention context. She discusses the unfairness of the therapist's prerogative to cancel an hour without evident penalty, and directly represents the secure frame: her own responsibility for missed sessions. The material also contains allusions to indicators—gross behavioral resistances in the form of plans to cancel several sessions. In addition, one quality of the therapist's intervention is minimally disguised in the patient's manner of response: She attempts projective identification (dumping) by making her own announcement abruptly, complaining directly about the therapist, and threatening to interrupt the treatment. (The therapist had no choice under the circumstances but to listen and wait; although the theme of the patient's missing sessions connects to the theme of the therapist's missing sessions, the disguise is so thin that the material cannot be regarded as a substantial encoded expression.)

This initial segment of material touches on a number of additional dimensions of the therapeutic interaction: (a) Ground-rule issues—The patient's plans to cancel hours represent anticipated deviations; the ground rule that permits the therapist to cancel hours (though ideally, not in abrupt fashion) represents the secure frame. (b) Mode of relatedness—The material alludes to the autistic mode of relatedness (the withdrawal of both patient and therapist), as well as to parasiticism—the exploitation of the therapist by the patient and of the patient by the therapist. (c) Mode of cure—The material centers on the action-discharge mode of cure. (d) Dynamics—The material expresses a strong sense of hostility. (e) Self and identity—Identity issues are implied in the patient's comparison of the role requirements and specifications that apply to herself with those that apply to the therapist. (f) Sanity and madness—There is a sense of inconsistency that speaks to the theme of madness.

2. The patient next displaces her communications from the therapeutic relationship on to the interaction with her husband. Here, the patient does indeed express a highly selected and encoded image of the therapist in light of his deviation. It should be mentioned in this regard that the therapist involved in this session had formulated a number of implications vis-à-vis the intervention context before the hour began. He had failed, however, to identify one implication that the patient's material faithfully reflected.

The key themes in the patient's associations are sexual exploitation and disregard for the needs of the other person. The patient's images portray the parasitic mode of relatedness and the action-discharge mode of cure. They record a sense of disturbed communication (note the allusion to the need for the patient to speak up) and dynamic conflicts related to hostility and perverse (almost masturbatory) sexual misuse. There are also implications of a lack of appreciation for the identity of the other person and the destructive use of the patient as a selfobject (narcissistically) by the therapist. Although the therapist had expected images that indicated a parasitic mode of relatedness and had anticipated allusions to dynamic issues involving sexual exploitation, he had not recognized or considered the perverse aspect of his deviation. This is how the patient's material provides supplementary information as well as validation with respect to the therapist's own formulations. The patient correctly perceived and expressed in her associations a meaning of the therapist's deviation that he himself had missed. The therapist should search for underlying countertransference factors in order to explain the block.

3. The patient's allusion to therapy meaning too much to her cannot be regarded as an encoded perception of the therapist in light of the cancelled session. Clearly, a therapist who suddenly abandons his patient is not expressing an overconcern for that individual. When an image does not fit as a view of the therapist, the therapist should pay attention to the patient's secondary responses—the patient's reactions to her own encoded perceptions. For the moment, we may take this particular image as a

model of rectification. It implies that the therapy should mean more to the therapist than he has shown by cancelling the hour. In other words, he should take the patient as his model.

4. The patient then states that she does not like being boxed in. Under other circumstances, if the frame were truly secure, we might consider this image a reflection of the patient's claustrophobic anxieties as mobilized by the restrictive character of the ideal frame. But in light of the therapist's cancellation of the hour, this material should be regarded instead as an encoded perception of the therapist. It is the therapist who has expressed himself as having claustrophobic anxieties. He is the one who does not like being boxed in by the ground rules of treatment. It is he who escaped by cancelling the session. Such a reading of cancelled sessions, of a therapist's late arrival, and of other modifications of the ideal frame is quite typical. The therapist is unconsciously perceived as escaping from a dangerous claustrum—the secure-frame therapeutic setting and situation. Notice that the perception of the therapist here is developed in terms of the patient's own manifest or latent claustrophobic anxieties and fantasies. Even when a therapist is faced with a real emergency and has no choice but to cancel an hour, the patient's perceptions are colored by the inevitable sense of relief experienced by a person who has a momentary opportunity to escape from a dreaded enclosure.

It should be recognized that the patient's manifest allusion to her own claustrophobic anxieties was used to represent the unconsciously perceived claustrophobic anxieties of the therapist for a number of reasons. This kind of image implies (a) an introjective identification with the therapist's perceived difficulty (modified to some extent in this case by the realities involved), and (b) a perceived correspondence for the moment between the pathology of the patient and the pathology of the therapist. Rectification and interpretation would be necessary in order to modify insightfully the pathology-related processes.

As the reader may have noted, this segment alludes to an anxiety and symptom (indicator) with strong dynamic implications, and therefore it belongs mainly to the category of dynamics and genetics. Of course, other dimensions may be involved as well; but they must be represented in the material before they can be reliably identified. The next segment of associations permits us to do this.

5. The final segment of material alludes to the father's abandonment of the family when the patient was four. It contains themes of death, madness, unreliability, and mistrust of men. The material reflects a clear unconscious perception of the therapist as having abandoned the patient in a manner strikingly similar to the disappearance of her father when she was a child. This loss is equated unconsciously with death, and the same element may well contain a reaction to the perceived loss of the therapist (father)—a wish that he were dead. Additional encoded perceptions involve the idea that an abandonment of this kind is an expression of madness and unreliability, and that it is a basis for mistrust. This last serves both as an encoded perception and a reaction to the perception (the broader mistrust of men).

This particular segment is organized around a genetic element—an early memory constellation that has been stimulated by the therapist's cancellation of the patient's session. This segment also has dynamic qualities and contains an allusion to an action-discharge mode of cure. In addition, it makes reference to madness, an autistic-parasitic mode of relatedness, and a break in the frame. This last is represented by the father's abandonment of his family and his responsibility to remain with them in his fatherly role.

This excerpt is an excellent example of the ideal communicative response to an intervention context. The associations have been shown to bear on virtually every aspect of the therapeutic interaction. In particular, the dynamic and genetic elements of the derivative complex are well-represented—a sign of a highly meaningful communicative response to an adaptive context. Also, the patient has shifted from one image or subject to another, each element of the material serving to convey a different aspect of her unconscious perceptions of the therapist in light of the main intervention context. This shifting about from one narrative or image to another is typical of a coalescing derivative complex that reveals multiple meanings in diverse spheres. The meanings are varied and cumulative, and the images coalesce into a comprehensive picture.

Exercise 8.3b

The above material lends itself ideally to interpretation. The patient's plans to cancel several sessions and possibly to interrupt her treatment is a strong indicator. The adaptive context of the therapist's cancellation of the patient's hour is represented manifestly. And, finally, there is a highly meaningful coalescing derivative complex. Although it is not the main purpose of this workbook to teach interpretive skills, this particular excerpt offers all of the elements necessary to attempt an interpretation. What could have been said to this patient at this point in the session? Remember that the goal is to explain the latent implications of the patient-indicator in light of the represented adaptive context and responsive encoded perceptions.

_____

_____

_____

_____

_____

_____

_____

_____

_____

_____

_____

_____

_____

_____

_____

_____

_____

_____

_____

It is usually best to begin an interpretation with a direct allusion to the adaptive context. This is always the fulcrum for interpretive comment. Thus, the therapist might have said the following:

> You have mentioned that you were upset when I called last week to cancel your session. You are thinking now of cancelling several sessions yourself and of possibly interrupting treatment (this is the main patient-indicator). You have spoken about your husband using you sexually for his own gratification and giving nothing to you. Indirectly, this must be the way you experienced my sudden cancellation—as my sexually misusing you. You spoke of therapy meaning too much to you, as if to imply it should mean more to me in light of what I did. You also mention not liking being boxed in. This too must be your image of me in light of my cancelling your session—getting out.
>
> All of this has led you to remember a time when your father suddenly abandoned you—a clear connection to what I did by cancelling the session. Just as you thought he was mad or dead, unreliable, and not worthy of your trust, these must have been your perceptions of me in light of my own sudden disappearance. It seems then that I have in some way repeated a very painful experience you suffered in your childhood and that in order to cope with it, you plan now to abandon or disappear from me (the patient's main reaction to the adaptive context and its underlying function).

This is how the listening–formulating process leads into the interventional efforts of the therapist. Rectification of the frame is impossible here, of course, in that the lost session is irrevocably lost. And the therapist cannot guarantee that he will never have to suddenly cancel the patient's hour again. All that can be done, then, is to offer a sound interpretation of the patient's material in light of the intervention context, making sure to draw out the meanings in each dimension of the patient's experience, particularly the dynamic and genetic dimensions. By concentrating on unconscious perceptions and their genetic repercussions, the therapist can at least demonstrate to the patient his ability to understand her pain and perceptions as well as her own action-discharge reponse to the therapist's action-discharge disruptive intervention.

Sometimes this kind of interpretive effort is insufficient to help a highly traumatized or separation-sensitive patient contain his or her own need to respond with action-discharge and maladaptive resistances. But ideally it enables the patient to introject an image of the therapist as understanding and controlled, and to use these qualities in reestablishing his or her own capacity to contain and manage without destructive action. But in either case, the interpretation must concentrate on the patient's encoded perceptions of the therapist. This is the only way to illuminate the unconscious aspects of the patient's response. If the therapist in this case, for example, were to explain the patient's material solely in terms of her own genetics and intrapsychic conflicts, omitting clear allusion to the intervention context and its implications, the patient would feel further dumped into and acted on, and would likely terminate the treatment prematurely.

CONCLUDING COMMENTS

In attempting to decode material from patients in light of prevailing intervention contexts, we have outlined the following process: The therapist subjectively evaluates the implications of each active adaptive context, supplementing these efforts by seeking images in the patient's material that support the initial formulations. The therapist must also remain open to derivative perceptions overlooked in the course of the initial evaluation, and to derivative images that do not fit at all with his or her formulations, perhaps leading to unrecognized intervention contexts.

Each identified derivative image should be categorized in terms of the seven-part scheme that identifies the dimensions of human experience and of the therapeutic interaction. A coalescing derivative complex will touch upon several of these dimensions, each with a meaningful encoded image.

Images that are simplistic and easily decoded tend not to be especially meaningful. Unconscious communication is carried by narratives and images of substance and depth. They do not lend themselves to easy or direct translation, and they are likely to express unconscious perceptions of an intervention context in a unique and surprising way, using strong displacement and a notable measure of symbolization and disguise. Such images are the poetry that stands in contrast to the prose of manifest expression. They must be decoded rather than skimmed for their evident inferences.

Encoded derivatives have meaning only in light of the specific stimuli of the therapist's interventions. At times, isolated decoding efforts may prove useful, if tentative, but only when the therapist has a sense that they may be organized eventually around a previously unrecognized intervention context. Ultimately, every formulation must take into account the implications of a definitive adaptive context and accordingly must identify specific derivative perceptions.

The patient's first and fundamental reaction to each intervention from the therapist is perceptual. The patient perceives the intervention context both consciously and unconsciously. Unconscious perceptions are selected primarily in terms of the patient's psychopathology and madness. This means that the very process of unconsciously perceiving an adaptive context will take into account and be a product of the pathology and healthy assets of both participants to treatment.

It is to be stressed that the patient's basic perception of stimuli conveyed outside of direct awareness is nontransference-based. The implications being perceived are really conveyed by the therapist's intervention. Nevertheless, the patient is selecting only certain of these implications for representation and reaction. This process of selection is significantly determined by the patient's psychopathology. This is why the patient's encoded perceptions can be interpreted; they express the patient's madness. On the other hand, the patient is selecting from perceptions that are themselves valid and sound. In fact, the genetic and dynamic aspects of the patient's encoded perceptions of an intervention context's implications will ultimately reveal the way in which the therapist has unwittingly repeated a past pathogenic interaction in the patient's life, thus engaging him or her unconsciously along the lines of least resistance. This interaction between the patient and the therapist is real. It is not an illusion determined by the patient's transference.

Transference reactions are extensions of the patient's initial perceptions; they are exaggerations and distortions precipitated by what has been perceived. Additional genetic factors emerge as the patient begins to react to his or her initial perceptions. These genetic factors form the basis for the distortions, misperceptions, or disturbed responses to the therapist that follow the patient's valid encoded representations of the intervention context.

The point here is that one need not seek out transference reactions in the patient's material as though the patient's pathology could be analyzed and resolved insightfully only on this basis. The patient's madness is expressed in both the nontransference and transference realms of response. Both types of communication deserve full formulation and, when possible, interpretation and rectification. Because they inevitably intermix in each sphere, it may well be that the very concepts of transference and nontransference have outlived their clinical usefulness.

As defined by most writers, a transference response is a patient's inappropriate reaction to a therapist based on pathological unconscious fantasy and memory systems. The concept of transference is thus invoked only in the presence of manifest allusions to the therapist. As we have seen, however, *every* association from the patient may be seen as a reflection of images related to the therapist. Furthermore, there is no room in the theory of transference for recognizing a patient's *valid* reactions to the therapist—for the understanding that a therapist may be evoking pathological responses in the patient by virtue of his or her interventions. The theory, in addition, does not recognize the patient's unconscious perceptions of the therapist—valid derivative images reflecting latent implications conveyed by the therapist's manifest interventions.

The entire concept of transference as presently defined is misguided and confused. It does not take into account the unconscious constellation involved in a patient's distortions when they are actually present, but assumes only that a manifest reaction has been shaped by unconscious childhood antecedents. Thus, it does not recognize encoded images of the therapist or of the therapeutic context in the patient's associations. In fact, these latter clinical referents are not understood as transference reactions at all. Compounding this confusion is the fact that veridical perceptions can be difficult to distinguish from unrealistic distortions. The unconscious implications of the therapist's interventions are so extensive that much of what was previously considered distorted and in error in a patient's reactions is actually quite valid and correct.

For these reasons, it may be clinically useful to drop the terms *transference* and *nontransference*. In their place, we may offer the fundamental conception that a patient responds initially to a therapist's intervention with valid encoded perceptions. These are conveyed in his or her associations and behaviors—key derivative communications. Such perceptions are selected for representation in terms of the patient's own psychopathology and madness. They are subsequently responded to in a variety of ways that will be described in the following chapter. Each step of this process is influenced by the actual nature of the therapist's interventions, the state of the current therapeutic interaction, and the genetic histories of both participants—but mainly that of the patient.

By intervening on the basis of this approach, there is little need to label any aspect of the patient's reaction as valid or distorted. The therapist will essentially detail the nature of the intervention context at hand, the manner in which the patient has selectively perceived its implications, and describe from there the patient's reactions to these perceptions. This process creates a truly neutral and comprehensive intervention that serves the interpretive and rectifying functions of the therapist. Much confusion would be eliminated thereby, and psychotherapeutic work would, as a result, be far more constructive and sound.

9
Responses to Interventions: Reactions to Perceptions

The patient reacts both consciously and unconsciously to an intervention context on the basis of his or her perceptions of its implications. We are concerned here with the patient's unconscious perceptions, on the basis of which a patient reacts in a variety of ways. There are six major categories of reaction to be monitored in the patient's material; these are discussed below.

CATEGORIES OF REACTION

The Intrapsychic Response

As we know, the patient's madness leads to selected veridical perceptions of an intervention context. Subsequent exaggerations, distortions, fantasies, and memories extend from these initial perceptions and can be identified only if the therapist has fully evaluated the conscious and especially unconscious implications of the intervention context at hand. Any derivative communication that does not meet the criteria of veridical unconscious perceptions of these implications may well be a distorted secondary response.

It is important to understand that unconscious fantasies and memories stirred by unconscious perceptions will often be represented in the patient's associations in encoded fashion. Memory elements are communicated not only in terms of consciously recalled incidents from childhood that have some connection to the intervention context; they are also communicated unconsciously through encoded images. Such images can be recognized as memories only when one has established a comprehensive appreciation of the implications of the patient's material in light of his or her life experiences.

For example, in the vignette presented toward the end of Chapter 8, the patient's communications regarding her wish to miss several future sessions contain encoded memory elements. In disguised form, the patient touches on one aspect of her mother's reaction to her husband's having abandoned the family: her refusal to accept him back into the home when his escapade had ended. In addition, this segment may encode an unconscious fantasy of talion revenge (abandonment for abandonment) harbored by the patient toward her therapist and her father.

The images involving the patient's sexual exploitation by her husband encode early memories related to the sexual conflicts existing between the patient's parents, along with unconscious sexual fantasies involving both her father and mother—the direct and negative oedipal constellations.

The patient's fear of being boxed in was later traced to primal scene experiences in which she unconsciously viewed her mother as entrapped and endangered by her father. The same image also contains one element of a series of unconscious fantasies within the patient related to these primal scene experiences.

Finally, the manifest genetic link portrayed by the patient between the intervention context of the cancelled hour and the earlier abandonment by her father involves the conscious thought that the father might have been dead. This thought contains within it unconscious violent death wishes toward her father. Even the allusion to the father's possible lapse into madness contains within it an encoded reference to the patient's own disorganized and mad response to the sudden loss of her father when she was a child.

As can be seen, once the patient has established a critical unconscious perception of the therapist selectively identified from the broad implications of an intervention context, it is likely that he or she will then reveal both direct and encoded versions of underlying memory and fantasy systems. It can be difficult, however, to clearly establish where the patient is exaggerating or distorting.

In a segment of the vignette under consideration, for example, the patient contends on an unconscious level that cancelling an hour is tantamount to sexual exploitation. Clearly, on the surface level, the therapist has not exploited the patient in any sexual fashion. On the other hand, a sudden cancellation of this kind is universally perceived as perverse and sexually exploitative. The intervention conveys a series of unconscious sexual fantasies and images that were perceived by this patient. The distortions in the patient's reading of these implications were determined mainly by earlier seductive experiences between the patient and her father, so the material reflects a transference-based communication; but the fact remains that sudden frame deviations of this type are universally unconsciously perceived in terms of their perverse quality.

The most important principle here is that the therapist must accept the patient's unconscious impression that a manifestly nonsexual deviation of this kind actually contains a latent unconscious sexual element. Consider it this way: If the patient had suddenly cancelled, the therapist would have viewed her behavior as an expression of her unconscious sexual and aggressive fantasies. It must therefore be acknowledged that a therapist who acts out in similar fashion (no matter what the rational justification) will be perceived unconsciously in those terms. When a therapist identifies a distorted or exaggerated element in the patient's material, there will almost always be a simultaneous grain of truth in those encoded communications. Conversely, every veridical perception, because it is selected and influenced by the patient's madness, contains some, however small, element of distortion.

Gross Behavioral and Affective Reactions

The patient responds to conscious and unconscious perceptions of the therapist with affects, behaviors, and enactments, expressed both within the therapeutic relationship and outside of it. The patient under discussion reacted to the cancellation of her session with plans to miss the two following hours, to cancel three or four weeks of sessions, and to terminate her therapy if she was held responsible for the missed hours. Such behaviors are generally understood as *acting out*, a term that implies the patient is living out both unconscious perceptions and responsive unconscious fantasies. The unconscious perception side of acting out has been greatly underestimated. The patient's actions must be regarded as indicators, but they should be understood in light of activated intervention contexts and the patient's derivative perceptions of the therapist.

The patient's plan to speak up to her husband is another potential behavioral response to the encoded perceptions of the therapist in light of the cancellation of the session. In reaction to the unconsciously perceived perverse sexual quality of the deviation, the patient's behavioral response was a distortion of the initial unconscious perception and its perceived unconscious meaning. Thus, it is important to recognize that patients react behaviorally not only to the evident qualities of an adaptive context but also to its unconscious implications. Following a version of the talionic law, an intervention context that constitutes an action directed against the patient and an action-discharge response by the therapist will tend to evoke similar behaviors in the patient. Communicatively, projective identifications and dumping by the therapist tend to prompt the same tactics from the patient. These unconscious influences of intervention contexts on the patient's behavior are quite strong and have gone relatively unrecognized.

Symptom Alleviation and Positive Characterological Change

Symptomatic improvement in the patient is a reaction that generally follows his or her constructive unconscious perceptions of valid interpretive and framework-management adaptive contexts. This positive sign is often accompanied by growth and maturation. The constructive underpinnings of such change is reflected in the patient's highly positive and constructively meaningful derivative perceptions of the prevailing intervention context.

But symptom alleviation may also follow deviant interventions by the therapist, and under these circumstances, an analysis of the adaptive context will reveal its erroneous and detrimental qualities. The patient's material will also reflect his or her unconscious perceptions of these negative attributes.

When this is the case, symptomatic improvement may stem from several sources. Among these, the patient's wish to present himself or herself as a model of emotional health to the sick (mad) therapist is often quite prominent (see below). It should be clear, however, that the underlying and unconscious basis for symptomatic remission can be determined only by identifying the prevailing adaptive context and the patient's selected derivative perceptions.

Symptomatic Exacerbation

In general, symptomatic exacerbation tends to occur when the patient unconsciously perceives and experiences the destructive elements in an erroneous intervention context and the unconscious pressure by the therapist toward an exacerbation of the patient's madness. It is critical to realize that the most important factor in symptom and characterological fluctuations in a patient in psychotherapy lies in the therapist's interventions. Just as these efforts can help the patient to insightfully resolve his or her madness, they can also greatly exacerbate the patient's psychopathology. Again, virtually the only means by which the underlying basis of symptomatic exacerbation can be formulated and understood is an analysis of the implications of the prevailing adaptive contexts and the patient's encoded perceptions.

Returning again to the excerpt under discussion, later in the same session, the patient referred to the return of her sexual frigidity during relations with her husband—a symptom that had greatly diminished over recent months. This exacerbation can be understood in light of the intervention context of the cancelled hour. Recall that the patient had unconsciouly perceived this particular intervention as constituting on a deep level a sexual exploitation. The patient responded to this unconscious perception with frigidity—a symptom that had as its underlying basis far more than the patient's resentment toward her husband. Without offering additional evidence, the material in the latter part of this session showed unmistakably that the major unconscious source of the patient's sexual disturbance derived from anxiety-provoking unconscious perceptions of the therapist in light of his deviant telephone call.

Positive Responses to the Therapist

Positive responses directed toward the therapist, such as the offer of models of rectification, efforts to help the therapist correct his or her errors, and unconscious curative endeavors are quite often seen. Perhaps the most frequent response to encoded perceptions of the therapist involves efforts by the patient to be curative and helpful (Little, 1951; Searles, 1975). The patient's unconscious curative powers are remarkably sensitive and strong.

Typically, once the patient has unconsciously perceived an errant intervention by the therapist, he or she automatically and unconsciously evaluates the implications of the deviant intervention. Quite frequently, the patient will then respond with unconscious (encoded) efforts to correct the therapist, to call to his or her attention the area that has been missed or misunderstood, and to set the therapist on the right track.

Such endeavors by the patient extend into actual unconscious interpretations—rather general and nonspecific encoded efforts designed unconsciously to help the therapist understand the sources of his or her mistake. The patient also offers models of rectification or corrective models, presenting to the therapist the type of intervention that should have been made, or more often, the nature of the framework rectification required by the situation. When a patient or therapist proposes a departure from the ideal ground rules of psychotherapy, the patient (who may consciously favor the deviation) will nearly always on a derivative level offer a correct model of how the situation should be handled— that is, the manner in which the frame should be maintained or secured.

In the vignette we are considering, the patient's reference to her husband's sexual exploitation has qualities of an unconscious interpretation made to the therapist. In effect, the patient seems to be suggesting that the therapist's cancellation of the session has an unconscious sexual and exploitative meaning for him. Similarly, the allusion to the patient's fears of being boxed in is an unconscious interpretation to the therapist, suggesting that his own claustrophobic anxieties might have contributed to his decision to cancel the hour. The genetic reference to the patient's abandonment by her father also may be an unconscious and general interpretation. It may have been designed to alert the therapist to his own earlier separation experiences as a possible factor in his decision to suddenly cancel the patient's session.

Although no clear model of rectification appeared in the material excerpted from that particular hour, later in the same session the patient spoke of her responsibility to be present at work. She alluded to a need to stay out from her job sometimes in order to go shopping, to see a dentist or a doctor, and even at times to be with someone in her family when he or she was ill. She went on to state that her role in the business was pivotal and that everything was enormously disrupted on the rare occasions when she had to miss work. She then admonished herself, saying that she should not miss a day at work unless she was flat on her back in bed.

This material is, of course, an encoded model of rectification in which the patient attempts unconsciously to propose standards by which the therapist should decide whether to attend his hours or cancel. The patient does leave room for emergency illness and the like, but the model stresses responsibility for being at the sessions even under such circumstances.

Attempts to Harm and Frustrate the Therapist

In response to errant interventions (and more rarely, and paradoxically, to sound interventional efforts), a patient will sometimes attempt to harm or thwart the therapist. In this case, the negative unconscious perceptions are registered and worked over, and they lead to reactions that are hurtful for the therapist.

In the session being cited here, the patient's decision to miss the next two hours, to miss several additional sessions, and to possibly interrupt the treatment possess such hurtful qualities. They are in part, of course, based on similarly hurtful unconscious (and conscious) perceptions of the therapist in light of his having cancelled her session.

The attempt is made to harm, to dump into (projectively identify into), and to otherwise frustrate the healing member of the therapeutic dyad. Not infrequently, this will involve lateness, silence, absence, direct and impossible questions asked of the therapist, and thoughts of or actual termination. These are all gross behavioral resistances provoked by errant adaptive contexts and the patient's resultant unconscious perceptions. Whenever a patient responds to a therapist directly in hostile and destructive fashion, a search must be made for the adaptive context and derivative perceptions that constitute the underlying basis of such responses.

REACTIONS TO UNCONSCIOUS PERCEPTIONS: EXERCISES

It is important while listening to material from patients in psychotherapy to attend to and formulate it in sequential fashion. Once the therapist has determined both patient-indicators and relevant adaptive contexts, efforts should be concentrated on determining the patient's selected encoded perceptions of the therapist. Each and every association from the patient should be taken as a potential encoded perception in light of an activated intervention context, and each should be evaluated for validity as such. A surprisingly large proportion of the patient's associations serve this function and will make sense in light of a full comprehension of the implications of a prevailing adaptive context.

By and large, then, it is only those images which, after repeated evaluation and testing, do *not* appear to make sense as encoded perceptions that one tests as reactions to perceptions. (The encoded perceptions to which the patient is reacting will, of course, be represented in other associations.) In short, one must first consider each association as a potential reflection of a perception before hypothesizing that it reflects a reaction to a perception. This sequence of listening and formulating is critical if one is to arrive at a valid and in-depth understanding of the patient's material.

While working on the following listening exercise, the reader should keep this sequence of tasks in mind—initially trying to identify patient-indicators and represented adaptive contexts in the material and, next, treating each element as though it encoded a valid perception of the therapist. Then, and only then, should an element be considered as a possible reaction to the patient's selected perceptions.

Exercise 9.1

The patient is a married woman with three children, two of whom are no longer living at home. One son, a young man in his twenties, has continued to live at home and has been of concern to the patient. She sought psychotherapy because of severe depressive episodes.

The patient has been seen for more than a year by a male therapist in a clinic setting. She pays a reduced fee to a secretary who gives her a receipt that she must show to her therapist before her weekly session can begin. In addition, because she lives in the same neighborhood as the therapist, she has come to know a great deal about him and his family. These modifications in relative anonymity eventually became a serious issue. The patient, who teaches Hebrew school, was assigned as the teacher of the therapist's son. Although the child did not know about the situation, both patient and therapist were aware of this contamination.

The patient, for her part, had befriended the son and had sought out and received additional personal information regarding the therapist's family. The therapist, too, had a great deal of difficulty when he discovered the existence of this particular contaminant. He tended to intervene on a manifest-content level, seemed rather critical of the patient, and had trouble working meaningfully with the patient's associations. Although he could have shifted his son into a different class and was aware of that option, he had failed to do so. The situation had become quite tense in the treatment setting. Both patient and therapist seemed to be at a loss as to how to resolve the anxieties and other disturbances that had arisen because of this coincidental event.

In a session three weeks prior to the hour to be partially excerpted, the patient had brought up thoughts of terminating treatment. Her associations made it clear that her depressive symptoms had not been resolved, and that the thoughts of termination were probably related to her continued contact with the therapist's son and her resultant sense of chaos in the treatment situation. Almost immediately after the patient had proposed termination, however, the therapist had intervened on a manifest-content level and suggested that the patient was right—termination should receive serious consideration. Though there were subsequent associations that gave derivative meaning to the patient's request and her perceptions of the therapist in light of his response, no interpretive intervention followed in this hour.

The next two sessions were flat and empty. Neither participant mentioned termination directly. The following hour began as follows:

> *Patient:* I've been unusually depressed this week. I got angry with my son and gave him a month to leave the house. My husband and his dear son stick together, eating foods they like as if I weren't there. My son primps up for his girl friend—she's his second cousin, you know. He left the house to see her without saying good-bye. He doesn't care if I live or die. My best friend's son provides his family with all kinds of merchandise. He works for a wholesale house. Naturally, I get nothing from my children. Maybe I'm being too abrupt in kicking my son out. On the other hand, it's about time he went out on his own. Maybe my problem is that I don't know how to handle separation and loss. I'm sure my mother's illness and hospitalization when I was six years old has a lot to do with it. Still, I shouldn't let the past influence my behavior in the present.

We will formulate this material in three steps, as follows.

Question 9.1a

Identify all of the patient-indicators in the introduction to this exercise, and then specify those patient-indicators that are reflected in the part of the session summarized above.

_____

_____

_____

_____

_____

_____

_____

_____

_____

_____

_____

_____

_____

_____

_____

_____

_____

_____

_____

_____

_____

_____

_____

_____

Answer

The following are the main background indicators as reflected in the introduction to this hour:

    1. The patient's depression, which led her to seek psychotherapy (symptom; moderate).

    2. The patient's knowledge about the therapist's family and personal life (gross behavioral resistance—frame deviation; strong).

    3. The patient's role as the teacher of the therapist's son (gross behavioral resistance—frame deviation; strong).

    4. The patient's asking questions of the therapist's son and obtaining additional personal information about the therapist's family (gross behavioral resistance—frame deviation; strong).

    5. The patient's wish to terminate her therapy (gross behavioral resistance

[largely because the patient's symptoms have not yet been insightfully resolved]; strong).

6. The flat and empty pair of sessions that followed the discussion of termination (gross behavioral resistances [assuming that the material was *manifestly* flat and empty]; moderate).

The patient-indicators reflected in the part of the session excerpted above are:

1. The patient's sense of depression (symptomatic; moderate).

2. The patient's anger with her son and her ultimatum that he must leave the house (a symptomatic, interpersonal disturbance; moderate).

3. The patient's complaints about her son and husband (an interpersonal disturbance; mild to moderate).

4. The patient's difficulty in handling separation and loss (symptomatic; moderate).

Question 9.1b

Identify all background and activated adaptive contexts. Indicate the two intervention contexts that best organize this material—that is, the two providing the clearest means of developing a coalescing derivative complex in terms of valid encoded perceptions of the therapist.

_____

_____

_____

_____

_____

_____

_____

_____

_____

_____

_____

_____

_____

_____

_____

_____

_____

_____

_____

_____

_____

_____

_____

_____

Answer

The main background adaptive contexts are:

1. The clinic setting, including the presence of the secretary (a deviant series of intervention contexts that modify the one-to-one relationship, the total privacy and confidentiality of the treatment, and offer the patient psychotherapy at a low fee; strong).

2. The therapist's role in the personal revelations regarding himself and his family that became available to the patient (a deviant intervention context that modifies the relative anonymity of the therapist and to some extent the locale of the contact between the two participants to treatment; strong).

3. The patient's contact with the therapist's son (a deviant intervention context that modifies the therapist's relative anonymity and provides the patient with extratherapeutic contact with the therapist outside of his office, though in displaced fashion; strong).

To comment further on this last intervention context, we may review its representation in the patient's allusion to the relationship between her son and his second cousin. This indicates, as the patient validly and unconsciously perceives, that this particular adaptive context is fraught with pathological incestuous gratification, pathological symbiotic and parasitic modes of relatedness, the possible use of the patient by the therapist (and the therapist by the patient) as a selfobject, an alteration in the usual interpersonal boundaries, and a means of effecting cure through action-discharge.

Despite the fact that the situation was somewhat beyond the control of the therapist (he had known that the patient taught at his son's Hebrew school, but not that she would be assigned to teach the boy), the patient will nonetheless respond to a situation of this kind as a powerful adaptive context, and will hold the therapist partly responsible for it. Certainly, both rectification and interpretation would be advisable, and both would have been feasible on the basis of the patient's direct and derivative material in these sessions. It was the therapist's failure to intervene in this regard that in significant measure led to the patient's thoughts of termination. On the other hand, it may well be that a contaminant of this kind ideally would be worked through in the patient's sessions such that termination and referral to another therapist would eventually be warranted if further therapy were needed.

4. The therapist's failure to intervene with interpretive and rectifying interventions in response to the deviation of the patient's contact with his son (an inappropriate silence and series of missed interventions; strong).

5. The therapist's statement to the patient that termination should be given serious consideration (a noninterpretive intervention with framework-deviation implications [the abrupt ending of the treatment experience]; strong).

This intervention context includes the therapist's manifest response to the patient, his failure to work with adaptive contexts and derivative responses in the patients' material, and his evident wish that the patient leave treatment. The context thus has qualities of an autistic and parasitic mode of relatedness, an action-discharge mode of cure, restriction of communication and understanding to the manifest level, dynamics related to hostility and separation, a sense of narcissistic manipulativeness, and a measure of madness—this last indicated by the abrupt and uncontrolled response of the therapist.

6. The final background adaptive context involves the therapist's failure to intervene interpretively in response to the meaningful material that followed the intervention regarding termination (the inappropriate use of silence and missed interventions; strong).

Question 9.1c

The two main intervention contexts that best organize this material appear to be: (a) the patient's contact with the therapist's son, and (b) the therapist's direct proposal that termination be given serious consideration. For each adaptive context, return to the excerpt and analyze the patient's associations in sequence. For each, identify those segments of associations that convey selected unconscious perceptions of the therapist in light of the adaptive context at hand. Next, identify those associations that involve reactions to these encoded perceptions. In doing so, state the nature of the response as a decoded raw message (i.e., undo the disguise and state the underlying and basic response) and indicate to which of the six categories of reactions a given response belongs. In all instances, be sure to use the implications of each adaptive context as the organizer of the patient's unconscious perceptions and reactions to these perceptions. As a first step, make use of the seven-part therapeutic interaction schema as a means of identifying the main implications of each of these intervention contexts. Although these have been mentioned briefly, attempt here a systematic analysis of these meanings. Use the fruits of these labors in organizing the patient's derivative perceptions and in carrying out the balance of this exercise.

_____

_____

_____

_____

_____

_____

_____

_____

_____

_____

_____

_____

_____

_____

_____

_____

_____

_____

Answer

The following appear to be the main attributes of the contact between the patient and the therapist's son. (This context will be treated in terms of the implication that the therapist's son is an extension of the therapist, and that the outside contact is in essence between patient and therapist.) On this basis, treating the contact entirely in terms of its function as an intervention context from the therapist, the following appear to be its main implications:

1. Frame: Deviant with blurred interpersonal boundaries, a basically mistrustful stance, and an impairment in reality testing (the nature of the relationship between therapist and patient is confused as to whether it is professional or student-teacher).

2. Mode of relatedness: Pathological symbiosis (an inappropriate form of merger).

3. Mode of cure: Action-discharge.

4. Communication: The creation of a basic disturbance in communicative relatedness with derivative communication focused on the deviant issue—the extratherapeutic contact.

5. Dynamics and genetics: Qualities of incest, oedipal issues, pregnancy fantasies, denial of separation, and specific genetic connections in terms of the patient's early life experiences.

6. Self and identity: The inappropriate use of the patient as a selfobject and a basic loss of clear identity as a therapist whose role with the patient becomes confused—an uncertainty as to whether he remains therapist or student-social companion.

7. Sanity and madness: The deviation is unconsciously experienced as an act of madness by the therapist.

We turn next to those meanings of this intervention context that were selected unconsciously by the patient for representation based on her own pathological needs and conflicts. In sequence, these encoded perceptions include the following:

1. The patient's allusion to being depressed contains an encoded perception of

the therapist's depressive disturbance, which has prompted him to become involved in a pathological symbiosis and fusion with the patient, using her as a selfobject to repair his sense of emptiness and aloneness.

2. The patient's reference to being angry with her son may be said to represent the adaptive context (her contact with the therapist's son), but it may also allude to a measure of unconscious hostility in this deviant intervention.

3. The patient's mention that her husband and "dear son" stick together is an encoded perception of the therapist's need to merge with the patient through the deviant intervention and establish a pathological symbiosis that undoes separation anxieties.

4. The allusion to the husband and son eating food is a derivative encoded perception of the oral devouring unconscious aspects of the extratherapeutic contact.

5. The son primping up for his girl friend probably alludes to the exhibitionistic qualities of this extratherapeutic contact.

6. The son's involvement with his second cousin contains an encoded perception of the incestuous qualities of the therapist's extratherapeutic contact with the patient.

7. The son's not caring if the patient lives or dies is an encoded perception of the hurtful and destructive aspects of the deviant context.

8. The allusion to the son who provides his family with all kinds of merchandise appears to portray an encoded perception of the gratifying aspects of the therapist's participation in this deviation.

9. The patient's allusion to getting nothing from her children may well represent the deprivation involved in the extratherapeutic contact—the patients' deprivation of a meaningful mode of relatedness with the therapist.

10. The allusion to the patient's difficulty in handling separation and loss is an encoded perception of the therapist's difficulties in these areas; it is based on his participation in the deviant intervention context.

11. The reference to the illness of the patient's mother involves a general encoded perception of some disturbance within the therapist.

Notice that the patient has portrayed several encoded meanings that were not included in our earlier formulation of the general implications of this intervention context. The patient chose these particular meanings because of the influence of her own psychopathology. It is the coordination of these two sources of information—the therapist's subjective impressions and knowledge, and the derivative communications from the patient—that produces a comprehensive understanding of the implications of an intervention context for a particular patient. The therapist should use his or her own understanding as a guide, but rely primarily on the patient's encoded material—especially when intervening. It is critical to work through, interpret, and rectify in terms of the patient's associations rather than rely on one's own unilateral understanding.

Our next task was to identify the patient's reaction to these encoded perceptions. In sequence, the following material appears to portray these responses:

1. The patient's depression is *a symptomatic response* to the intervention context.

2. The patient's anger with her son, although alluding by way of displacement to the therapist's son, is an *affective reaction* to the intervention context.

3. The ultimatum to the son that he leave the house within a month's time may be seen as an encoded reaction to the intervention context, first, in terms of the patient's *wish* that the situation could be corrected and, second, as a *model of rectification.*

4. The son's leaving the house without saying good-bye may be an additional *model of rectification:* The patient and the therapist's son should part.

5. Through condensation, the image of someone not caring if the patient lives or dies may be a further aspect of the patient's *depressive reaction* to the derivative complex, and may well reflect the patient's own *sense of guilt.* The patient may be holding up this guilt and a *self-punitive attitude* as a *model* for the therapist, suggesting that he too should feel guilty and depressed for his participation in the deviant context.

6. The allusion to the friend's son who provides the family with all kinds of merchandise may be an additional *model of rectification.* It would allude to more appropriate satisfactions that the therapist should be providing to the patient instead of the deviant and pathological gratifications involved in the extratherapeutic contact.

7. The comment that it is time the son went out on his own is another *encoded corrective* suggesting to the therapist that he should establish his relative autonomy from the patient by correcting the situation between the patient and his son.

8. The patient's proposal that she does not know how to handle separation and loss may be viewed as an *unconscious attempt to interpret* to the therapist some of the underlying pathology that has led him to continue to participate in the deviant contact. As such, it may be seen as an encoded or disguised (unconscious) interpretation.

9. The reference to the illness of the patient's mother and her hospitalization when the patient was six years old is a further attempt to *interpret unconsciously* to the therapist. This genetic interpretation suggests that early separation problems may be a factor in the therapist's need for the pathological extratherapeutic contact between his son and the patient.

10. The proposal that the patient should not let the past influence her behavior in the present is a final general recommendation or interpretation and a *model of rectification* offered through derivatives to the therapist.

We turn now to the encoded perceptions of the therapist reflected in this material in light of the termination intervention context. The following, listed in sequence, seem pertinent:

1. The patient's allusion to her increased depression is, through condensation, an encoded perception of the therapist in light of his proposal that the patient prematurely terminate her treatment. A sense of depression within the therapist is probably one of the factors that prompted his intervention, especially in view of the fact that it was made on a manifest-content level. The therapist was indeed subjectively depressed over this treatment situation and his dilemma of how to handle the patient's involvement with his son.

2. The patient's allusion to her anger with her son may be decoded, in light of the therapist's proposal, as an unconscious perception of the therapist's anger with her. Again, subjectively, the therapist was able to confirm this particular view of his attitude.

3. Next, there is the patient's ultimatum that her son leave the house within a month. The reader has likely recognized that this image is probably the best encoded representation in the excerpt of the adaptive context of the therapist's termination intervention. But it also suggests, through condensation, that the intervention functioned as an encoded ultimatum to the patient. This attribute came across to the patient so prominently because the therapist's response was direct, immediate, and given on a manifest-content level. If the circumstances had been different—if, say, the idea of termination had been proposed by the patient's derivative images as a constructive and appropriate course of action, and if the therapist had intervened in light of that material—the patient's subsequent image of his intervention as an ultimatum would have to be regarded as a distortion. The patient would have been exaggerating one of the perceived implications of a termination intervention on the basis of her own pathology.

4. The allusion to the alliance between the patient's husband and son, and their treating her as if she were not there, contains further encoded perceptions in light of the termination intervention context. The image essentially proposes that the patient's needs are being disregarded and that she is being ignored or gotten rid of. The image of the alliance is more directly related to the son's presence in the patient's class, so that it actually contains the patient's raw impression that the therapist's allegiance to his son has led him to wish to terminate treatment abruptly with the patient.

5. The allusion to the son's involvement with his second cousin does not seem to fit as an encoded perception of the therapist in light of the termination intervention context, though the son's leaving the house without saying good-bye does characterize once again the abruptness of the therapist's termination response and wish to be rid of the patient.

6. The allusion to the son's not caring if the patient lives or dies is an encoded perception of an implication of the intervention context: The therapist, in wishing to be rid of the patient quickly and directly, shows his lack of concern for the patient's survival.

7. The image that the patient gets nothing is an unconscious perception of the therapist's termination intervention and of his failure to work meaningfully with the patient's represented adaptive contexts and derivative material. Failures to generate adaptive-context interventions are seen as enormously depriving by patients on an unconscious level.

8. The next allusion, in which the patient wonders if she is being too abrupt in

kicking her son out of the house, contains again an encoded representation of the intervention context and of the patient's unconscious perception of the therapist—here, once more, that he is abruptly getting rid of her and excluding her from the treatment situation.

9. The final segment of associations contains a genetically represented encoded perception of the therapist as abandoning the patient in a manner comparable to her mother in her own childhood.

Discussion

As we can see, this highly traumatic intervention context has generated a powerful derivative complex containing many encoded perceptions of the therapist. Before turning to reactions to perceptions, we will pause here to categorize each of these perceptive elements in terms of the seven dimensions of the therapeutic interaction. On this basis, the reader should decide whether this is a meaningful and coalescing derivative complex, or if it significantly lacks depth, diversity, and dimensionality. What then are the categories into which each of these derivative images falls?

_____

_____

_____

_____

_____

_____

_____

_____

_____

_____

_____

_____

_____

_____

_____

_____

_____

_____

_____

_____

_____

_____

_____

_____

_____

To state the answer briefly:

1. The patient's depression is difficult to categorize for the moment without additional associations. It may have meaning in any or all of the spheres of human experience, especially the autistic mode of relatedness, and dynamics and genetics.

2. The patient's unconscious perception of the therapist's anger with her and the ultimatum to leave treatment falls into the realm of frame deviation, the autistic and parasitic mode of relatedness, the action-discharge mode of cure, projective identification mode of communication, hostile and separation-issue dynamics, and possibly madness—if the ultimatum was sudden and irrational.

3. The patient's image of being treated by the therapist as if she were not there involves mainly the pathological autistic mode of relatedness.

4. The therapist's abrupt wish to terminate touches on issues similar to the termination ultimatum described above (see #2).

5. The image of the therapist as not caring if the patient lives or dies appears to involve an autistic and parasitic pathological mode of relatedness, depressive dynamics and genetics, a failure to acknowledge the patient's identity and necessary narcissistic needs, and a possible sense of madness.

6. The patient's image that she gets nothing from her family implies a pathological autistic mode of relatedness and depressive dynamics and genetics.

7. The patient's allusion to her mother's hospitalization and illness is a strong dynamic and genetic statement of earlier events that influenced her direct and encoded responses to the therapist's termination intervention. It also embodies references to a possible frame break, a pathological autistic mode of relatedness, a disturbance in communication, and a damaged sense of identity and narcissism.

It seems evident that this is a highly meaningful, strongly coalescing derivative complex that touches on virtually every dimension of the therapeutic interaction, with the exception of the realm of dynamics (although it does have a strong genetic component). That is, the material offers little in the way of instinctual-drive representation other than a general sense of hostility and a hint at incestuous issues in the relationship between the patient's son and his second cousin. But as it pertains to the termination adaptive context, there is as yet little in the way of instinctual-drive derivative response—perceptions or reactions.

In all, these encoded perceptions tend to emphasize the patient's sense of sudden abandonment, her experience of a pathological autistic mode of re-latedness between herself and the therapist, a sense of the action-discharge mode of cure, communicative disturbance, separation issues, and the lack of a clear sense of identity. The encoded perceptions of the therapist appear to be organized around the patient's own depressive needs and constellation. Valid interpretation and rectification would therefore influence this important seg-ment of the patient's pathology.

We turn finally to the patient's reactions to the encoded perceptions stimulated by the termination intervention. To identify these responses in sequence, they are:

1. The patient's increased depression. Typically, patient-indicators are symp-tomatic exacerbations structured as unconscious responses to unconscious percep-tions of activated intervention contexts. This is why patient-indicators are interpreted in light of these latter two elements. We have here, then, a major symptomatic reac-tion to negative and hurtful unconscious perceptions of the therapist in light of his termination intervention. It would be the therapist's responsibility during the actual session to eventually interpret this depressive response in light of the patient's en-coded and depressively selected unconscious perceptions of the intervention context. Similar considerations apply to the patient's reactive anger.

2. The patient's ultimatum to her son may be seen as a behavioral reaction to the therapist's ultimatum to her. It is in this fashion that the interventions of the therapist tend to influence the patient's outside life. Often, an intervention context and its implications are unconsciously perceived and introjected by the patient, who then enacts a similar trauma with an outside figure. Of course, these external reactions may be more complex than illustrated here. Still, the ultimatum to the son appears to be a powerful reaction to the unconsciously perceived ultimatum the patient experienced from the therapist.

3. The allusion to the husband and son sticking together may be an unconscious fantasied response to the patient's perception of the therapist in light of the termina-tion intervention. Thus, this particular image may represent an encoded fantasy within the patient of being close to or sticking with the therapist. In this way, an intervention context unconsciously perceived as a wish to get rid of the patient prompts the patient to respond with fantasies of fusion and merger, extending into wishes to be fed as well. Even the allusion to being treated as if she were not there may represent the unconscious fantasy-wish that the therapist would more clearly acknowledge her existence.

4. The allusion to the son's primping for a date with his second cousin may also represent an unconscious fantasy. Here, the patient may well be expressing the wish to be attractive to or to seduce the therapist. These wishes are once again a response to the traumatizing unconscious perceptions of the therapist in light of his interven-tion.

The reason we are testing out these last two images as expressions of unconscious fantasy and wish systems is that the associations fail to decode as meaningful en-coded perceptions of the therapist in light of the prevailing intervention context. We are therefore shifting from the search for encoded perceptions to a consideration of possible reactions to such perceptions. When an image does not allude to a genetic element or a direct behavior of the patient, it is likely to contain either an encoded fantasy (wish) or a model of rectification. It is important, as always, to eventually identify the instinctual-drive qualities of such fantasy-wish systems.

5. The images of the son's leaving the patient without saying good-bye and his not caring if the patient lives or dies may, in addition to other functions, contain additional unconscious fantasies and wishes of the patient in response to the encoded perceptions already identified. Thus, the patient herself may be entertaining conscious and especially unconscious wishes to abandon the therapist before he abandons her. The image may also reflect the patient's not caring if the therapist lives or dies—that is, may reflect the patient's wishing him harm as an unconscious response to the intervention (though for the moment not acting directly on those wishes).

6. The image of the son who provides for his family may well contain the unconscious fantasy-wish that the therapist would better provide for the patient. The patient may also be responding to her perception of the therapist's underlying depression and hostility—wishing that she could provide better for the therapist.

7. The patient's allusion to the possibility that kicking her son out of the house may be too abrupt contains within it a curative element and a model of rectification. In its raw sense, the patient is advising the therapist in a rather confronting and slightly interpretive fashion that he should reconsider his thoughts of abruptly terminating the patient's treatment. There is an unconscious effort here to help the therapist understand the precipitous quality of his intervention and an effort as well to direct him toward reconsideration.

8. The patient's recognition that it is time for her son to function on his own contains within it a more constructive encoded unconscious recommendation— namely, that it may be appropriate for her to terminate her psychotherapy and to function on her own. It may be understood in this sense as an effort to obtain a perspective in response to the hurtful encoded perceptions already identified.

9. The patient's comment that she may be behaving in too abrupt fashion with her son because she herself is sensitive to loss may be taken as an effort at unconscious interpretation to the therapist. The patient may be saying in encoded form to the therapist: *You are responding precipitously to my thoughts of termination by wishing to be rid of me; perhaps you had this reaction because of an earlier loss that you suffered.*

10. In the patient's comment that she shouldn't let the past influence the present lies another model of rectification. Thus, if the patient's speculations are correct, and the therapist is indeed having difficulty in handling separation issues because of his own early traumatic experiences in this area, she is suggesting that he should attempt to minimize this disruptive influence. Of course, in addition, the encoded perceptions of the therapist have stirred up the patient's early memories related to separation traumas—in particular, the absence of her mother because of illness.

In all, then, the patient has responded to her unconscious perceptions of the therapist with fantasies, memories, behaviors, symptoms, efforts at cure and rectification, and fantasies of harming the therapist. This is a rather full set of reactions, one that includes an important symptomatic response that will require interpretation. It would also be possible to interpretively influence the patient's behavior with her son through an understanding intervention and rectification (i.e., allowing the patient sufficient time for an appropriate termination experience). An awareness of the unconscious influence of the therapist's interventions and of her own responsive unconscious perceptions would help the patient to bring into perspective this particular factor in the manner in which she is handling her son's reluctance to leave home.

Granted, the full listening process is complex, but communicative findings suggest that most encoded perceptions tend to coalesce around one or two basic images, and the patient's reactions to these perceptions are similarly organized. There is generally a flow and rhythm to the patient's material in each session. By identifying the key intervention contexts and their implications, it is possible for the therapist to develop a sense of the main encoded perceptions that have been generated in the patient and to identify the two or three major responses to these perceptions.

It requires considerable practice to listen in this fashion in a relaxed manner and to readily organize the patient's material in terms of its actual functional meanings. Nonetheless, it is our responsibility as therapists to tap the most crucial elements of this elaborate network of communications in order to generate the most meaningful and constructively helpful interventions possible.

Exercise 9.2

For the following vignette, we will carry out the basic listening–formulating process from beginning to end. Although the focus will be on reactions to encoded perceptions, the material will also serve to provide a brief review of the fundamental steps in the listening process.

The patient is a young man being seen by a female therapist. He sought psychotherapy because he was foundering both on his job and in his social relationships. He had episodes of both anxiety and depression. The present therapist first saw him for a period of psychotherapy several years ago in a treatment situation that involved many departures from the ideal ground rules. The current period of treatment had been going on for about a year and a half when the session to be discussed took place. In this psychotherapy the frame had been secured except for an occasional break or lapse by the therapist. The patient was showing improvement in both his work capacities and his love relationships. But he was still working on issues in both areas.

Treatment now took place on a once-weekly basis in the therapist's private office. Two sessions before the one to be discussed, the telephone had rung while the patient was in the therapist's office. Although she was greatly concerned about a significant family problem, the therapist did not answer the phone. But as the session went on, she found herself increasingly distracted and anxious and was unable to devote her attention fully to the patient. She therefore decided to call home. She interrupted the session, told the patient that she had to make an urgent telephone call, put the call through, briefly asked if everything was all right, and listened silently to the response (her child was ill, but the situation was under control). She then hung up the telephone and apologized to the patient, who, of course, had been present during the entire conversation.

In the balance of that particular hour, and in the session that followed, the patient made no direct allusion to the interruption of his session. There were, however, some moderately strong derivative perceptions of the therapist in light of the interruption, though the therapist failed to make an adequate interpretation. The next hour began as follows:

> *Patient:*   Things have been good with my girl friend and on the job. I do my job now, even though I still hate it. I can't stand being confined to the office. I've been thinking of stopping therapy. Things are better now. You may think otherwise, and I'd like to know your reaction. I'm going to stick with my girl friend because I've made a commitment. She clings to her former boyfriend; she should be able to let go of him. Leaving treatment is changing a commitment too. I have this friend in treatment with a therapist who tolerates and even promotes telephone calls at all hours. He gives my friend extra sessions. They're too tight with each other. I wouldn't stay in a treatment like that. It reminds me of how my mother treated my sister: She would never let her out of her sight. Some therapists can't let go of their patients. They seem to be too needy. It's plain wrong. I had some diarrhea during the week, but I don't think it's psychological. Anyhow, I don't see it as a serious problem.

The reader should come to terms with this material by first identifying, categorizing, and rating the strength of each background indicator. Next, do the same for each therapeutic context alluded to in the material excerpted. Then state the active adaptive contexts for this hour. Select the intervention context that is most critical for the moment. State the major implications of this central adaptive context in terms of the seven dimensions of the therapeutic interaction. Indicate if the context is represented manifestly; if it is not, select the clearest derivative (displaced) representations (there are at least seven). Of these, decide which is the best such portrayal. With this completed, identify the major selected unconscious perceptions of the therapist in light of this particular intervention context. Indicate which of the seven dimensions of human experience is reflected by each major perception. Overall, is this a strong and meaningful, coalescing derivative complex or one that is relatively weak? Finally, identify the patient's main reactions to his encoded perceptions. Here, too, specify the dimension of experience into which each reaction falls. Carry out this particular exercise step by step, revising your thinking and your answers if any error is discovered as we review the solutions to these questions and adding to your initial response if need be.

_____

_____

_____

_____

_____

_____

_____

_____

_____

_____

_____

_____

Answer

The main background indicators are:

1. The patient's job and social problems (interpersonal difficulties and possible symptoms; moderate).

2. The patient's anxiety and depression (symptoms; moderate).

The main patient-indicators in the abstracted portion of this hour are:

1. The patient's anxiety over his confinement to his office (symptomatic; weak to moderate).

2. The patient's thought of stopping therapy (a gross behavioral resistance and alteration of the frame; strong). This proposal is a critical patient-indicator, even when termination is introduced at a seemingly appropriate juncture in treatment. It is a far more serious indicator when it is introduced suddenly and prematurely. In this situation, there is every indication that this particular idea is indeed a premature though not unreasonable thought, one that would require considerable exploration and interpretation.

3. The episode of diarrhea (a psychosomatic symptom; moderate).

In all, then, the major indicator in this hour is the patient's decision to consider termination. The therapist would interpret this decision in light of the main activated adaptive contexts and derivative complex; and, ideally, the intervention would include some measure of understanding of the patient's claustrophobic anxieties and the episode of diarrhea. In view of the fact that the patient is not threatening to terminate immediately (i.e., in that hour), the decision whether or not to intervene would depend on how directly the patient had represented the most active adaptive context, and on the degree of meaning of the derivative complex. If at all possible, it would be advisable to intervene interpretively during this hour, but lacking suitable material, the therapist could wait for a subsequent session without undue consequence.

The major intervention context for this interlude is the therapist's interruption of the session two weeks earlier in order to make a telephone call. This is a blatant and traumatic therapist-indicator and adaptive context. Making a call during a patient's hour is highly disruptive and inadvisable except in dire emergency. Similarly, the therapist should not answer his or her telephone during sessions. The best way to handle calls is to use an answering device so that no third parties are involved in accepting messages. Calls can be returned between patients.

A second and less significant intervention context is the therapist's failure to intervene adequately in the prior session despite a strong and coalescing derivative complex. Because an intervention was in fact attempted, the actual adaptive context is constituted by a poor or limited effort at interpretation. Such contexts are seldom clearly represented in the material from patients and are difficult to interpret with respect to the patient's encoded perceptions of the therapist. In principle, it is best under these conditions to let the patient redevelop the material so that a fresh opportunity is created for sound interpretation of the patient's reactions to the primary adaptive context—in this case, the therapist's telephone interruption. Rectification, if necessary and feasible, can also be accomplished at that point.

In addition to these main patient-indicators, the patient's report of improved functioning with his girlfriend and in his work must be understood in light of the prevailing adaptive contexts and derivative complex. As we know, symptom remission should be understood in a manner similar to the way in which we understand symptom exacerbation—in light of the ongoing therapeutic interaction and the unconscious implications of adaptive contexts.

The following appear to be the main universal implications of the major activated adaptive context for this hour—the therapist's telephone interruption:

1. Frame: The intervention is a major frame deviation fraught with all of the implications of such alterations in the ideal frame—the generation of basic mistrust, disturbances in reality testing (the patient's belief that the hour is exclusively his is considerably damaged), impairments in the therapist's holding and containing capacities, and uncertainty regarding interpersonal boundaries.

2. Mode of relatedness: Autistic and parasitic in that the therapist has selfishly withdrawn from the patient for the moment; pathologically symbiotic in that it involves the patient in an extratherapeutic transaction and concern of the therapist.

3. Mode of cure: Clearly action-discharge.

4. Communication: Disrupted, takes on a dumping or projective identification quality. The basic communicative interplay will be disturbed and impaired.

5. Dynamics: Issues of separation, exploitation, hostility, seduction, abandonment, and helplessness are likely to emerge. (Genetics are still to be represented by the patient and will probably involve related issues.)

6. Self and identity: There will be a view of the therapist as suffering from some type of identity disturbance (her uncertainty as to whether she is therapist or parent), disturbed tension regulation, and narcissistic imbalance. The patient will also feel used as a selfobject by the therapist and a sense of narcissistic neglect along with possible reactive narcissistic rage.

7. Sanity and madness: The telephone call will consciously and/or unconsciously be seen as an act of madness—an unpredictable loss of control and a major failure of the therapist to maintain her role requirements. (Such failures are consistently experienced by patients as forms of madness.)

Subjectively, the therapist should realize that this framework deviation has major implications. Interventions of this kind usually produce strong and coalescing derivative perceptions and powerful reactions to those perceptions. Because of the dangerous image of the therapist created by the deviation, the adaptive context will often not be represented on a manifest level, though usually there will be a suitable encoded portrayal of the intervention. Under such circumstances, the therapist is confined to a playback of selected derivatives. The intervention would begin with the best encoded representation of the adaptive context, recognize a non–specific bridge to therapy, and then touch upon the patient's main, selected encoded perceptions in light of this unmentioned context. The therapist should not introduce the context manifestly, but should maintain the intervention at a derivative level and at the level of the patient's communicative resistances (in essence, he or she should use only that which the patient provides, giving it shape and form as needed). Quite often, such an intervention receives validation in the form of a modification of the patient's defenses and a shift to a direct (manifest) allusion to the adaptive context, accompanied by fresh and surprising meaningful additional derivative material.

What, then, are the best *encoded* portrayals or representations of this intervention context in the patient's material? Several are rather evident:

1. The patient's dislike of being confined to his office.

2. His thoughts of stopping treatment.

3. The image of the girlfriend clinging unnecessarily to her boyfriend.

4. The images related to commitment.

5. The therapist who unnecessarily calls his patients.

6. The inability of the patient's mother to allow her daughter out of her sight.

7. The image of a therapist who can't cope.

We see, then, a series of equipotential representations of the therapist's sudden decision to make a telephone call during the session. The best derivative portrayal of the adaptive context appears to be the patient's allusion to the therapist who permits himself to be called excessively by his patients and telephones them in return, because this image contains the themes of telephone calls and overinvolvement. All of these portrayals also encode valid selected unconscious perceptions of the therapist in light of her intervention. In selecting the best representation of this context, we are simply deciding how to begin a playback of selected derivatives, given the decision to intervene in the absence of direct representation.

In sequence, the following are the main encoded perceptions of the therapist, selected by the patient in terms of his own pathology in response to the intervention context of the telephone interruption:

1. The patient's allusion to hating his job and being confined to his office is a self-referential encoded perception of the therapist. It could be decoded as follows: *You* [the therapist] *hate doing psychotherapy and being constricted to your office; this is why you made the telephone call, which reflects these feelings.* The meanings of both images were readily validated by the therapist in terms of her subjective awareness. The allusion, then, reflects the patient's selected view of the therapist's claustrophobic anxieties and of her resentment regarding the strictures of her work— of being a psychotherapist. There is a frame reference in the patient's comment about his confinement to the office; this image also suggests hostility and other dynamics related to the claustrophobic anxieties, which have not yet been expressed in derivative form. The patient's allusion to hatred of his job carries a sense of disturbed identity and narcissism, and there is a possible quality of madness to the expressed anxiety about being confined to the office.

2. The patient's thoughts about stopping therapy contain an encoded version of the therapist's interruption of treatment. This is mainly a frame allusion.

3. The image of the girl friend clinging to her former boyfriend encodes an unconscious perception of the therapist's clinging unduly to her family (based on other experiences, the patient knew that the therapist had probably telephoned her husband or a babysitter) and to the patient as well. Here we have a pathological symbiotic mode of relatedness.

4. In the allusion to leaving therapy as a change in commitment, we have another encoded perception of the therapist's alteration in her commitment to the patient— her implied promise to afford him a private space for the 50-minute hour. This change in commitment touches on a disturbance in mode of relatedness and possibly in mode of cure.

5. The image of the therapist who freely calls and is called by his patients, offers them extra sessions, and seems to be "too tight with" (close to) them contains an extended selected perception of the therapist's overinvolvement with her family, and especially with her patient whom she forced to observe an extratherapeutic transaction. Here, the pathological symbiotic and parasitic modes of relatedness seem most prominent, though there is an action-discharge mode of cure and a quality of madness as well.

6. In the allusion to the mother's overinvolvement with the patient's sister, there is another encoded reference to the therapist's overinvolvement with her family and patient. Here, there is a strong genetic component and a vague hint of perversity in the form of latent homosexuality (instinctual-drive derivatives are notably absent as yet from this material). There is a suggestion as well of pathological narcissism in the mother's use of the sister as a selfobject. Again, there is a hint of madness.

7. In the patient's reference to therapists who can't let go of their patients there is an encoded allusion to the therapist's inability to separate from her family and patient. Pathological symbiosis is again emphasized.

8. The patient's mention of his diarrhea may contain an unconscious perception of the therapist's loss of control, or perhaps it records an unconscious perception of the therapist's concern about illness in someone else. These are heavily disguised and remote derivatives that would require further associations for validation of their meaning.

In the main, then, this patient, based on his own psychopathology, has emphasized the pathologically symbiotic qualities of the therapist's telephone call. Additional selective perceptions suggest that the patient viewed the therapist as exploitative, as using the action-discharge mode of cure, as lacking commitment to the patient, as being overly dependent and in need of pathological fusion, as hostile and having difficulty in separating from others, as narcissistically inclined to use others as selfobjects, and as conveying a measure of madness. On the whole, this is a meaningful, coalescing derivative complex. It touches on most of the dimensions of the therapeutic experience, lacking only a clear representation of instinctual-drive derivatives.

To this point, then, we have a strong indicator—the patient's thought of terminating treatment. Although there is no direct allusion to the central adaptive context—the telephone interruption—several relatively close and thinly disguised derivative representations are present in the material. Among these, the allusion to the therapist who is overly involved with his patients on the telephone appears to be the least disguised. The material also contains a highly meaningful and coalescing derivative complex; it has important components and touches on virtually all of the dimensions of the therapeutic interaction, including genetic factors—for the most part lacking only instinctual-drive derivatives. In all, then, there is a low to moderate level of communicative resistances that have blocked direct representation of the adaptive context and selected aspects of the derivative complex. Even so, there is sufficient material available for interpretation and rectification in this session—a demonstration of the unconscious reasons for the patient's wish to terminate treatment (and for his claustrophobia and diarrhea) in light of the telephone interruption and the patient's resulting selected encoded perceptions of the therapist.

We move next to the patient's reactions to his encoded perceptions of the therapist. Here, we are seeking images that do not make sense as perceptions of attributes of the intervention context. In this material, such images are as follows:

1. The comment that things are good with the girlfriend and on the job appears to be a reaction to the therapist's disturbing intervention context. The most likely sequence involves the patient's having unconsciously perceived the therapist as wishing to fuse and merge with him, prompting the patient to distance himself and improve his own autonomous functioning. There is a sense that the therapist wishes the patient to function in infantile fashion so as to be available for a pathological symbiotic relationship. In asserting his own sound functioning, the patient appears to

be conveying to the therapist his wish not to be involved in this type of pathological symbiosis and his preference for a commensal mode of relatedness (equal gratification on both sides). In addition, the patient's constructive functioning on the job may be seen as a corrective or model to the therapist, who has not functioned well in the recent hour.

2. In the patient's allusion to his doing his job even though he hates it, we have another corrective or model of rectification to the therapist. The key raw message is that the therapist should do her job properly despite her distaste for it.

3. In the patient's thoughts of stopping therapy we have a potential behavioral reaction to the adaptive context. On this level, termination can be viewed as a talion response to the therapist's abandonment of the patient. It is also a vengeful attempt to harm the therapist, in that the plan is premature and hurtful to her.

4. In the reference to the patient's decision to stick with his girlfriend because of the commitment he made to her, we have another model of rectification. The raw message is that the therapist should remain loyal to the patient rather than having deserted him by making the telephone call.

5. The patient's comment that it is wrong for a therapist and patient to be overinvolved with telephone calls and extra sessions, along with his stated disinclination to stay in such a treatment situation, contains still another model of rectification. The patient is repeatedly encoding the message that the therapist's overinvolvement with her family and patient is destructive to the therapy and to the patient and should desist.

6. In the patient's recollection of his mother's overinvolvement with his sister, he is on one level making a general attempt at an unconscious (encoded) genetic interpretation directed to the therapist. Thus, the raw message is that perhaps some overinvolvement between the therapist and her mother (or more concretely, between a sibling and the therapist's mother) has led to the therapist's difficulty in separating from her family. Potentially, this comment could lead the therapist to evaluate the genetic factors in her countertransference-based deviation.

7. Similarly, the remark that some therapists have difficulty letting go of their patients is an encoded general interpretation to the therapist. In substance, the raw (decoded) message is that the therapist is having difficulty in separating from her family and patient. The patient further adds that the therapist is therefore too needy and in error.

8. The diarrhea is a symptomatic response to the adaptive context, which has taken a psychosomatic form. In terms of the patient's associations, the diarrhea seems to express a pathological need for symbiosis and the action-discharge mode of cure. It also involves some measure of projective identification and may have additional dynamic elements.

In this instance, the patient has responded behaviorally to his encoded perceptions of the therapist—with both an increase and decrease in symptoms, and with efforts to both harm and cure the therapist. There are also suggestions of reactive unconscious fantasy formations related to entrapment in a claustrum, fusion and merger, and some type of pathological sexual involvement.

Discussion

We are now in a position to explain the unconscious basis for the patient-indicators and the patient's momentary improvement in his social and work endeavors. The reader is asked to venture this kind of explanation in light of the patient's best representation of the intervention context, his selected encoded perceptions of the therapist, and his reaction to these perceptions. The result should be an interpretation of the indicators of the patient's improved functioning, his thoughts of terminating treatment, his claustrophobic anxieties, and the episode of diarrhea. Such an intervention, as indicated, would begin with the patient's best representation of the adaptive context, identify the general bridge to therapy (the thought of stopping therapy), and then touch on its main represented implications in the derivative material, using the entire complex as a means of helping the patient to understand the prevailing indicators. In the actual session, the therapist would probably wait, allowing the patient to associate further. An ideal intervention would require a better representation of the adaptive context than the material offers at the moment, along with a measure of instinctual-drive derivative expressions. But given the material as we have it, how might the therapist best intervene at this point?

_____

_____

_____

_____

_____

_____

_____

_____

_____

The following appears to be the best potential intervention based on the material from the patient to this point in the hour:

> The conditions of your treatment are very much on your mind. You are talking about a therapist who is involved with others by telephone in a way that is "too tight" with them and wrong. You have said that you would not stay with such a therapist. This may well have something to do with your thoughts of stopping treatment with me. There are other images—of carrying out a job though it's hated, of anxieties about confinement to an office, and of the need to maintain commitments. There are also allusions to your girlfriend's overinvolvement with her previous boyfriend and your mother's overconcern with your sister. It is this kind of overinvolvement—somehow connected to the telephone and somehow connected to me—that has created images for you of someone who is made anxious when confined to a situation. Perhaps these images are a factor in the neediness and loss of control expressed by your diarrhea. Something I have done of late, which appears to have expressed this overneediness and which seems to have involved the telephone, has generated images of me as overinvolved with others and perhaps yourself, and as changing my commitment to you. Apparently you see this as reflecting some type of poor functioning on my part, and you have reacted to it with improvement on your own. But these images have also prompted some type of anxiety, which seems to have been expressed in your concerns regarding confinement and your diarrhea. These two symptoms express in some fashion your view of me in light of a disturbing intervention I have made recently.

To be sure, this intervention is crude and would be difficult for the patient to understand. One can see why a therapist should wait for a clear representation of the intervention context before interpreting. Further, although some of the derivatives do help to explain the patient's improved functioning and symptoms, they do not establish a clear unconscious basis for either response. The kind of intervention formulated here would be developed silently within the therapist and understood as preliminary and inadequate for the moment. It might serve in that way as a reference point in listening further to the patient's free associations. Should the adaptive context be more clearly represented and should the derivatives coalesce further and better clarify the unconscious meanings of the patient's symptomatic exacerbation and remission, the therapist could then undoubtedly offer a definitive interpretation to the patient. It would also be quite important to acknowledge the patient's models of rectification, which are so abundant in this material, including his unconscious directive that commitments must be maintained and reasonable separateness from others established. On the basis of these models of rectification and in the context of a clear interpretation, it would be possible to assure the patient that there would be no further emergency telephone calls during his hours. This type of rectification would be essential to restoring the patient's trust of the therapist and to reestablishing the necessary sound therapeutic hold.

CONCLUDING COMMENTS

In general, reactions to encoded perceptions are revealed through material in a given session that does not accord, after repeated testing, with the implications of known intervention contexts. The therapist must bear in mind that such material may well contain encoded perceptions related to an adaptive context not yet recognized, but once this possibility has been discounted, the therapist can begin to assume that such associations are indeed responses to encoded perceptions. These reactions usually have a considerable measure of logic in light of the implications of an activated intervention context.

As we have seen, many of these responses to encoded perceptions are also patient-indicators, including disturbed behavioral reactions, symptomatic remissions, gross behavioral resistances, and efforts to harm the therapist. Thus, responses to perceptions bring us full circle—back to the patient-indicators that we wish to understand unconsciously in terms of activated intervention contexts and the patient's derivative responses. Symptomatic and resistance reactions to encoded perceptions are indeed among the most important responses to the patient's images of the therapist in light of prevailing adaptive contexts. The basic goal in psychoanalytic psychotherapy is to understand these reactions in terms of the unconscious perceptions that have evoked them and the intervention contexts that have, in turn, given rise to those perceptions. In interpreting, we simply identify the adaptive sequence that began with an intervention context, led to responsive and selected encoded perceptions, and resulted in symptomatic reactions to these perceptions. We explain the latter in terms of the former.

This completes the detailed specifications of the listening–formulating process. The interested therapist should from time to time write out process notes after a session (not during a session, because this is a major break in the frame) and make use of them for the types of exercises developed in this volume. Once a session has been recorded, it is possible to study the material for patient-indicators, known adaptive contexts, representations of these adaptive contexts, responsive encoded perceptions, and reactions to these perceptions. Familiarity with each of these elements can soon make this particular listening–formulating process a smooth one. For better or worse, there is no other way to understand quite specifically the structure and functions of the patient's communications. The goal, then, must be to develop the empathic and intuitive ability to utilize this cognitive sorting process as easily and unobtrusively as it is humanly possible. Many exciting insights tend to follow.

III
INTEGRATED LISTENING

10
Some Precepts
of Listening

In the final section of the book, we will apply the listening–formulating process to three entire sessions. With two, the background and prevailing intervention contexts will be identified; for the third (Chapter 12) we will use the material from the session (the derivatives) in an attempt to identify an unmentioned deviant context.

In preparation for this final attempt to listen and to formulate, the present chapter will be devoted to identifying selected precepts of listening. There is no intention here to offer a detailed presentation of principles, but only to identify some of the more common problems in listening and formulating, and to propose a number of basic guidelines for their resolution. This chapter may be considered a basic compendium of some of the most important precepts and pitfalls in listening and intervening.

INDICATORS

The following should be noted with respect to patient-indicators:

1. There are two major categories of patient-indicators: symptoms and efforts by the patient to alter one or more ground rules of psychotherapy. The latter constitute the major proportion of patient-indicators in psychotherapy. Such endeavors are almost always forms of gross behavioral resistance.

2. The therapist should identify the indicators reflected in the patient's behaviors and associations early in a session. Be certain to generate formulations that explain the unconscious basis and implications of a patient-indicator. All indicators are responses to adaptive contexts and have an interactional foundation.

3. Indicators are expressions of patient-madness and psychopathology. Each interpretation or framework-management response that deals with a patient-indicator

constitutes a form of minianalysis. It is the accumulation of minianalyses of this kind that constitute sound psychotherapy.

4. Be certain to include the major patient-indicators in your intervention. These are what must be explained in terms of the prevailing adaptive contexts and derivative complex.

ADAPTIVE CONTEXTS

Important precepts regarding the handling of the adaptive or intervention contexts, which are the stimuli for the patient's adaptive and communicative responses, include the following:

1. A clearly represented adaptive context, especially one that is portrayed on the manifest level (i.e., quite directly and without disguise), will generally facilitate a meaningful interpretive or framework-management response from the therapist.

2. Be sure to work with *specific* intervention contexts rather than with general impressions of the therapist and treatment experience. Every finished formulation and intervention should begin with the best representation of a particular adaptive context and expand from there. Interventions are the specific stimuli for the patient's conscious and unconscious reactions as they illuminate his or her madness.

3. Pay attention to every intervention you make as a therapist. Among these, management and infractions of the ground rules are especially significant. Keep in mind your last intervention—whether a lengthy silence or an active response.

4. Attempt to silently formulate the major implications of each notable intervention context. Think of these in terms that are quite specific, rather than using generalities (such as having made a countertransference-based reaction or having generated an empathic failure). Understand the definitive areas of human interaction in which you have failed, and attempt to trace out each error's countertransference-based sources. Make sure that you understand the nature of your erroneous active interventions: Ask yourself what specific pathological unconscious communications and inputs have I expressed to the patient? Also, examine the material from the patient that has prompted an erroneous intervention. These associations and behaviors often serve as the immediate adaptive context for the therapist's pathological communicative response. In all, then, understand as definitively and extensively as possible the causes and implications of each erroneous intervention.

5. Keep an ear open for the best representation of each currently active intervention context. When a manifest portrayal is present, the remaining material can be studied mainly in terms of derivative perceptions and reactions to these perceptions. In the absence of a manifest representation of the adaptive context, seek out the best encoded representation available. If this portrayal is relatively thinly disguised, be prepared to begin your interventions with that particular encoded representation. Remember, you will also need a general bridge to therapy in order to show the patient the encoded material is related to the therapeutic interaction. Do not bypass the patient's communicative defenses and do not allude directly to an intervention context when the patient has not done so in that particular hour. Analyze resistances rather than attempting to bypass them or set them aside. Failure to respect a patient's de-

fenses will generally lead to denial by the patient—an expression of the so-called "denial barrier." Attempt relatively early in the session to settle on good representations of the most important intervention contexts so that much of the remaining listening effort can be concentrated on the derivative complex.

6. In evaluating the implications of intervention contexts, attempt to account for meanings in each of the seven dimensions of the psychotherapeutic experience. In view of the fact that the therapist's most natural resistances are usually directed against realizations of frame issues, instinctual-drive implications, genetics, and madness be certain to include these in your formulation. Remember to stay open to new ideas and formulations as you are listening and decoding.

THE DERIVATIVE COMPLEX

Much therapeutic listening involves the attempt to decode the derivative complex in light of the implications of an activated intervention context. The following are important precepts:

1. Be sure that you are engaged in *decoding*—the undoing of displacement and symbolization. Manifest content is important in conveying indicators and adaptive contexts, but the manifest level cannot reveal the unconscious meanings and functions of the patient's material.

2. Be wary of making direct inferences from manifest material. Although understanding at this level may serve some preliminary function, it is no substitute for the decoding process. Unconscious communication is not conveyed through implication but through disguise—the use of displacement and symbolism and other representations.

3. Be wary of easily decoded or linear derivatives. These tend to be relatively simplistic even when organized around a meaning of an intervention context. Their use seldom leads to a validated intervention. True unconscious communication is more complex, convoluted, indirect, heavily or moderately disguised, and symbolically represented—something like poetry as compared with prose. It always involves unique meaning and nuances. Whatever is self-evident and intellectual can be used in a preliminary fashion; but such communications do not represent unconscious expression as it illuminates the active and critical unconscious basis of madness.

4. In studying the derivative complex, the key process lies in identifying manifest themes that connect to—are shared by—those that are latent. Meaningful manifest associations consistently represent the patient's encoded perceptions of the therapist in light of his or her therapeutic efforts. Thus, whatever the manifest theme, *the latent theme pertains to an intervention of the therapist.* Clinical sensitivity involves identifying the particular thematic level and content that give the most pertinent meaning to the patient's derivative or encoded communications.

5. Alternate between loose listening with empathic and intuitive qualities and attempting to develop specific formulations.

6. Remember that the patient's madness influences both sound encoded perceptions as well as reactions to these perceptions. Thus, an understanding of a *selected*

perception may reveal as much about the patient's underlying madness as a reactive extension or distortion of these perceptions. In other words, the patient's madness is expressed in both nontransference (valid) and transference (distorted) expressions, and should be understood accordingly.

7. Make sure to initiate all of your formulations of encoded communications in terms of disguised perceptions selected from the universal and personal meanings of an intervention context according to the patient's madness. The formulation of valid encoded perceptions is a burdensome task for the therapist, whose natural defenses direct him or her away from his or her own perceived madness and from this aspect of the patient's unconscious understanding. Nonetheless, there are many meaningful and valid perceptions communicated in disguised fashion by patients, and these must be recognized and interpreted well before unconscious distortions. Such perceptions are fraught with genetic implications and touch upon all of the dimensions of the therapeutic experience. Again, because these encoded perceptions are the patient's first reaction to an intervention context, it is here that every formulation by a therapist must begin despite their anxiety–provoking aspects for the therapist.

8. Allow as much time as possible for the patient to express instinctual-drive material, especially sexual, primitive, and genetically connected material. A full and coalescing and therefore meaningful derivative complex will touch on most of the seven dimensions of human experience.

9. Formulate encoded perceptions first (that is, derivatives in keeping with the implications of an adaptive context), then formulate reactions to these perceptions (derivatives that do not reflect the meanings of an intervention context). Formulate perceptions of the therapist before self-perceptions of the patient. Both are always present in the material from patients, but the former tend to be uppermost.

10. A valid understanding of an intervention context and indicator should involve the most compelling and instinctual-drive-related derivative material. If these cannot be accounted for, there may well be a missing adaptive context. Perhaps a formulation has been incorrectly organized around a context that is already known and worn thin. Attempt to reformulate when strong derivatives do not make integrated sense.

11. Be sure when formulating and intervening to utilize only the material in a particular session and to validate an impression and formulation silently before intervening to the patient. Be sure to seek further derivative validation once an intervention has been made.

12. Useful derivatives do not have to be pursued or forced to suggest disguised meanings. Nor do the formulations generated from these derivatives need to be forced or overstated. Most valid listening involves material from the patient whose unconscious implications are relatively evident, if convoluted and indirect. Allow derivative meanings to virtually insist on their existence rather than actively pursuing and digging for underlying implications.

13. In decoding a derivative, the therapist has two tasks: (1) to translate the derivative into a decoded perception of the therapist, and (2) to identify the specific adaptive context that contains an implication that is correctly perceived (identified) in the derivative image. Thus, the therapist states both: "This is a correct perception of me as such and such," and "This is what I did (how I intervened) to deserve this particular perception."

In conclusion, several other principles of listening and formulating are worthy of note:

1. On the whole, psychotherapy is a ground-rule issue treatment experience. The therapist's management of the ground rules and the patient's responses to these efforts constitute the main arena for the expressions of the patient's madness. *Secure-frame therapy* will generate anxieties about restriction, while offering a special form of inevitable support. *Deviant-frame therapy* offers pathological defenses, while disrupting sound holding and interfering with the other functions of the ideal frame. In either case, it is the therapist's management of the ground rules that constitutes the overridingly most important intervention contexts to which patients respond communicatively, symptomatically, with new health, and adaptively or maladaptively. Analysis of patient-indicators in light of these adaptive contexts and the patient's derivative responses constitutes the optimal psychotherapeutic experience. In such efforts, interpretive work is always supplemented by framework-management responses—virtually always in the direction of securing or establishing the ideal frame.

2. The secure frame is viewed unconsciously by both patient and therapist as a somewhat dangerous claustrum. The major sources of anxiety involve the experience of death anxieties (we are all born into an ultimately annihilating claustrum), separateness or aloneness within the claustrum, the dread of the intruder who will enter the claustrum and destroy those within its confines, and the uncontrolled upsurge of instinctual-drive impulses and images. It would appear that claustrophobic anxieties are among the most basic human concerns and are undoubtedly an important aspect of the basic paranoid-schizoid position described by Melanie Klein.

3. In communicating, patients portray and react mainly to the *actualities of the therapeutic interaction*. Their primary responses are to the definitive interventions of the therapist or to those important interventions clearly anticipated (e.g., requested) in the near future. Patients, as is true of all human beings, work over these realities in terms of their unconscious implications as they touch upon their madness. Although there is a definite measure of primary unconscious fantasy that determines the selective nature of the patient's unconscious perceptions of an intervention context, and a measure of conscious and unconscious fantasy activity that occurs in response to these unconscious perceptions, the perceptions themselves are realistic and appropriate. Most of what a patient communicates in therapy does not involve fantasies and wishes about the therapist, but encodes unconscious perceptions of the therapist in light of his or her interventions, the implications of which are experienced as anxiety-evoking and dangerous.

4. Perhaps the most important single question a therapist should ask himself or herself in listening to a patient is as follows: "What intervention have I made (and what are its implications?) to account for this material as an encoded and valid perception of myself?"

5. Learn to tolerate without undue anxiety or special need to intervene those sessions in which the patient does not generate truth or meaning. For most therapists, the most difficult intervention is that of appropriate silence. In the absence of a well-represented adaptive context and an accompanying, meaningful derivative complex (mainly encoded perceptions), remain silent and allow the patient to work out his or

her communicative resistances. If there is indeed an important traumatic intervention context, the patient's need to communicate and to insightfully get well will eventually lead to modification of the communicative resistances and to an especially meaningful psychotherapy hour. If there are no especially active intervention contexts, the absence of meaning is not usually pathological, but expresses a need within the patient to lie fallow and to work over internal and interpersonal issues on his or her own. Although such efforts tend to be carried out in terms of manifest contents and obvious inferences, they nonetheless help the patient to modify his or her pathological defensive formations in a manner that is salutory and that may lead to symptom alleviation.

In all, then, do not press to find meaning in the patient's material and accept silently sessions in which meaning does not appear to have been generated. The constructive use of silence is an intervention difficult to master; its use with a patient is by no means wasteful, but is instead an extremely helpful (and all too rare) therapeutic intervention. The disciplines of psychoanalysis and psychotherapy tend to an overemphasis on the use of active interventions, in part, because there is no implicit reward within their value systems for appropriate silence. Such hours are extremely meaningful and constructive for a patient, however, and at times, they permit him or her to pause before dealing with new levels of anxiety and madness. Unneeded interventions are particularly disruptive at such times.

6. Listening is greatly enhanced by a knowledge of the flow of the most recent sessions and material. The therapist gains an important perspective in recognizing the adaptive contexts that have been recently worked over—deviations that have been rectified or carried out, validated interpretations, and the areas of human interaction with which the patient has been dealing.

It is generally quite easy to recognize just what is needed in order to intervene in a particular session. Often, it becomes possible to simply wait for the patient to produce the missing ingredient(s). For example, when there are two critical intervention contexts and the patient has represented and responded in derivative fashion to one, the therapist should be well aware that he or she requires the representation of the second critical intervention context and several responsive derivatives before being in a position to offer an ideal intervention. Similarly, when an adaptive context is known, the therapist simply waits for the derivative complex to unfold—especially encoded perceptions. Or when the derivative complex is available, the wait is carried out for a clear representation of the main intervention context. Along different lines, there are sessions in which the therapist recognizes a critical implication of a particular adaptive context, and waits for the patient to portray the meanings involved. As noted, it is important to delay intervening whenever possible until instinctual-drive derivative representations and genetic material appear.

In time, then, a therapist develops an understanding of the attributes of an ideal interpretation or framework-rectification response under a particular set of conditions. In general, he or she will wait for the patient to communicate the necessary direct and derivative material before intervening. Should the patient fail to complete the communicative network, the therapist may then intervene in incomplete fashion, hoping to stimulate further expression from the patient. Still, silence is often the best intervention when the communicative material is incomplete.

7. Among the many complex reactions to a patient's encoded perceptions of the therapist in light of an intervention context, it is especially critical to watch for corrective models and models of rectification. Such models, conveyed in derivative form, are absolutely essential in the presence of a framework deviation. They are also quite common in the presence of erroneous verbal (meaning) interventions as well. Just as it is critical to be certain to interpret the unconscious meanings of major patient-indi-

cators in light of the adaptive context and derivative complex, it is essential not only to include acknowledgment of the patient's models of rectification when intervening, but also to attempt to actualize such correctives whenever feasible.

8. Patients are deeply disturbed and driven mad by unconscious perceptions of significant splits within the therapist. Among these, the most common is the therapist's rectifying certain aspects of the frame, while maintaining deviations in others. Or the therapist may be capable of securing the frame in its entirety, but fail to interpret the patient's subsequent derivative material. Conversely, a therapist may be capable of interpreting the patient's material in light of an activated adaptive context, but then fail to take necessary available measures of rectification.

9. In general, the main consequences of any deviation in the ideal frame are a basic mistrust of the therapist, a fundamental communicative disturbance, a sense of relatively unclear interpersonal boundaries, disturbances in reality testing, and a basic feeling of being held and contained in poor fashion.

10. A highly meaningful derivative complex is characterized by a working over of significant indirect implications of an intervention context. When a patient responds to an erroneous interpretation or break in the frame with manifest reactions and/or with encoded derivatives that are straightforward, simplistic, and almost exclusively concerned with the surface nature of the deviation, the patient is in a state of relative communicative resistance. Optimal unconscious communication involves encoded perceptions of specific meanings of an intervention context and a working over of these implications through additional derivative reactions. In essence, then, meaningful derivative communication involves encoded responses to unconscious meanings of deviant intervention contexts.

11. It is well to recognize the various vehicles through which the patient communicates—words, affects, behaviors, bodily movements and postures, and somatic expressions. Each should be regarded as a *communicative* component of human experience.

12. Perhaps the therapist's most critical job is to undertake a full and deep exploration of the implications of an activated intervention context. This type of understanding requires both an extensive knowledge of psychodynamics and interpersonal functioning, as well as a sound grasp of one's own inner mental world. Most errors in listening and formulating begin either with a failure to recognize the presence of a critical activated intervention context or with a failure to appreciate an important implication and meaning of such a context. Most errors in listening and formulating involve significant unrecognized expressions of therapist–madness.

11
Formulating
an Entire Session:
Part I

CASE PRESENTATION

Let us now apply the listening–formulating process to two complete sessions taken in sequence from the same once-weekly psychotherapy. The patient is a young married woman who sought psychotherapy because of depression, an inability to make a firm commitment to her husband, and episodic work difficulties. The treatment was carried out by a male therapist at a private clinic. The patient paid an average fee, but was billed by and made the check out to the clinic, not to the therapist. It was evident that patient-records were kept. In addition, the patient registered with one of the clinic secretaries before each visit.

In the sessions before the hours that will be excerpted in full, the patient had been working over her feelings about being seen in a private clinic. She had a strong conscious sense that the therapist felt deep misgivings about seeing his patients in the clinic setting. She suspected that disputes had arisen between him and the clinic directors, and that he was uncertain about remaining at the clinic as a therapist. The patient had shown special sensitivity to these issues of boundaries and secure holding because her father had been unfaithful to her mother when the patient was a child, and the patient herself had been unfaithful to her husband, much as he had been with her. Eventually, with the assistance of interpretive interventions from the therapist, the patient was able to express her manifest anxieties about the records being kept at the clinic and the presence of third parties to treatment; simultaneously, she had conveyed important derivative material that revealed many of the unconscious meanings of these deviant intervention contexts for her personally.

But of late, the patient had shown a mounting sense of frustration. The therapist was repeatedly interpreting her valid unconscious perceptions of the damage done to her because of the clinic conditions, and yet, no rectification was forthcoming. On this basis, a strongly split image of the therapist had developed: On the one hand, he was capable of understanding; on the other, he had failed to follow up his interpretations with relevant actions. At the time of the sessions under consideration, the therapist had not yet been able to interpret the images reflecting the attributes of this adaptive context.

The first session will be presented in summary form up to the point of the therapist's intervention. At that juncture, and before indicating the nature of his effort, we will review the material for (1) patient-indicators (type and strength), (2) aspects of the adaptive contexts, (3) derivative perceptions based on the main intervention contexts, and (4) reactions to these perceptions (nature and type of response). We will also attempt to shape these listening efforts into a potential intervention—an interpretive and/or framework-management response.

In an actual session, the therapist tends initially to listen freely and attempts to organize the material into categories only from time to time. Thus, the reader should pause at two or three junctures in reading the first half of the session to jot down in the space allotted below his or her main impressions and formulations. As an alternative, at the point where we pause in the report, the reader should engage in the formal listening exercise proposed. The goal is to encourage loose listening alternating with periods of definitive formulation.

THE FIRST SESSION: EXERCISES

The session that we will study unfolds as follows:

> *Patient:* The dentist I work for hired a new receptionist who quit the next day. He called a meeting and asked us why nobody wants to work for him. We told him the hours are too long, the pay too little, and the responsibilities too great. He asked each of us to submit what we thought was a fair salary. He said he would try to make some changes in the office, but I'm afraid that he won't follow through with them. He's made promises before, but he never keeps them. I doubt if he'll ever make the changes; it's all become just a word game with him. [Silence]
>
> I had this dream of a baby in a crib crying for its mother. It had the body of a one-year-old infant and the face of a four-year-old child. I tried to get to the baby but I just couldn't do it. I was so frustrated. I felt helpless because I couldn't do anything about the situation.
>
> I think the dream was stimulated by a talk with a social worker and an attorney who told us it would take a couple of years to adopt a handicapped child. The problem is we have our own biological children. It seems fair, but somehow it just shouldn't take that long. I think those bureaucratic agencies just hold on to their children to get government funds and subsidies. They're going to charge us $10,000 to adopt a child. Where are the costs? A few clothes and food. They just want your money. It's a rip-off.
>
> I had another dream the other night. My husband was having an affair with a girl friend of mine from college. I felt terribly sad. Last session we talked about how I don't entirely trust my husband around this neighbor of ours even though I know she would never get involved with him. My

husband received a card from a former mistress the other day. They exchange humorous cards all the time. There is nothing to it, I know that.

The night after I had the dream, my husband wanted to have sex. I found myself full of hatred toward him and was totally unable to respond to his sexual overtures. That old coldness that I thought I had divested myself of had returned with a vengeance. I can see that the rage is still there, barely beneath the surface.

The next night I called the wife of this man I had had an affair with. In the past, I'd feel too anxious and guilty to do it. We had a very good conversation. But that night I woke up feeling anxious, my heart was pounding. I know it had to do with calling her. Maybe it has something to do with my relationship with you as well. It all seems kind of obscure to me.

This material occupied approximately three-quarters of the patient's session. It was at this juncture that the therapist intervened. We will therefore now engage in our specific listening exercise.

Listening–Formulating: Exercise 11.1

Please answer the following questions in sequence. (They are listed alphabetically, to correspond with the answers that follow). Try to answer each of these questions without turning to the responses offered in the text. If the response to a particular question seems to be elusive, however, read the answer to the prior questions and then attempt to answer those that have as yet not been completed:

A. Name the background indicators (those reflected in the introduction to the session), classify them, and define their strength.

B. Name the indicators present in the material from the session, classify them, and define their strength.

C. Identify all background and active intervention contexts (those in the introduction as well as any reflected in the therapist's activities in the session itself).

D. Indicate the main universal implications of this collection of adaptive contexts. Use the seven-part schema reflecting the dimensions of the therapeutic interaction.

E. Are there any manifest representations of an adaptive or intervention context?

F. Are there any derivative representations of the adaptive context that are active for this hour? Do you detect a general bridge to the therapeutic situation? Specify the most important intervention contexts for the session. Indicate as well those adaptive contexts that are most clearly represented in the patient's derivative material.

G. Reviewing the session in sequence, what are the best selected encoded perceptions of the therapist in light of the prevailing adaptive contexts? Identify the manifest material that contains these perceptions and indicate the decoded or raw image latent to each manifest association. In addition, identify the area within the seven dimensions of the therapeutic interaction to which the image applies.

H. Identify the madness and psychopathology in the patient reflected in her selected encoded perceptions of the therapist. Consider each perception in sequence, and delineate the area of disturbance in terms of the seven dimensions of the therapeutic interaction. Identify as well the patient's encoded self-perceptions.

I. Identify all of the patient's major reactions to her selected unconscious perceptions of the therapist. Do so in sequence, and state the type of response and its meaning or function.

J. Finally, write out what appears to be the best possible intervention based on the material in this session to this point.

_____

_____

_____

_____

_____

_____

_____

_____

_____

_____

_____

_____

_____

_____

_____

_____

_____

_____

_____

_____

_____

_____

_____

_____

_____

_____

_____

_____

_____

_____

_____

_____

_____

_____

Answer

A. Background Patient-Indicators

The following appear to be the main patient-indicators reflected in the introduction to this session:

1. The patient's depression (symptom; moderate).

2. The patient's lack of commitment to her husband (interpersonal difficulty; moderate to severe).

3. The patient's work problems (interpersonal and symptomatic difficulties; moderate).

4. The patient's previous affairs (interpersonal difficulties; moderate to severe).

5. The patient's concerns regarding therapy, the existence of records, and third parties to treatment (an appropriate resistance; moderate to severe).

6. The patient's frustrations with the therapist (an appropriate resistance; moderate to severe).

B. The Main Patient-Indicators in the Session

To this point in the hour, the following appear to be the most significant patient-indicators reflected in the material:

1. The patient's frustration and anxiety in her dream of the baby (symptom; mild because it occurred in a dream).

2. The patient's mistrust of adoption agencies (symptom; mild).

3. The patient's sadness in her dream of her husband's affair and her mistrust of her husband (symptom and interpersonal difficulty; mild to moderate).

4. The patient's hatred toward her husband and inability to respond to his sexual overtures (symptom and interpersonal difficulty; moderate to strong).

5. The patient's call to the wife of a former lover (interpersonal difficulty; mild to moderate).

6. The patient's anxiety attack after this telephone call (symptom; moderate to strong).

There are, then, no major frame-break indicators in this material—that is, the patient is not attempting to alter the basic ground rules of treatment in this hour. There are, however, allusions to frame issues in the patient's initial description of the dentist for whom she works and the receptionist who quit her job. Were this patient and treatment situation better known, it might have been possible to conclude that these associations reflected *encoded* indicators. In any case, the patient's wish to modify the frame would require clearer representation before it could be used as a patient-indicator in intervening.

The session is best characterized as containing a series of mild to moderate symptomatic and interpersonal patient-indicators—disturbances and expressions of madness. The most compelling indicator—the episode of anxiety—appears relatively late in the hour (an unusual occurrence in a psychotherapy session). In all, this is the type of session where the therapist should intervene only if there is a strong representation of an intervention context and a highly meaningful derivative complex—that is, a low level of communicative resistances. The therapist might also intervene if there were a well-represented and strong therapist-indicator—a recent traumatic intervention context—conveyed in the material, one that organized the patient's derivative associations in meaningful fashion.

C. The Background and Active Intervention Contexts

We may identify the following background and still active intervention contexts:

1. The presence of secretaries and other third parties to treatment (frame deviation that modifies the one-to-one relationship and the confidentiality of the psychotherapy).

2. The existence of records and reports (a deviation with similar implications).

3. The receipt of a bill from clinic personnel and the payment of the fee directly to the clinic (a deviation in the area of fee, total privacy, the one-to-one relationship, and confidentiality—all of which are significantly modified).

4. The therapist's recent ability to respond with validated interpretations to the patient's encoded perceptions of him in light of the above-listed frame alterations. No rectification had been proposed or attempted however, so there was also a missed or failed intervention.

In sum, then, the main active background adaptive contexts for the moment involve frame deviations in the form of third parties to treatment, the existence of reports on the patient, payment to a third party, and the like. We should also keep in mind the mixed qualities of the therapist's efforts—interpreting well, but failing to rectify the frame. Implied here is a powerful split image of a therapist who functions well in one respect, but fails to do so in another. Such a therapist is seen as communicating contradictory messages and as placing the patient in a double bind—viewed as both mad and as driving the patient mad.

D. The Main Universal Implications of the Adaptive Contexts

To concentrate now on the most significant universal implications of these deviant intervention contexts, we will characterize them in terms of the seven-part schema related to the therapeutic experience:

1. Frame: Major frame deviations, such as occur in a clinic setting, create a basic sense of mistrust within the patient, an experience of inadequate interpersonal boundaries, and a failure in the therapist's holding and containing functions. These deviations also disturb the patient's capacity for reality testing. The patient will view the therapist as afraid to be alone with her, have a sense that he requires the help of others in order to function, and a picture of him as subservient to others. There is an intrusion of third parties into treatment, with the patient's consequent view of the therapist as incapable of holding her independently in an exclusive two-person relationship. The frame deviations may also create an immediate sense of exploitation of the patient by the therapist.

2. Mode of relatedness: The therapist will be seen as establishing mainly a parasitic and pathological symbiotic mode of relatedness with the patient. There will also be a sense of pathological autistic qualities in the therapist's abandonment of his responsibility to secure the frame and in his neglect of the patient's therapeutic needs (the deviations are unilaterally self-serving for the therapist). Specific aspects of these deviations will also contribute to the experience of an autistic mode of relatedness with the therapist, especially those aspects involving the therapist's abandonment of his responsibility to write out the patient's bill (if the patient is indeed to receive a bill; ideally, no bill should be used) and to receive the fee through a check made out to him personally. There are thus indications of major pathology in the object-relationship sphere.

3. Mode of cure: Action-discharge.

4. Communication: The therapist's deviations have qualities of projective identification as well as the destruction of meaning. The basic communicative relationship is likely to be impaired, and the patient's derivative expressions undoubtedly will concentrate and organize mainly around these deviant intervention contexts.

5. Dynamics and genetics: Dynamically, third parties to treatment create oedipal and preoedipal rivalries, primal scene qualities to treatment, and issues of exhibitionism and voyeurism. The fee problem may involve oral (greed), anal, and phallic aspects. In the aggressive sphere, issues of mistrust and betrayal loom large. Genetics are not as yet represented, but will probably fall into these areas.

6. Self and identity: There will be a sense of narcissistic and identity impairment in the patient's images of the therapist under these deviant conditions.

7. Sanity and madness: There will be a quality of madness perceived in the therapist's inability to function on his own and in his need to create a confusing setting. The patient will also perceive madness in the contradiction of the therapist's being able to interpret the implications of these deviations and yet failing to rectify the situation.

Keeping these implications of the prevailing intervention context in mind, we must remain open for the patient's communication of as yet overlooked meanings. We must also be prepared for the implications of other intervention contexts that serve well to organize the patient's encoded material and responses.

E. Manifest Representations of the Adaptive Contexts

We turn next to the representations or portrayals of these intervention contexts. The closest the patient comes to a manifest representation of an adaptive context is her comment, following the dream of her husband's affair, that she and the therapist had talked last session about her mistrust of a woman neighbor. In actuality, this is an aspect of an intervention that the therapist had made regarding the patient's inability to trust him because of the frame deviations contained in the treatment setting. As such, the comment may be seen as a relatively weak but direct representation of this particular adaptive context.

Beyond that allusion, there is no other direct representation of an adaptive context in the patient's material to this point. There is, however, a general bridge to the therapeutic relationship in the patient's comment toward the end of this excerpt that her anxiety attack in the middle of the night might have something to do with her relationship with the therapist. This type of general allusion to the treatment situation or the therapist is sometimes used in intervening in the absence of a specific manifest representation of an adaptive context. It serves as a means of connecting the patient's derivative material in some general way to the therapeutic situation and interaction, though it does, of course, fall short of providing a specific link between a particular adaptive context and the derivative complex. This type of bridge enables the therapist to connect the patient's material in a general way to himself or herself (and the therapy) when playing back selected derivatives related to an unmentioned intervention context. There is an implied expectation that the patient will validate the intervention by then providing the specific intervention context to which the derivatives that have been pointed out are connected.

F. Derivative Representations of the Adaptive Contexts

What then of the patient's encoded representations of deviant intervention contexts—her portrayals of the therapist's efforts at interpretation, unaccompanied as yet by rectification? Indeed, there are several strong and thinly disguised representations of these intervention contexts. In sequence, the major portrayals appear to be the following:

1. In the patient's initial associations regarding the problems with conditions at work, we have a basic representation of a disturbed frame (a poor hold and container).

In addition, there is a strong displaced and symbolized portrayal of the therapist's mixed responses to the deviations—offering interpretations (the dentist's realization that changes were necessary), but failing to rectify the situation (making promises that are never kept). These are excellent derivative representations.

2. The clinic itself, and by implication the deviations involved, is well represented in the patient's allusion to bureaucratic agencies that are exploitative.

These, then, appear to be the best representations of the main intervention contexts. Most clearly conveyed in these portrayals is the latent issue of the fee (receiving a bill from and making a check out to the clinic); this theme is contained in the initial manifest allusion to the dentist and in the theme of money problems (the salaries that are too low). It is also expressed in the reference to the bureaucratic agencies that are exploitative financially, and in the mention of the cost of adopting a child. Thus, this particular aspect of the deviant frame should receive special attention when intervening.

It is critical to be as specific as possible when offering an interpretation in light of an adaptive context. In listening to and formulating material from the patient, there are two basic concerns for the therapist: first, the clarity of the communication and, second, the nature and meaning of what is being expressed. The first issue is especially important when studying derivative portrayals of intervention contexts. The therapist must determine whether the derivative representation is sufficiently clear to support a playback of the derivative complex that the patient will understand. The key question, then, is whether the derivative portrayal is thinly disguised and therefore likely to evoke conscious (and unconscious) recognition within the patient as to the intervention context involved. Communication issues (and then frame) must be dealt with before all other considerations.

In the material of the patient under consideration, we have evident bridging themes that link manifest content to latent perceptions of attributes of the deviant adaptive context and of the contradiction in the therapist's efforts. The manifest allusion to the dentist easily ties to the therapist. The allusion to the receptionist is a simple displacement from the receptionist at the clinic. The meeting of the dentist's personnel appears to connect to the latent theme of the third parties to treatment and to the records that the secretaries and therapist keep. The allusion to the low pay connects to the somewhat reduced clinic fee and especially to the clinic billing and payment procedures.

The dentist's proposal to make changes in the office conditions connects to the therapist's interpretations concerning the meaning of the clinic deviations and their strong implication that rectification is required. The therapist's failure to rectify the frame is well portrayed in the manifest allusion to the dentist's tendency to make promises and never keep them.

In the second portrayal segment, the social worker (manifest content) is readily connected to the therapist (latent content). The presence of an attorney (manifest content) is another bridge to the presence of third parties to treatment (latent content). A bureaucratic agency (manifest theme) readily portrays the clinic setting (latent theme). The images of funds, subsidies, the cost of adopting a child, and of a bureaucracy that just wants your money (manifest contents) readily connect to the fee issues in the treatment setting (latent content).

In all, we have a relatively good example of manifest themes that clearly bridge over into latent images and perceptions—latent themes. This type of bridging is, as noted, a sign that intervening has been facilitated on the *communicative level*. In the presence of a clear indicator and a strong, meaningful, coalescing derivative complex, the therapist would be likely to intervene—here, in the form of a selected playback of encoded perceptions of the therapist in light of an encoded portrayal of an intervention context. It would be important to maintain the intervention at the level of the patient's communicative expression and resistances, that is, to use the derivative portrayals of the adaptive context available without alluding to their latent contexts directly.

In this situation, it is well to realize that although the patient-indicators are moderate, the therapist-indicators or traumatic qualities of the prevailing intervention context are quite strong. This creates a relatively powerful need for intervention within the patient, who is experiencing and attempting to deal with, communicatively and adaptively, the deviations in the treatment conditions and the therapist's failure to rectify them. Such rectification would, of course, require the therapist's shift from the clinic setting to private practice. Actually, at this particular time, the therapist was struggling with this very issue. In principle, even in the absence of relatively strong patient-indicators, a therapist should intervene when he or she is involved in major frame deviations.

There are additional portrayals of intervention contexts reflected in this material. In sequence, they appear to be the following:

3. The meeting between the dentist and his staff appears to represent the therapist and other clinical personnel.

4. The allusion to the work conditions represents the conditions of the treatment setting.

5. The dentist's efforts to make some changes in the office setting is a disguised portrayal of the therapist's efforts to secure the frame.

6. The dentist's failure to follow through is an encoded portrayal of the therapist's failure to rectify those aspects of the frame that have been interpreted and seem to require correction. (Numbers 3–6 are elaborations of the first portrayal identified earlier.)

7. The baby in the crib is a relatively disguised portrayal of the infantilizing treatment setting.

8. The contact between the social worker, the attorney, and the patient and her husband is a portrayal of the treatment setting, which includes third parties to the therapy. (This is an elaboration of the second portrayal identified above.)

9. The card received by the husband from his former mistress may be a strongly encoded portrayal of the bill the patient receives from the clinic.

This listing of the main portrayals of specific intervention contexts has been confined to those appearing both to represent an adaptive context and to convey some of its implications. It is important to identify these portrayals; they will become the basis for a playback intervention. This analysis reveals that the patient is strongly portraying the deviant conditions of treatment and the therapist's mixed efforts by focusing on the therapist's continued identification of the need for rectification and his continued failure to follow through. Most of these derivative portrayals can be readily connected to the treatment situation, suggesting the feasibility of intervening.

G. The Patient's Selective Encoded Perceptions

We turn now to the patient's selective encoded perceptions of the therapist in light of the prevailing intervention contexts. In identifying these perceptions, we will include attributes of the portrayals of the intervention context as well as other derivative material. If the reader has not as yet completed this part of the listening exercise, he or she is advised to go back over the material and to record additional impressions. In sequence, the following appear to be the patient's main encoded perceptions of the therapist, along with the dimensions of the therapeutic experience that are involved:

1. The receptionist who quit her job appears to be an unconscious perception of the therapist who has not secured the ideal frame—has not carried out or has quit his job. This is primarily a frame allusion, but it also implies an action-discharge mode of cure.

2. The allusion to the staff meeting contains an encoded perception of the therapist's involvement with other clinic personnel. It reflcts some measure of frame issue, a pathological symbiotic mode of relatedness, and dynamics related to third parties to treatment (e.g., public exposure).

3. The allusion to the low salary and to the responsibilities that are too great contain encoded perceptions of (1) the fee issues in this treatment and (2) the low salary that the therapist is paid in the clinic—something the patient appears to sense or know about. The great burden of responsibility is an encoded perception of the therapist's failure to carry out the treatment on his own—an image of the therapist as suffering from too great a burden in this regard. There is a sense here of frame issues and possibly a parasitic mode of relatedness.

4. The dentist's offer to consider changes and the patient's concern that he will not follow through is, as noted, a representation of the patient's unconscious perception of the therapist's constructive intentions as reflected in his interpretive interventions, accompanied by a perception of the hollowness of these interventions because of the absence of follow-up through rectification. The more positive part of this image reflects a healthy therapeutic symbiosis and efforts to secure the frame, and implies cure through insight and understanding. There is also a sense of openness of communication and of meaningful expression. A positive sense of identity and sanity is also implied.
The latter part of the image, however, suggests a failure to secure the frame, an autistic mode of relatedness (promising something but then withdrawing before the promise is fulfilled), an action-discharge mode of cure, a failure in communication, the use of language to destroy meaning and to generate lie-barrier systems, a disturbed

sense of narcissism (the use of employees—the patient—as selfobjects) and of identity, and a sense of madness.

As can be seen, this initial excerpt is rich with derivative encoded perceptions of the therapist that touch on all of the spheres of the therapeutic experience. It already has strong meaning and suggests a richly coalescing derivative complex. The images to follow are similarly endowed. A therapist might anticipate as much by recognizing that this patient is communicating through rich narratives and images—stories laden with meaningful and highly evocative detail. It is communication of this kind—involving dreams, recent incidents, and memories of the past—that are most likely to convey rich derivative meaning, especially in the realm of selected encoded perceptions.

To continue now with the further selected unconscious perceptions of the therapist:

5. The baby in a crib crying for its mother is an unconscious perception of the therapist, developed in light of the deviant frame adaptive contexts, so that he is viewed as an infant in need of others. Here, separation and depressive dynamics are suggested, as well as the pathological autistic and pathological symbiotic modes of relatedness.

6. The body of a one-year-old and the face of a four-year-old suggest a split image of the therapist, one that is probably based on his use of interpretations without rectification. Narcissistic and identity disturbances seem implied.

7. Attempting to get to the baby but not being able to do it, and the feelings of helplessness and frustration, may well involve unconscious perceptions of the therapist wishing to change the deviant treatment situation but being, as yet, unable to do so. The image implies a failed mode of cure, an autistic mode of relatedness, and depressive dynamics and genetics.

There is a sense of coalescing meaning in this second segment of material that touches upon several important dimensions of the therapeutic experience, including hints of bodily concern as portrayed in the allusion to the infant child in the dream.

Continuing our sequential analysis of the patient's encoded, selected perceptions of the therapist:

8. The image of the handicapped child appears to be an unconscious perception of the therapist in light of the deviant conditions of treatment and his failures to achieve rectification. Here, too, dynamics related to bodily impairment and neediness (infantilism) seem central.

9. The conflict between having biological and adopted children appears to involve an unconscious perception of the therapist's split loyalty—part to the clinic and part to the patient.

10. The images of the bureaucratic agencies that hold on to their children to get

funds and subsidies, and of the excessive fee for adopting a child, appear to involve unconscious perceptions of the therapist holding on to the clinic because of the salary he earns or the ease with which he is able to obtain patients. These images would also seem to encode the patient's perception of being exploited by the therapist financially both through the manner in which the fee is collected and through the therapist's failure to achieve the necessary rectification of the frame. The images involve the parasitic mode of relatedness and dynamics related to exploitation and abuse, as well as to dependency and neediness.

To this point, the patient has represented a series of unconscious perceptions of the therapist as infantile, split or divided, handicapped, and overly needy. Communications from the patient that involve different derivative expressions of the same underlying theme are useful in intervening, because they carry special weight and conviction. In an actual session, the therapist would begin to make silent hypotheses and formulations based on the patient's initial associations. He or she would then discover that these ideas were being validated by the patient's continuing associations on a *derivative* level. This validation would lend strong support to the therapist's initial formulations and begin to provide the wherewithal for an interpretive and perhaps framework-rectifying intervention.

The next segment of material contains these additional encoded perceptions:

11. The image of the husband's affair appears to contain an unconscious view of the therapist as unfaithful to the patient in his involvement with the clinic. Through condensation, the same derivative may contain a view of the therapist as latently sexually involved with the patient in light of his deviant interventions and failures to rectify the ground-rule conditions of treatment. The image contains a frame break, an action-discharge-merger mode of cure, a parasitic mode of relatedness, and dynamics that suggest unresolved sexual conflicts with incestuous qualities.

12. The patient's sadness may well contain an unconscious perception of the therapist's own depressed state in light of his deviant interventions and his interpretation without rectification. The dynamics would be depressive in nature.

13. The image of mistrusting a woman neighbor, accompanied by the knowledge that she would not get involved with the patient's husband, contains another encoded and split image of the therapist: The patient is unable to trust him because of the deviations, and yet, based on his interpretive efforts, the patient understands that the therapist knows where to draw the line. These images contain frame allusions and the mistrust that arises under deviant-frame conditions. In addition, the uncertainty of reality and the presence of a deviant frame is also conveyed. There may as well be important dynamics regarding mistrust and incestuous sexuality.

14. The allusion to the exchange of cards between the patient's husband and his former mistress may well involve an unconscious perception of the therapist's seductive qualities in light of the information that he exchanges with clinic personnel. It may also in derivative fashion represent the billing and record keeping practices at the clinic. There are qualities here of pathological symbiosis and parasiticism and dynamics related to sexuality and defensive denial.

In this section, the incestuous sexual implications of the deviant frame are expressed. This provides a fullness to the developing derivative complex that also facilitates intervention and its likelihood.

To continue:

15. The husband's wish to have sex with the patient may involve another unconscious perception of the therapist in light of his deviant exploitation of the patient. Although the image might well convey a wish for a healthy symbiosis or for a commensal (equally satisfying) relationship, the patient's subsequent associations reveal that the parasitic quality of this desire looms large for her.

16. The patient's hatred of her husband and inability to respond to his sexual overtures seems to convey an unconscious perception of the therapist as vengeful toward the patient as reflected in the basically deviant frame and in his failure to rectify this frame. Here, there is stress on the parasitic mode of relatedness and sexual and aggressive dynamics. The unexpected quality of this rage also suggests a measure of perceived madness in the therapist.

In this section, the vengeful qualities of the continuing deviant conditions of treatment are expressed in vivid derivative form. There is an encoded perception of the therapist as failing to understand himself and as overlooking the destructive aspects of his failure to rectify the frame. This segment adds still more diversity to this highly complex and coalescing derivative complex.

As for intervening, the material is so rich in derivative perceptions that a therapist might well be inclined to offer an interpretation at this very point. The major drawback is that the patient has not clearly (or very directly) represented the critical adaptive context to which she is responding. The material regarding the dentist, however, provides an extremely usable representation of the main intervention contexts at hand and can be used to initiate an interpretation at any point in the session. A clear bridge to therapy is also present (the patient's allusion to her relationship with the therapist). Some therapists might, nonetheless, wait a bit longer, hoping that the patient would provide a quite specific and manifest portrayal of one of the crucial intervention contexts currently active.

The final segment contains the following additional encoded perceptions of the therapist:

17. The patient's call to the wife of a former lover appears to portray an unconscious perception of the therapist's involvement with clinic personnel—most of whom are women. There is a pathological symbiotic and parasitic quality to this image, as well as a sense of some type of frame deviation.

18. The patient's anxiety attack seems to involve an unconscious perception of the therapist's conflict and anxiety in maintaining a deviant frame and in being unable to rectify the conditions of treatment. It is here again that issues of intrapsychic conflict come into play. The contact with the former lover's wife may also hint at homosexual dynamics that are not otherwise clearly conveyed in this material for the moment.

It was at this point in the session, at about 35 minutes into a 50-minute hour, that the therapist chose to intervene. He did so at this juncture largely because the patient had provided him with a general bridge to treatment. Aware of the many rich derivatives and of the representations of the adaptive contexts, the therapist opted for an interpretation. Before considering his intervention, other matters must be clarified.

For one thing, it should be recognized that many of these derivatives contain images of the patient herself—self-perceptions. As a general rule, the unconscious perceptions of the therapist take precedence over those of the patient herself. Still, these self-referential aspects of the material should be taken into account by the therapist and formulated in secondary fashion.

A sequential summary of the patient's unconscious view of herself would appear to involve her own unreliability as portrayed in the images of the dentist; her difficulties in making the changes necessary in her treatment and in her life; her own infantile and split qualities as reflected in the dream of the baby; her helplessness in the face of need; her view of herself as handicapped, overly needy and exploitative, as conveyed in the material regarding the adoption; her wishes for affairs and her untrustworthiness and seductiveness as conveyed in the section with the dream of her husband's affair; her disregard for boundaries; and her latent homosexual needs as reflected in the contact with her former lover's wife. It is well to be clear that the patient's sense of her hatred toward her husband is a conscious rather than unconscious perception.

H. The Dimension Reflected in the Patient's Selection of Encoded Perceptions

Our next task is to review the patient's selected unconscious perceptions of the therapist. This will permit us to identify the nature of the patient's madness or psychopathology as reflected in the selection process. The following seem most pertinent:

1. Frame: The patient is expressing wishes for the secure frame, as reflected in the material about the dentist; but strong, conflicting wishes for the deviant frame are reflected in the dream of the patient's husband's affair and in her allusion to the contact with the wife of a former lover. The patient therefore appears to have significant psychopathology in the area of ground rules and interpersonal boundaries, and seems as well to be quite divided in regard to her needs in this respect.

2. Mode of relatedness: There are many signs of pathological modes of relatedness in this material. There are also indications of wishes for a healthy therapeutic symbiosis and for outside commensal relatedness. Nonetheless, there are repeated images of abandonment and therefore of the pathological autistic mode of relatedness; of a pathological symbiosis, as reflected in affairs and in the contact with the former lover's wife; and of parasiticism, as best portrayed in the dentist's salary policy and excessive job responsibilities for his employees, and in the allusion to the bureaucratic agencies. There are significant indications, therefore, of major psychopathology in the area of object relationships for this patient.

3. Mode of cure: There are, again, signs of a significant split in the patient. The material regarding the dentist's constructive efforts best represents cure through in-

sight. On the other hand, the dream of the affair, the sexual repudiation of her husband, and the contact with the wife of a former lover point to action-discharge and merger as modes of cure and relief. This is an extremely divided patient with signs of positive functioning as well as deep madness and malfunctioning.

4. Communication: The material itself is highly meaningful, but not without communicative resistances—these mainly in the form of a failure to represent manifestly a significant intervention context. In general, the associations contain images of open communication, notwithstanding some disturbance in communication with respect to the sexual problems between the patient and her husband. On the whole, this patient appears to have a deep unconscious need to express herself meaningfully and to be understood.

5. Dynamics and genetics: There are no genetic allusions in the material to this point. Dynamically, the central issues appear to involve bodily anxieties, depressive issues, incestuous sexual involvement, and concerns with aggression and exploitation.

6. Self and identity: There are indications of issues of identity and narcissism, conveyed especially in the dream image of the baby, the wish for a handicapped child, the sexual conflicts between the patient and her husband, and the contact with the wife of the former lover.

7. Sanity and madness: There are aspects of madness in the material regarding the dentist, but they are not especially clear. In addition, there are qualities of madness in the image of the infant, the irrationality of the bureaucratic agencies, the conflicted and uncontrolled feelings within the patient toward her husband, and the call to the wife of a former lover.

In all, the analysis of the patient's material in terms of the dimensions of human experience provides a valuable diagnostic profile. This type of understanding can be used to supplement the more commonly used diagnostic considerations that, because of the limited material from this hour, will not be discussed here. The reader should appreciate that the basics of the listening–formulating process apply to patients in all diagnostic categories, ranging from those who are schizophrenic to those who are neurotic, though variations will appear in keeping with the patient's psychopathology and other factors.

I. Reactions to Unconscious Perceptions

We turn now to the indications of the patient's reactions to her encoded perceptions of the therapist. They fall into the following categories: behaviors, intensification or diminution in psychopathology or madness, conscious or unconscious fantasies and memories, and efforts to help (mainly through encoded interpretations and models of rectification) or harm the therapist. In sequence, the main reactions appear to be as follows:

1. The first segment of material regarding the dentist contains an evident encoded conscious or unconscious fantasy, represented indirectly. It may be decoded or reduced to the following raw image: The patient will respond to the deviant conditions of treatment and to the therapist's failures to rectify the situation by quitting

treatment. The manifest vehicle for this expressed response is the allusion to the secretary who quit her job.

As the reader may recall, it was possible earlier to formulate the same segment of material as an encoded perception of the therapist who failed to carry out his functions in the treatment of the patient. Thus, it is possible that a particular element of material may, through condensation, convey a selected unconscious perception of the therapist as well as a reaction to such a perception.

The balance of this sequence appears to contain other conscious or unconscious fantasies concerning the way in which the therapist might actually go about correcting the conditions at the private clinic or affecting other changes in the treatment setting. This reaction shades into strong and useful models of rectification, which represent the patient's major response to encoded perceptions of the therapist. The manifest material here decodes as follows: The therapist should rectify the deviant frame and follow through for once on his promises, instead of making it all a word game.

2. The image of the infant child may touch unconsciously on early memories of maternal deprivation or abandonment, as set off by similar attributes in the failures related to the therapist's missed interventions (especially, his failure to fully secure the frame.) Additional material would be required to clarify this hypothesis. By and large, however, this dream appears to involve unconscious perceptions more than it does reactions to such perceptions. On the other hand, the patient's sense of helplessness in the dream may, through condensation, be both a perception of the therapist and a reaction to that perception.

3. It is unclear from this single session as to whether the patient's plans to adopt a handicapped child is on some level a response to unconscious perceptions of the therapist as handicapped and in need of care. Of course, additional self-perceptions, generated as responses to the failings in the therapist's efforts, may also be involved. For the moment, these may be taken as likely hypotheses.

4. It is also probable (though uncertain) that the patient's dream of her husband having an affair is on one level an encoded unconscious fantasy regarding similar wishes within the patient toward the therapist. This is a not uncommon response— sometimes acted out—to a therapist who maintains a deviant frame and/or fails to intervene in keeping with the patient's therapeutic needs—interpretively and in regard to framework management. The sense of loss and hurt is repaired through some type of conscious or unconscious erotic fantasy.

Thus, in addition to conveying a valid unconscious perception of the seductive aspects of the therapist's efforts, this material may also contain an encoded unconscious fantasy directed toward the therapist—that is, it may embody both an element of nontransference (the perception) and of transference (the erotic *wish*). On an object-relationship level, the autistic qualities of the therapist's deviant interventions will tend to stimulate sexualized fantasies of union with the therapist, which constitute wishes for some form of pathological symbiosis, merger, and repair.

5. The patient's hostile response to her husband's sexual overtures appears on one level to be a behavioral and somewhat symptomatic response to the encoded perceptions of the therapist. Here, wishes to harm the therapist are displaced onto the husband. In addition, the perceptions of the therapist may have strongly influenced the patient's reactions to her spouse in more general fashion. This type of interplay between the therapeutic interaction and a patient's outside life is quite typical of the psychotherapeutic experience.

6. The patient's contact with the wife of a former lover also appears to be a behavioral and interpersonally symptomatic response to the encoded perceptions of the therapist.

7. Finally, the patient's anxiety attack appears to be a symptomatic exacerbation that is related in part to the same constellation of encoded perceptions of the therapist that has been defined above.

In all, the patient's reactions to her unconscious perceptions of the therapist do not appear to be especially powerful. This accounts for the relatively moderate indicators represented in these reactions. For the most part, these reactions are behavioral, symptomatic, fantasied, and possibly mixed with elements of unconscious memory formation, with clues that the patient wishes to harm the therapist.

J. The Best Intervention

It remains now to define the best intervention available from this material. Once this has been spelled out, we will return to the case presentation and consider the intervention actually made by the therapist. We will then be in a position to analyze this intervention, though entirely from a listening–formulating vantage point. The patient's response to the intervention is also available, and efforts will be made to predict and then evaluate selected attributes of this response.

In principle, the intervention should have the following structure in light of the absence of a manifestly represented intervention context: It should begin with the best encoded representation of the main intervention context, point to the bridge (connecting link) to the therapy, then deal selectively with the best encoded perceptions of the therapist in light of the intervention context, and finally, it should use the foregoing as best as possible to explain the most compelling indicators. In the absence of a manifestly represented adaptive context, the goal is to selectively identify the most compelling images of the therapist for the moment in light of one or two critical intervention contexts. The therapist may then represent manifestly the most important activated intervention contexts with which he or she is dealing. At that juncture, a specific and full interpretation of the main indicators usually proves feasible.

A brief perspective on the timing of active interventions is in order. This discussion applies to the use of interpretation–reconstructions, the playback of selected derivatives organized around a critical but unmentioned intervention context, and framework–management responses.

There are two basic patterns of communication in psychotherapy sessions:

(A) The patient offers a strong manifest or derivative portrayal of the adaptive context early in the hour, and the therapist awaits the development of a meaningful coalescing derivative complex. When this complex appears to be sufficiently meaningful and diverse, an intervention is made, either as the patient returns to the portrayal of the adaptive context or provides a general bridge to the treatment situation. Failing to find such fresh links to treatment, the therapist may intervene when an especially compelling additional derivative appears in the patient's associations.

(B) The patient conveys meaningful and coalescing encoded perceptions of the therapist in light of an intervention context (known to the therapist), but that context is not initially well-portrayed either through derivatives or in manifest form. The therapist is subjectively aware of the critical intervention context and listens to the patient's derivative perceptions in light of this context in order to validate the hypothesis. As these encoded images of the therapist begin to form a meaningful coalescing derivative complex, the therapist then awaits a clear representation of the intervention context—in direct or derivative form. In general, once this portrayal has emerged, the therapist should wait for a few additional associations, because they often contain important and fresh encoded perceptions of the therapist. Once these have been expressed, the intervention is made.

In contrast to these two meaningful types of sessions in which communicative resistances are relatively low, there are many hours in which there is no clear representation of an intervention context and/or no coalescing derivative complex. The therapist must learn to test our various activated adaptive contexts as organizers of the patient's material and to accept the experience (and hypothesis) of nonmeaning. He or she should then be comfortable in maintaining a therapeutic silence and hold, awaiting the emergence of more meaningful material.

What appears to be the most cogent intervention available in terms of this material? Interventions from the communicative approach tend to be somewhat lengthy, because they must identify an intervention context, allude to a series of encoded perceptions and the patient's responses to them, and then integrate this material into an understanding of a patient-indicator. The following appears to be the best intervention available, using the patient's associations:

> You suggest that your anxiety attack may have something to do with your relationship with me, and this may be your way of saying that much of what you are talking about today is also connected to our relationship. You have been talking about your job with the dentist and many of the problems that exist in the basic conditions under which you work. You have also indicated that the dentist seems aware of these difficulties and has made promises to change them in the past, but has not followed through on such changes. You are concerned, then, with problems relating to the basic conditions of a situation, realizations of problems in these conditions, and the failure to follow through with the necessary changes.
>
> There are also images of a helpless baby crying for its mother in a crib. In the dream, you yourself are unable to do anything about the situation. Another image involves bureaucratic agencies and people who hold on to children just to get funds and subsidies. There are also allusions to conflicts of loyalty, to affairs, to mistrust, and to questionable kinds of involvements—between your husband and your neighbor, between you and the wife of your former lover. There is an uncertainty regarding the boundaries of the relationship between yourself and others. The same problem is reflected in your image of others and those with whom they are interacting. It is this uncertainty that seems to have been a factor in your anxiety attack, which you connect to your relationship with me—indicating that here, too, you have doubts and anxieties regarding the conditions of treatment, our own involvement, and my involvement with others.

All of this is connected as well to your coldness and rage toward your husband and your need to repudiate his sexual overtures. In some way this, too, must be connected to me and to your sense of anxiety. At issue appears to be past and present involvements with others in a manner that is seductive and inappropriate. Perhaps the bottom line in some way involves the conditions of treatment and our relationship—along with promises you have sensed from me to set straight the problems at hand. You feel that, like the dentist, I have failed to make the necessary changes.

In an effort to provide further clarification of the structure of this intervention, it will now be repeated with remarks in brackets offered to explain the strategy of listening and intervening. The intervention along with the comments follows:

You suggest that your anxiety attack may have something to do with your relationship with me, and this may be your way of saying that much of what you are talking about today is also connected to our relationship. [The intervention begins with the bridge to therapy as a way of stressing to the patient that the themes to be identified in some fashion relate to the treatment situation and relationship.] You have been talking about your job with the dentist and many of the problems that exist in the basic conditions under which you work. You have also indicated that the dentist seems aware of these difficulties and has made promises to change them in the past, but has not followed through on such changes. [We move next to the best representation of the two main intervention contexts: the deviant conditions of treatment and the therapist's recent efforts at interpretation without rectification.] You are concerned, then, with problems relating to the basic conditions of a situation, realizations of problems in these conditions, and the failure to follow through with the necessary changes. [These general themes are offered as bridges between the manifest and latent levels—the direct (manifest) concern with the dentist and the latent concern with the therapist and the conditions of treatment.]

There are also images of a helpless baby crying for its mother in a crib. In the dream, you yourself are unable to do anything about the situation. Another image involves bureaucratic agencies and people who hold on to children just to get funds and subsidies. [The intervention now shifts to some of the most compelling unconscious perceptions of the therapist in light of his involvement at the private clinic and his difficulties in modifying the conditions of the patient's therapy.] There are also allusions to conflicts of loyalty, to affairs, to mistrust, and to questionable kinds of involvements—between your husband and your neighbor, between you and the wife of your former lover. [We move now to additional encoded perceptions of the therapist in light of the prevailing intervention context. These are played back to the patient as selected themes in a manner that hints at the connection between the manifest level and the treatment situation—this latter established earlier by suggesting that all of the patient's associations on some level touch upon the therapeutic relationship.] There is an uncertainty regarding the boundaries of the relationships between yourself and others. The same problem is reflected in your image of others and those with whom they are interacting. It is this uncertainty that seems to have been a factor in your anxiety attack, which you connect to your relationship with me—indicating that here, too, you have doubts and anxieties regarding the conditions of treatment, our own involvement, and my involvement with others. [Here an attempt is made to interpret unconscious factors in the anxiety-attack—the main patient-indicator—using the earlier comments as background factors. Proposed here is the idea or implication that the therapist's involvement with clinic personnel and his failure to secure clear boundaries between himself and the patient in light of the deviant conditions of treatment stand important among the unconscious sources of the patient's anxiety experience.]

All of this is connected as well to your coldness and rage toward your husband and your need to repudiate his sexual overtures. In some way this too must connect to me and to your sense of anxiety. At issue appears to be past and present involvements with others in a manner that is seductive and inappropriate. Perhaps the bottom line in some way involves the conditions of treatment and our relationship—along with promises you have sensed from me to set straight the problems at hand. You feel that, like the dentist, I have failed to make the necessary changes. [The intervention concludes by a return to the best derivative representations of the adaptive context and the most important unconscious perceptions of the therapist. It is well to bring the patient back to these central issues—the ones with which he is currently dealing—and to bridge the manifest material once again to the treatment experience.]

As the intervention proceeded, it was possible for the therapist to make more and more clear the connections between the patient's manifest associations and that latent level of meaning pertaining to the therapeutic interaction. Considerable use was made of bridging themes that connected the surface with the depths—the latter, of course, the patient's relationship with the therapist.

The intervention seemed advisable in light of the moderately strong indicators and the relatively clear and meaningful derivative material. Above all, the well-represented, though encoded, portrayal of the adaptive contexts facilitated the intervention process.

The playback of selected encoded derivatives conveyed in this intervention may be seen as an interpretation offered to the patient without allusion to a specific adaptive context. The patient's communicative resistances are respected. It may be anticipated, however, that the patient's unconscious awareness of the therapist as prepared to deal with the adaptive contexts at hand and the issues they have created will lend unconscious support to her need to communicate. It is likely that she will modify her communicative resistances as a result. There is a strong probability that an intervention of this kind would be validated either by the emergence of a specific and manifestly portrayed intervention context and/or fresh associational material that would embody interpersonal and cognitive validation of the intervention. Interpersonal validation occurs when positively functioning figures emerge in the patient's associations. Cognitive validation is witnessed when the patient's material contains associations that embody derivative perceptions and other responses to the intervention context previously unreported by the patient. If validation of this kind were not to appear, it would be absolutely essential for the therapist to remain silent and to attempt to reformulate the material. First and foremost, he would search for adaptive contexts that had been overlooked, attempt to reorganize the derivative material in light of such a context, or reformulate it in terms of those contexts already known.

The Therapist's Intervention: Exercise 11.2

We will now return to the actual session and consider the intervention made by the therapist. It was as follows:

> *Therapist:* You mention that the conditions at work had not changed despite the promises of the dentist whom you worked for to do something about them. You said that in the final analysis he would probably do nothing because he trades in words only. That situation would certainly seem to have a parallel here where we have talked about the conditions of your treatment but nothing has really been done to change them. The dreams seem to indicate that on one level you experience the conditions here as a kind of maternal failure on my part, a failure to provide you the kind of care and treatment that you need and over which we are hopelessly frustrated as far as our being able to do anything about it. On another level, despite your often-expressed denial, you continue to experience me as well as your husband as disloyal, as engaged in an illicit relationship with another woman. I think that you took out some of your anger toward me against your husband the other night when he wanted to make love to you.

We will consider this particular intervention in terms of the listening–formulating process. Thus, we will attempt to answer the following five basic questions (and two others) regarding the intervention—questions that can be applied in principle to each intervention made in psychotherapy and psychoanalysis. Using the space below, please respond to the following:

1. Did the intervention deal with the major indicators and attempt to illuminate their unconscious basis? Which indicators, if any, were overlooked?

2. Did the therapist utilize the best available representations of the adaptive context at hand? If not, which were missed? Was there any other error in the use of the representation of the main adaptive context?

3. Did the therapist make use of the most compelling selective encoded perceptions of himself in light of the active intervention contexts? Were the main reactions to these perceptions identified as well? What of significance, if anything, was left out?

4. Did the therapist introduce anything into his intervention which the patient had not herself communicated in this particular hour?

5. Was anything else of significance missed in the intervention?

6. Is there any other major criticism or value to the intervention? What is your overall appraisal?

7. What is the likelihood of derivative validation? Clarify the basis for your answer.

_____

_____

_____

_____

_____

_____

_____

_____

Answer

The following appear to be the best answers to the questions raised above:

1. The intervention deals with the patient-indicator of the interpersonal problem between the patient and her husband. By implication it deals with the patient's difficulties in maintaining clear interpersonal boundaries and a secure framework to her interpersonal relationships. It does not, however, deal at all with the patient's major symptom—her anxiety attack—nor does it attempt to clarify her questionable call to the wife of a former lover. In regard to indicators, then, the major failing is the omission of an attempt to understand the unconscious basis for the anxiety episode.

We must consider, too, whether the therapist attempted to explain the unconscious basis of the main indicator with which he dealt—the patient's anger at her husband. He did attempt in a somewhat limited way to connect the anger at the husband to anger with the therapist, thereby suggesting that on an unconscious level the husband was used as a stand-in for the therapist. By implication, the anger was also connected to unconscious perceptions of the therapist as disloyal and as involved in an illicit relationship with another woman (here, implying the clinic secretary). The anger was also implicitly connected to the therapist's general failure to secure the conditions of the treatment. In all, then, there is a fairly substantial effort to indicate to the patient that her anger toward her husband had an important unconscious source in her anger toward her therapist in light of specific interventional failures and other meanings conveyed by active intervention contexts.

2. The therapist does make use of the patient's best representations of the adaptive contexts by focusing on the situation with the dentist as a portrayal of the conditions of treatment. He also makes use of the same material as it portrays his recent efforts in interpretation accompanied by his failure to rectify the treatment situation.

Although this effort appears sound, there are several problems with it. First, the therapist alludes directly to the conditions of treatment when the patient has not done so herself (see below, #4). Second, he refers to the patient's unconscious perceptions of himself as disloyal and engaged in an illicit relationship with another woman without indicating to the patient the best representation of the particular adaptive context involved. These images portray a specific deviant condition of treatment as constituted by the presence of a secretary, with whom the patient has seen the therapist talk. It is important that the therapist indicate clearly to the patient the specific associations on which a particular perception or other response is based and to thereby indicate to the patient the source of a particular formulation.

3. The intervention touches on images of the therapist that are encoded in the allusion to the dentist, conveyed in the dream of the infant/child, mentioned in the patient's dream of her husband's affair, and alluded to in her mention of the exchange of cards between the husband and a former mistress. Although the therapist does not

specify the particular derivatives he was using in each instance, he does nonetheless touch on the main encoded perceptions of himself conveyed in this material. Perhaps the therapist's major oversight was the significance of the patient's associations regarding her wish to adopt a handicapped child and of her comments about bureaucratic agencies. The therapist also overlooked the patient's telephone call to the wife of her former lover as a carrier of encoded perceptions of himself.

As for reactions to these perceptions, the therapist deals with one of the patient's two major responses—her anger with her husband. Omitted, as already noted, is the patient's anxiety attack.

4. In making the intervention, the therapist added the fact that he and the patient had talked about the conditions of her treatment and specifically stated that nothing had really been done to change them. This comment goes well beyond the communications of the patient and introduces a specific adaptive context on the manifest level that the patient has portrayed only in derivative form. Bypassing communicative defenses and resistances of this kind, however, is not likely to evoke the kind of denial usually prompted by too direct a reference to an adaptive context not yet manifest in a patient's associations. In this instance, the patient herself is close to stating the parallel indicated by the therapist, and the issues related to the conditions of treatment have been under exploration for some time. So it seems unlikely that the patient would entirely negate the therapist's comment at this juncture.

On the other hand, the intervention as stated may decrease the likelihood that the patient will validate the therapist's comment with strong derivative material. There may be instead a concentration of associations on the manifest level pertaining to the conditions of treatment. These will convey no critical encoded or unconscious meanings. But derivative validation is not impossible. Despite the therapist's destruction of the patient's denial barrier, he is quite correct in what he has overstated.

A more subtle addition to the patient's associations can be seen toward the end of the intervention, when the therapist characterizes the husband's sexual overture as "wanting to make love" to the patient. A review of the patient's material indicates that the patient characterized this effort as her husband's wanting "to have sex" and as making sexual overtures. There was no image of lovemaking in the patient's associations. The therapist must be careful to characterize a particular interlude in terms of the patient's own sense of it and not modify the patient's portrayal due to some inner, mad (countertransference-based) need.

5. We have already touched upon the main omissions in the therapist's intervention—the failure to use the material related to the adoption, the omission of the patient's telephone call to the wife of a former lover, and the patient-indicator of the anxiety attack.

6. On the whole, the intervention may be characterized as an attempt at interpretation and an acknowledgment of the patient's model of rectification. It touches on framework issues, mode of relatedness, mode of cure, some measure of dynamics, and includes instinctual-drive expressions. It therefore has a sense of breadth and depth and is relatively sound.

7. There is a strong likelihood here of derivative validation. The therapist has already provided aspects of the missing adaptive context, though the patient may become more explicit. We might well expect the emergence of an image of a positively functioning individual, reflecting an introject of the well-functioning therapist. The patient will also unconsciously perceive the pressure within the therapist to add

the missing adaptive context to his comment, and this, too, may be portrayed in derivative form. Confirmation might also take shape through fresh derivative perceptions of the therapist in light of the intervention contexts at hand. The major mitigating factor is the therapist's continued failure to achieve actual rectification of the frame deviations.

The Patient's Response: Exercise 11.3

In psychotherapy, much as in everyday life, one seldom deals with a simple, linear sequence of events. Again and again, in carrying out clinical research, no sooner does a therapist isolate a single adaptive context and derivative response from the patient, than some complicating factor comes along to render the situation difficult to sort out. This particular treatment sequence, already complicated to some degree, takes on an additional and unexpected contaminant at this point. It appears that neither the patient nor the therapist was aware of the problem during the time it was happening, although the therapist recognized his error almost immediately afterwards. It may well be—and we will soon look for evidence in the patient's associations—that the patient, too, was unconsciously aware of the difficulty.

To clarify, immediately upon ending this particular hour with the patient, the therapist realized that *he had extended the session by ten full minutes.* Thus, the associations that we are about to evaluate for the presence or lack of validation as an immediate response to the therapist's intervention are, on another level, a reaction to an adaptive context of which both participants were probably consciously unaware—the fact that the session was being continued beyond the time at which it should have been terminated. It is the therapist's impression that the hour should have ended at the point when he had completed his intervention, or after the patient's very first responsive associations. In any case, the following material embodies the patient's associations after the therapist had intervened:

> *Patient:*   You know, I can see that. I remember as a child I felt my father was terribly unfair and arbitrary in his disciplining me. For minor mistakes he would take the hairbrush and spank me really hard. He would become even violent at times. My parents could really be kind to me at times, but their marriage was a terribly unhappy and violent one. They drank too much, argued incessantly and really hated each other most of the time. They separated when I was 15 years old, and I can remember pleading with my father not to leave us. I cried and actually hung onto his leg as he left. Frankly, my parents are crazy at times. I can recall the time my father found me in this van with another guy after I was supposed to have come home. He jerked me out of the van, slapped me back and forth across the face, and threw me back in the van. I don't know if I actually could have murdered him or not at the time, but I know I certainly felt like it.

> *Therapist:* Our time is up now.

We are confronted with several tasks in evaluating this material. Indicate below the responses to the following questions:

1. Are there signs of interpersonal and/or cognitive validation of the therapist's verbal intervention? If so, what form do they take? If not, what is the most likely source of the patient's nonconfirmatory response? In addition, state whether the material contains fresh indicators, a new—direct or encoded—representation of a known intervention context, and fresh derivative perceptions in light of this context—as well as reactions to these perceptions. Identify the factors within the patient that account for these selected perceptions of the therapist in light of his intervention.

2. State the patient's unconscious *commentary* on the therapist's intervention— her encoded perceptions and responsive fantasies in light of his effort.

3. Name the adaptive context(s) that we must now consider in addition to those that existed prior to the therapist's verbal intervention.

4. Finally, make use of the adaptive context of the therapist's extension of the patient's hour in formulating this material. Is there a manifest representation of this context? Is there one or more encoded representations of this particular intervention context? List in sequence the selected encoded perceptions of the therapist in light of this particular adaptation-evoking context. In this regard, identify the categories of the seven dimensions of the therapeutic interaction into which these perceptions fall.

_____

_____

_____

_____

_____

_____

_____

_____

_____

_____

Answer

1. The patient's comment that she can see what the therapist means is manifest and direct and therefore cannot be taken as psychoanalytic validation. Direct agreement may be followed either by derivative confirmation or by lack of it. The derivative response is the only true test of the validity of an intervention. It is well to note, however, that in most instances where a patient directly denies or negates the intervention from a therapist, derivative validation does *not* follow. And when the patient offers direct agreement, the situation is rather unpredictable.

The patient does not represent a specific validating intervention context in this material. The associations, however, treated as derivatives related to the areas touched on in the therapist's interpretation, do appear to extend the therapist's efforts in new and unique encoded (indirect) fashion. The main addition reveals a genetic component to the patient's unconscious perceptions of the therapist's inconsistency and his involvement in the deviant conditions of treatment. The patient offers a link to her father, and less so to her mother. She adds a sense of unfairness in regard to discipline, an image that touches on maintaining ground rules and frames. There is now a superego quality to the patient's associations; she conveys her perception of the deviant conditions of treatment as an extremely hurtful form of punishment for minor transgressions.

In addition, the patient represents the conditions of treatment in terms of a new attribute—their violence—and provides a new portrayal of her sense of abandonment—the autistic mode of relatedness. The therapist is unconsciously perceived as clinging to the clinic and is therefore represented in the pathological symbiotic mode. The madness of the situation is portrayed, as is the inappropriately seductive nature of the deviations, with an additional allusion to their punitive quality. The patient's main reaction to these deviations is now one of murderous rage.

There is, then, rather extensive derivative validation of the intervention, even though the material does not crystallize around a specific adaptive context or lend itself to definitive additional interpretation. There is also a sign of a positive introjective identification with the therapist in the patient's allusion to her parents' occasional kindness to her. In all, however, the sense of validation falls somewhat short of the type of additional material that would have lent itself to more explicit interpretation and, especially, toward the undertaking of measures to rectify the deviant frame.

It is well to realize that the genetic validation in this last segment of associations is essentially nontransference-based. The material involves valid and selected unconscious perceptions of the therapist as someone who is *repeating on some level* the arbitrariness, harsh discipline, abandonment, loss of control, and punitive attitudes of her father. Although there may be some measure of exaggeration conveyed here—and this impression is open to question in light of the fact that the hour had now run over—these images are in substance valid perceptions of the therapist in light of the prevailing intervention contexts.

The factors that appear to be determining the patient's selection of unconscious perceptions of the therapist at this time are (a) a harsh, arbitrary, and punitive superego, which is coloring the patient's perceptions of the therapist in light of early experiences with her father, and (b) the patient's introjection of her father's poor controls and murderous rage, which she then turns against both herself and her parents. In all, this additional material appears to add significant unique dimensions to the therapist's understanding of the meanings for the patient of many currently active intervention contexts.

2. Next, we must consider the patient's unconscious commentary on the therapist's intervention. On this level, the patient's associations are treated as encoded perceptions of the therapist in light of the immediate intervention, and as her reactions to these perceptions.

Initially, we may observe that the patient consciously agrees with the therapist, but then immediately offers a derivative image of the therapist in terms of her father, who is unfair and arbitrary in his discipline of her. This latter image suggests that the intervention is unconsciously perceived as having qualities of this kind. In reviewing the therapist's comment, this perception may be based on his need to introduce an adaptive context not directly alluded to by the patient and on the therapist's comments about the patient taking out some of her anger toward him against her husband. This latter part of the intervention attributed the destructiveness and rage entirely to the patient, without acknowledging her unconscious perceptions of these qualities in the therapist.

Notice that we have made every attempt to justify this first association as an encoded perception of the therapist. Because the formulation appears a bit forced, it may well be at this point that the major determinant of these associations is the patient's dawning realization that her session is being extended—a point to which we will turn in a moment. For now, we may recognize that the next allusion to the father's violence and to his spanking the patient for minor mistakes implies that the intervention has been perceived as an attack. Keeping in mind that the therapist has acknowledged his failings to the patient, there is little in the intervention beyond those qualities already noted that could account for these encoded perceptions.

The patient's images continue this theme, insisting on a view of the therapist as highly uncontrolled and destructive. The allusion to the father's abandonment suggests that in some fashion the therapist's intervention was out of touch with the patient's communications. The critical meaning link between patient and therapist, so essential to a sound therapeutic relationship, appears to have been destroyed.

Here, too, the images do not appear to tally with our evaluation of the intervention and of the patient's derivative validation in the material now under study. The hypothesis that these derivative images have been significantly determined by the 10-minute extension of the patient's session appears to be more and more likely. Here before us we have an opportunity to study an attempt by a therapist to explore the patient's associations in light of one adaptive context (his most recent interpretation) only to find that the derivative images do not appear to tally with his best understanding of the implications of the intervention context at hand. It therefore becomes essential to reappraise the intervention or to seek out another intervention context that may better organize the material. As the reader may already sense, the adaptive context of extending the patient's hour far more clearly and meaningfully lends substance to the patient's associations as derivative perceptions of the therapist than does the implications of his last intervention.

The same sense applies to the perception of the therapist's madness and to the derivatives contained in the reaction of the patient's father to finding her in a van with a young man. We must therefore conclude that a powerful adaptation-evoking context, the extension of the patient's hour, has now virtually captured all of the patient's unconscious attention, and her adaptive and communicative responses as well.

To comment further, there are no new indicators in this material. The adaptive context of the therapist's verbal intervention appears to be portrayed in moderately disguised fashion in the allusions to the disciplinary actions of the patient's father, the incessant arguments between the patient's parents, and the punitive behavior of the father toward the patient as described at the end of the session. These representations, as noted, do not appear to fully convey the implications of the therapist's verbal intervention.

3. The fresh adaptive context is, of course, the ongoing extension of the patient's session.

4. If we now consider the adaptive context of the extension of the patient's session, we find that the material contains fairly clear derivative representations of this context, though there is no direct allusion to its occurrence. First, there is the unfair and arbitrary discipline by the patient's father—this undoubtedly connected to the arbitrariness involved in not ending the session on time. Next, there is an allusion to a minor mistake that deserves punishment. There then follows—and this derivative is indeed a quite striking portrayal—the image of the patient hanging on to her father and pleading that he not leave her. Finally, there is the reference to the patient's staying on with a young man in a van after she was supposed to have come home— another excellent encoded portrayal of the adaptive context.

The increasing clarity of these portrayals of the extension of the patient's hour constitutes a form of silent validation that lends considerable support to the thesis that this particular intervention context is now most critical for the patient. For this reason, it behooves us to more clearly specify the patient's unconscious selected perceptions of the therapist in light of this particular intervention. The main images, stated in sequence, appear to be the following:

1. Despite the evident seductive and gratifying qualities, the extension of the patient's hour is seen as arbitrary and harsh. This first image has some measure of frame allusion, a genetic tie between the therapist and the patient's father, a parasitic quality to the mode of relatedness, and reflects an action-discharge mode of cure. Dynamically, it is here that superego issues loom large; these emerge because of the inappropriate, deviant, forbidden qualities of the therapist's errant intervention.

2. The patient next indicates that the therapist is making a minor mistake— though in principle, the error may be more major than minor. The violent qualities are again portrayed. Here, too, the harsh superego qualities continue to find expression on a dynamic level, as does the parasitic mode of relatedness. Issues of anger and violence are also receiving significant representation.

3. The patient's allusion to her parents' unhappy and violent marriage may, first, embody some sense of the violence that is done to the patient when her hour is not stopped on schedule. In addition, however, this image may contain an encoded per-

ception of the therapist as unhappily married, as a way of attempting to account for his unfolding seductive error. As such, this particular image could qualify as an unconscious interpretation by the patient to the therapist—this last a reaction to the patient's perceptions of the therapist in light of this particular intervention context.

4. The next images involve drinking too much, an incorporative and destructive act. This, too, may involve an unconscious perception of the therapist in light of his need to hold the patient beyond her time—here perceived as orally devouring and destructive.

5. As noted, the patient's clinging to her father appears to be a valid unconscious perception of the therapist's need to cling to the patient. The patient portrays and interprets the therapist's separation anxieties, which he has unconsciously attempted to modify by extending the hour with the patient. Involved here are frame issues, pathological symbiosis, pathological autisim in the form of abandonment, the action-discharge mode of cure, genetic factors, and issues of separation.

6. The allusion to the craziness of the patient's parents is an encoded perception of the therapist's madness at a point where he has lost contact with reality—the time at which the session should end.

Many of these images could be viewed as unconscious confrontations and interpretations to the therapist, efforts to call to his attention on an unconscious level the nature and implications of his mistake. It is striking, too, that although these derivatives are quite clear, the patient does not permit herself to *consciously* recognize that the hour is being extended. The pathological gratification afforded to the patient through this deviation may be an important factor in this defensiveness.

7. The incident in which the patient's father found her in a van with a young man—after she was supposed to have come home—portrays the seductive qualities of the extended hour. Unconsciously, the patient indicates a need to punish both herself and the therapist. She also proposes that there is a punitive quality to this extension which has murderous attributes and which is evoking murderous feelings within her. At the same time, this material seems to indicate that the patient wishes, as does the therapist apparently, to continue their tryst uninterrupted. Implied is that ending the hour or the discovery of the hour's extension by someone else would evoke murderous rage in the patient.

Here, too, issues of rage, a harsh superego, primal scene with a third-party observer, and murderous fantasies are evident. So, too, is the parasitic mode of relatedness, disrespect for ground rules and frame, and the action-discharge mode of cure.

In substance, the patient appears to selectively view the therapist's lapse regarding the length of her session as a highly punishable, uncontrolled, hostile, seductive, and mad act. The patient appears to feel victimized by the therapist in a manner quite similar to the way she felt when she was punitively treated by her father. She is also evidently gratified by finding that the therapist is having difficulty leaving her, along with being disturbed by his need to cling and hold on to her.

Several aspects of the listening and formulating process and of the nature and structure of the patient's associations are called to our attention by this shift. The patient is no longer producing reactions to a series of ongoing intervention contexts, but to a single, immediate and specific adaptation-evoking context that impinges upon the ground rules of treatment. The extension of the patient's session beyond its appropriate time has a number of universal qualities or attributes. In addition, this deviation has meanings that are highly personal to the patient, personal to the therapist (some of which will be unconsciously perceived by the patient), and quite particular for this treatment situation and this moment in the psychotherapy.

The patient's communicative responses will be influenced by each of these dimensions. Much of her reaction will involve vectors from the universal attributes of this deviation (its seductive, entrapping, out-of-reality-contact attributes, for example) along with the patient's own genetically and pathologically determined selective perceptions. Indeed, it seems evident already that this particular adaptive context has evoked and brought to the fore specific dimensions of the patient's encoded perceptions of the therapist and the influence of aspects of her own madness that were only vaguely portrayed prior to the therapist's verbal and then deviant interventions.

In this way we learn again that the material from a patient is an interactional product with critical inputs from both participants to treatment. Associations never exist in a vacuum and never function communicatively in isolation. They always face in both directions, toward patient and therapist, serving as conscious and unconscious commentaries on both participants to treatment and on their immediate, recent, and past meaningful transactions.

On this note, we complete our discussion of this most interesting treatment hour. In the next chapter, we will consider the session that followed the next week.

12
Formulating an Entire Session: Part II

We turn now to the next session that took place between the patient and therapist presented in the last chapter. The reader will recall that after the previous week's session was over, the therapist realized he had inadvertently extended the allotted time period by 10 minutes.

Exercise 12.1

In the second session, the therapist chose to speak first. He said:

> Therapist: After last session, I realized that I had inadvertently extended your session by 10 minutes beyond the 50 usually allotted for our work. I hadn't realized what I had done, and I apologize for the confusion.

What are the main attributes of this particular intervention? The reader should briefly evaluate the implications of extending the session, along with the implications of this particular intervention. In this way, the therapist would be prepared to organize the patient's material in light of the meanings of both interventions—though the extension of the hour would undoubtedly prove to be the more powerful of the two adaptive contexts. For the moment, using the seven-part schema, what are the patient's likely universal unconscious perceptions of the therapist in light of each intervention?

_____

_____

_____

_____

_____

Before turning to our answers, a brief comment is in order. A therapist who consciously or unconsciously becomes involved in an intervention such as the one that begins this session is likely to be feeling quite disturbed, guilty, and concerned about the underlying countertransference issues involved in his original deviation. As I have pointed out, it is well for the therapist who has made an error to engage in a period of self-analysis in an effort to identify the unconscious factors in the lapse. Personal adaptive contexts must be considered, including issues in the therapist's outside life. In this particular case, the therapist should explore his relationship with the clinic personnel and the clinic situation, his basic relationship with and feelings toward the patient, and the specific material of the session in which the deviation occurred. The therapist should free associate in response to these intervention contexts, subsequently attempting to analyze his spontaneous thoughts, memories, feelings, fantasies, and so forth.

In the session with the patient, however, whatever the results of the therapist's self-analysis, the patient should be permitted to set the tone of the hour. The primary devotion of the therapist is to the patient's therapeutic needs, and this includes allowing a session to unfold on the patient's terms. When a therapeutic error has occurred, this strategy gives the therapist an opportunity to observe whether the patient is alluding directly to the intervention context or in encoded form, and whether the incident is being dealt with meaningfully through derivatives. Furthermore, interpretation of the patient's responses to a deviation and rectification of the frame should ideally be carried out at the behest of the patient's own derivative material.

The most difficult issue where the present therapy is concerned is the question of whether the frame should be rectified after this kind of error. Rectification, of course, would entail shortening the following session by the amount of time the last one was wrongfully extended. Although the patient might complain consciously that such an act is harsh and punitive, unconsciously, patients recognize the justice and necessity of the measure. In most instances, the patient's derivatives would advise this very course of action as a way of rectifying the deviant frame. Failure to handle the situation this way leaves the patient with an unpaid or free portion of a session and with a continued sense of the therapist's pathological needs as expressed through the deviation. This type of rectification should at least be considered and the patient's derivative material used as the ultimate guide.

We will begin our answer by considering the intervention with which the therapist opened the hour. It may be characterized as follows, using the seven dimensions of the therapeutic interaction:

1. Frame: In a sense, the intervention modifies the frame, because the ideal frame requires that the patient begin each hour rather than the therapist.

2. Mode of relatedness: There is a pathologically symbiotic and parasitic quality to this premature intervention.

3. Mode of cure: The therapist's inability to delay his intervention until facilitated by the patient's material expresses cure by action-discharge.

4. Communicaton: By alluding directly and manifestly to the deviation, the therapist encourages communication restricted to manifest meanings and may interfere with the patient's expression of derivative responses.

5. Dynamics: There is a pathological need in the therapist to confess and exhibit himself to the patient as reflected in this intervention.

6. Self and identity: The therapist's effort also reveals a disturbance in narcissism and identity. The therapist presents himself as the functional patient for the moment, losing sight of his role as a therapist. He thereby misuses the patient as a selfobject to gratify his own pathological narcissistic needs. Poor tension regulation is also implied.

7. Sanity and madness: There is a measure of madness in the same confusion— the designated therapist operating as the functional patient.

In all, a premature intervention of this kind expresses a therapeutic need on the part of the therapist which will be perceived by the patient as taking precedence over her own treatment requirements. The intervention imposes additional madness on the patient who has already experienced a powerful act and projective identification from the therapist in his extension of the hour. The therapist would have been well advised to sit back and to attend silently to the patient's material, containing and metabolizing its contents and pressures until he saw an appropriate point at which to interpret and manage the frame.

As for the extension of the hour, the following qualities seem most prominent:

1. Frame: The frame break has all of the implications of frame deviations—mistrust, loss of sound containment and holding, disturbed interpersonal boundaries, and the like. The specific deviation is likely to be perceived by the patient as entrapping and highly seductive. There is a striking lapse in the therapist's contact with reality.

2. Mode of relatedness: Pathologically autistic, symbiotic, and parasitic.

3. Mode of cure: Action-discharge-merger.

4. Communication: Emphasizes projective identification and the destruction of meaning. Action, pathological gratification, and evacuative needs appear to take precedence over the wish to establish meaning and insight.

5. Dynamics and genetics: The dynamics of this type of deviation are likely to involve separation anxieties, merger wishes, themes of seduction, and anxieties related to entrapment. Derivatives related to these themes have already emerged toward the end of the previous hour, during the very time the session was being extended. The genetics will touch upon early experiences related to these themes.

6. Self and identity: The deviation reflects a sense of impaired identity in the

therapist who loses sight of his therapeutic functions. It also reflects use of the patient as a selfobject for the pathological narcissistic gratification of the therapist. In part, there is also a disturbance in tension regulation.

7. Sanity and madness: Mainly because of the therapist's lapse in contact with reality, the patient will see the deviation as an uncontrolled act of madness.

The material from the previous session already indicates that this particular deviation context has powerful implications, in that the patient's associations are organized extremely well around encoded representations of the intervention context and responsive and selective derivative perceptions of the therapist.

On the other hand, because ground-rule issues are of critical importance to both this patient and this therapist, listening and intervening can be quite productive for this psychotherapy. How productive is really a question of balance. Even if the therapist proves capable of interpreting and rectifying the deviant interlude, an element of mistrust and uncertainty is bound to linger in the patient's image of him. It is here that the actualities of the therapist's behaviors, which convey both conscious and unconscious implications, have their effects, some of which cannot be entirely modified by verbal interpretations and correctives. Even so, if the therapist proved capable of maintaining this aspect of the frame for the remainder of the psychotherapy, and if he were, in addition, able to establish a private treatment setting and relationship with this patient, virtually all of the significant consequences of this particular deviation could be effectively analyzed and modified as to their impact on the patient.

In all, much effective therapeutic work can take place after a lapse of this kind, and although some residuals are likely to remain, with sound intervention, the balance can fall mainly to the constructive side of the picture.

Exercise 12.2

We will turn now to the patient's material in this session. The excerpt will include a summary of all of the patient's associations up to the point where the therapist intervened toward the latter part of the hour. The material contains sequences with relatively little functional meaning—that is, with heavily disguised derivative expressions. Interspersed we may expect to find important indicators, representations of adaptive contexts, and derivative material—perceptions and otherwise.

In view of the fact that this material will be presented at some length, the reader should develop silent hypotheses along the way and attempt to subject them to derivative validation as the material unfolds. The goal is to decide whether an intervention is called for and to specify its nature—doing so in terms of patient-indicators and the therapist-indicator constituted by the traumatic adaptive context with which the prior session ended. After going through the first part of this excerpt, we will engage in a formal discussion of the material.

The patient spoke next:

Patient: I want to take up where I left off last session. I've been thinking of many different doctors with whom I've had negative experiences. There is this one doctor in particular—someone I saw months ago when I was very upset. He was quite good with me, even though he gave me a whole mess of medication and some unsolicited and unwanted advice. He gave me tranquilizers and antibiotics, none of which I took as he prescribed them. It was as if the drugs were supposed to cure what I knew were psychological problems. But this all seems repetitious, boring, and old to me. I've gone over this so much, I'm tired of it. I might add, Amen.

There's something I want to talk about that I really never entirely told you about before. There was this incident when I was out late and my father jerked me out of a van I was staying in with a boyfriend. He slapped me across the face and injured me. About that time I became pregnant out of wedlock. I wonder if I did it to get my parents' attention. I was very naïve at the time, and I really didn't know what all of that was about. The doctor talked primarily with my mother and gave me very little in the way of feedback about the pregnancy.

I've been thinking about the fact that there is a lack of confidentiality in your office because the secretaries have access to my records. That concerned me for a long time, because it made my case into a public document, a situation I don't like. I reassured myself that the secretaries probably aren't interested in my records anyhow, no more than I'm interested in the patients that see the dentist I work for.

When I was 15 years old, my parents got into a violent quarrel, separated, and my father moved into a home in Minneapolis. It was his hope that my mother would eventually come with me to live with him, but she didn't do it. My father would call home, talk with me about my mother, cry over how lonely he was, and try to get me to convince my mother to move back in with him. There I was in the middle of the proverbial triangle between mother and dad.

Then, when I was about 17 years old, I was having trouble with my work in high school. My parents decided I should move in with my dad and go to a very ritzy private girls' school. They didn't like the friends I had made in public school. They thought I would make better friends at this other school. They would have been shocked had they seen what was going on at the private school.

We smoked and drank all the time. We would often start drinking at 5:00 on Fridays and wouldn't stop until Sunday night. We'd sneak out of the dorms and go to Chicago and get into all kinds of mischief. It's a wonder we didn't all become alcoholics.

I cooked, cleaned, and was the woman of the house for my father. I felt so grown up and sophisticated. Seventeen years old. Can you believe it? Dad had mistresses who stayed overnight at the house all the time. He drank a lot, either alone or with his friends. There were cocktail parties. I used to invite girls from school over to the house for the weekend. We'd have a few beers, sit around, smoke, talk, and drink.

It was about this time that I lost my virginity. One night my father came upstairs when he was drunk as hell and sat on the edge of my bed in his underwear. I noticed as we talked about my boyfriends and sex that he had an erection. I couldn't believe it. Then he said to me, "Let's give each other an orgasm." I thought for a minute, "Now what does that mean?" I thought, "He couldn't possibly mean what I think he means." I love my Dad, and I really didn't want to hurt him, but that was too much. I was terrified. So I said, "I'm tired, Dad, I want to go to sleep now." When he left, I smoked one cigarette after another, trying to figure out what he was doing. Here I was, a naïve 17-year-old girl who had as much sex appeal as a wet blanket, and my father had made some kind of sexual overture toward me. The next morning he was so terribly embarrassed that he apologized to me, but it was really eerie around the house all that day.

For 10 years I never talked with my father about that incident. Then on a visit home and after going through some kind of cathartic experience in my earlier psychotherapy, I confronted him about it. He became extremely defensive and tried to blame me for the incident. He said that I had been provocative. I told him he was the parent and it was his responsibility to manage his own urges. He disagreed with me. I guess if he hung from the chandelier, that would be my fault too.

[Glances down at her watch] I had this long dream that I wanted to tell you, but I don't want to go over tonight. The essence of the dream is that I'm on a double date with Burt Reynolds and Candice Bergen and her boyfriend. I have to reassure myself in the dream that Burt Reynolds is really not you, because in the past we have often talked about other people in my dreams as being representative of you. After almost going out of control in an automobile, we arrive at a motel where we climb into bed but can't have any kind of sex because we are all at right angles to each other. Suddenly I find myself in Minnesota without Burt Reynolds, lost and in search of him. There are people all over the place. I am smoking one cigarette after the other. I finally go into a shop where there is this really fat black woman seated. The woman hands me a pack of cigarettes, which has only butts in them, and tells me to smoke them. She hands me a brochure about Smokenders. Then she thinks that I'm out too late; the day has started to break and my father is going to be furious at me. I say, "No, I'm 39 years old and I can stay out as late as I want. I only have to account to myself and my husband."

For those who have not already done so, let us now formally analyze this material in terms of the listening–formulating process. Our tasks are:

A. To name and classify all indicators.

B. To identify all manifest representations of intervention contexts or clear derivative representations, in the absence of a manifest allusion. (We have already identified the main implications of the central intervention context, and we considered in the previous chapter the implications of the background deviant intervention contexts.)

C. Identify the patient's main selected encoded perceptions of the therapist in light of the extension of her previous session. State the dimensions of the therapeutic interaction that are touched on in these perceptions. (Those readers who wish to attempt ot trace out the patient's encoded perceptions in light of the therapist's initial intervention in this session may do so as a separate and personal exercise. Only the adaptive context of the 10-minute extension will be considered in detail here.)

D. Identify the patient's major reactions to these encoded perceptions.

E. Indicate whether you believe there is a meaningful and coalescing derivative complex, and further, whether an intervention is called for and feasible. State the basis for your conclusion.

F. State the best possible intervention available to the therapist at this juncture in terms of the associations of the patient in this particular hour.

_____

_____

_____

_____

_____

_____

_____

_____

_____

_____

_____

_____

_____

_____

_____

_____

_____

_____

_____

_____

_____

_____

_____

_____

_____

_____

_____

_____

_____

_____

_____

_____

_____

_____

_____

_____

_____

_____

_____

_____

_____

_____

_____

_____

_____

_____

_____

_____

_____

_____

_____

Answers

We will begin the answers to the foregoing listening–formulating questions with a discussion of the indicators reflected in the patient's material to this point in the hour.

A. *Indicators*

1. The major indicator in this hour (that is, the major cause of emotional disturbance within the patient and a reflection of the patient's need for intervention) is the therapist-indicator of the adaptive context of the extension of the patient's previous hour. In all likelihood, the intervention from the therapist will center on implications of this deviation for the patient and on the need for rectification.

2. The historical material is fraught with recollections of symptomatic and interpersonally pathological behaviors in the patient and in her family members. But these do not constitute immediate patient-indicators. Such material is virtually always evoked by a current and usually traumatic adaptive context. Thus, these past disturbances are a type of background patient-indicator, whose unconscious factors might well be clarified for the patient now through a sound interpretation that deals with current indicators and is organized around an immediate intervention context.

3. The session is striking for its relative lack of immediate patient-indicators. The clearest expression of a therapeutic context is the patient's concern about the lack of confidentiality in the clinic setting. More broadly, this patient-indicator involves her participation in the deviant-frame therapeutic experience. Such an indicator, of course, touches on critical adaptive contexts as well.

It is not uncommon in the presence of a major deviant therapist-indicator (traumatic adaptive context) for patient-indicators to be absent or to appear only minimally in the patient's material. In general, evidence of patient sanity increases in direct proportion to the increase of therapist-madness—though only within limits. Patients tend to unconsciously attempt to cure their therapists of their general underlying pathology so that the therapist may in turn cure the patient. Such activities unconsciously provide the patient with some measure of satisfaction and integration.

Obviously, an intervention in this session will focus primarily on the therapist-indicator, the deviation committed by the therapist himself, and only secondarily on patient-indicators as they connect up to the deviant intervention context. The genetic experiences reported by the patient in this hour, as noted, do not constitute patient-indicators in the usual sense of the term. They suggest that the present deviant intervention context—the therapist-indicator—in some way links up with earlier traumas suffered by the patient in her relationship with her parents, especially her father. These critical genetic experiences will become illuminated by the patient's current unconscious communications and available insights in light of the present intervention context. The influence of past genetics on the patient can be understood only in terms of the stimulus that is helping to determine the present interaction. Linking the past with the present must be done in a way that is currently meaningful and dynamically active, emotionally critical past inputs interpreted with a full appreciation for the present interaction to which they are related.

To summarize, then, the main patient-indicator in this hour is the patient's concern about and participation in a treatment situation in which her confidentiality has been somewhat violated by the presence of third parties to treatment, such as secretaries. In part, the relative thinness of patient-indicators in this hour can be accounted for by the existence of a major therapist-indicator—a traumatic adaptive context involving the unwitting extension of the patient's previous session. The therapist's intervention will therefore center around this latter stimulus as the main source of the patient's unconscious perceptions and internal madness, and it will fan out into other issues from this central nodal point.

B. The Adaptive Context

As indicated, this discussion will focus primarily on the main adaptive context for the patient—the therapist's extension of the previous session. One might suggest the following, however, with regard to the therapist's initial intervention in this hour: (1) The patient does not allude directly to this context in the associations that follow the intervention. (2) She does, however, begin her associations with a derivative representation of this intervention context. (The patient alludes to her wish to take up where she left off in the previous session; this is an encoded representation of her unconscious perception of the therapist's need to do exactly that.) (3) The patient's encoded and derivative associations begin with an allusion to negative experiences with doctors, including an internist who offered unsolicited and unwanted advice; this is the beginning of the patient's encoded perceptions of the therapist's premature, unsolicited and unwanted intervention.

We will now turn to the main adaptive context. The therapist's direct allusion to his 10-minute extension of the previous hour spares the patient the responsibility for any manifest reference to that deviation in her own associations. Nonetheless, it is best to identify the patient's clearest direct or encoded representations of each context. Here, we have the patient's comment just prior to introducing her dream—that she doesn't "want to go over tonight." This can be seen as a manifest portrayal of the therapist's having gone over (beyond the time of) the previous hour. As such, it is an essentially manifest representation of the adaptive context, one that will readily facilitate both the listening–formulating process and intervention.

There is, of course, a manifest representation of a second intervention context in this material as well: the lack of confidentiality for this psychotherapy and the existence of third parties to treatment—the secretaries. Here, too, the reader might trace out the balance of the patient's associations—both before and after this particular direct allusion—and organize the material as derivative perceptions of (and subsequent reactions to) this particular intervention context. It is important to realize, however, that it would be inappropriate and defensive for the therapist to organize his intervention around this secondary adaptive context rather than around the extension of the hour. In a way, the allusion to the confidentiality issue is being used in the patient's material as a representation in derivative fashion of the other and more serious deviation issue—the therapist's lapse. So the therapist's listening and formulating should concentrate on this latter context and endeavor to link up in ancillary fashion the subsidiary intervention contexts. That is, the secondary contexts should not be ignored. Both listening–formulating and intervening should take as the central focus the most critical adaptive context at a given moment, including as secondary organizers all other subsidiary intervention contexts.

When there is a manifest allusion, however glancing, to the most critical intervention context, all other representations are included in the derivative complex—in particular, the delineation of the patient's selected encoded perceptions of the therapist in light of the adaptive context. Rather than maintaining a continuing concern for finding another good representation of the intervention context, the therapist's efforts should be concentrated on the decoding of derivative meanings. For this reason, we may now turn to the derivative complex conveyed by this patient in this particular hour.

C. *The Derivative Complex—Selected Encoded Perceptions*

Because this particular adaptation-evoking stimulus (the extended hour) was very powerful for the patient, her response in this session is quite strong and diverse. To cite the main selected encoded perceptions of the therapist in light of the deviant intervention context, the following, in sequence, seem most pertinent:

1. The patient begins her associations by alluding to negative experiences with doctors. She mentions in particular an internist who overmedicated her and offered unsolicited and unwanted advice. She encodes here her perception of the therapist as responsible for creating a negative or hurtful experience and then offering her a curative measure that she herself did not seek out—the extension of the time.

This encoded perception touches on the pathological symbiotic and perhaps parasitic needs of the therapist, falling into the realm of mode of relatedness. The image also reflects the action-discharge mode of cure and the pathological narcissistic need of the therapist to use the patient as a selfobject. In other words, he on some unconscious level feels merged with the patient and manipulates her as if she were part of himself. (This is an important implication of this deviant context in the realm of narcissistic psychopathology.) Implied, too, is a disturbance in communication and the therapist's expression of unmanaged madness. (The patient's allusion to the internist being quite good with her probably reflects the patient's perception of other positively toned intervention contexts.)

2. The patient's comment that the internist gave her tranquilizers and antibiotics, none of which she took as prescribed, is a rather meaningful encoded perception of the therapist's failure to adhere to the prescribed ground rules. The image contains a critical frame allusion, indications of a pathological autistic mode of relatedness, an uncertain mode of cure (the patient's behavior may involve action-discharge or it may contain wisdom designed to prepare the way for insight), and problems with communication.

3. The patient's allusion to the drugs being offered as a means of curing what were psychological problems is an encoded perception of the therapist's efforts to provide both himself and the patient with relief from emotional tension through the action-discharge measure of extending the patient's hour. They are also suggestions of identity confusion, communicative disruption, and madness.

4. The patient's comment that the material seems repetitious (and boring) may involve an encoded perception of the therapist's having deviated in this or similar fashion in the past.

5. The patient's review of the incident with her father, who discovered her in the van with a young man, contains an encoded perception of the therapist conveyed through an image having strong genetic implications. Because these were discussed in a previous section, the image will not be reformulated here.

6. The balance of this particular segment of material makes reference to the patient's out-of-wedlock pregnancy, a question on her part as to whether she wished to get her parents' attention, her naïveté, and the doctor's contact with her mother while offering the patient herself little feedback. Here, we may decode unconscious perceptions of the therapist's modifying a ground rule, being involved in something that is unconsciously sexual and impregnating, and seeking the attention of the patient. There is an image of therapist-ignorance and naïveté.

The allusion to the mother's involvement with the physician appears to pertain more to the lack of confidentiality and the presence of secretaries (as mentioned in the patient's following associations) than it does to the extension of the patient's hour. (It may be, however, that the common theme between this manifest material and the encoded perception of the therapist is the general one of the failings and insensitivities in the patient's physicians.) This material thus introduces in a very general way the theme of sexuality and the connection between the time extension and other breaks in the frame committed by the therapist. The material appears to touch on some measure of pathological symbiosis, disturbance in communication, the action-discharge mode of cure (the pregnancy out-of-wedlock), some type of dynamic (oedipal?) threesome, a possible narcissistic disturbance, and a hint of madness.

7. The associations regarding the lack of confidentiality and the presence of the secretaries in the therapist's office expresses in encoded form the frame deviation aspects of the adaptive context of the extended hour. Here, a set of associations serves simultaneously as a patient-indicator (the patient's concerns regarding the conditions of treatment), a manifest representation of an intervention context (third parties to treatment and lack of confidentiality), and a derivative perception of the therapist (as having modified the basic ground rules of treatment). In addition to the frame allusion, there are implications of the pathological symbiotic and parasitic modes of relatedness.

8. The next cluster of associations involve the arguments between the patient's parents, her father's move to his own home, his efforts to have his wife and daughter live with him, and his crying to the patient regarding his wife. Encoded here are a series of unconscious perceptions of the loss of the therapist (who had inadvertently withdrawn from the patient in forgetting the time at which the hour was to end), as well as the more compelling image of the therapist's need to cling to and misuse the patient for his own pathological needs. Involved are some ground-rule qualities (the image implies a break in the boundaries between father and daughter and the former's inappropriate use of the latter) and the pathological symbiotic and parasitic modes of relatedness. The associations also contain a dynamic image of violence and conflict. They also establish a genetic connection between the present deviation and an earlier experience or set of experiences between the patient and her father. An action-discharge mode of cure is implied along with some sense of narcissistic pathology—the patient was being used as a selfobject by the father (and therefore by the therapist). This narcissistic misuse is certainly a notable implication of the therapist's extension of the patient's session, one that is selectively and unconsciously perceived by the patient in light of her own narcissistic needs and pathology.

Of note here is the unconscious perception that the extension of the hour expresses the therapist's desire that the patient come to live with him. This perception is quite valid, but as we will discuss shortly, it contains a measure of exaggeration. It is therefore a mixture of nontransference and transference. Implied, too, in this imagery is a disturbance in communication (between the patient and her father, which is to say, between the patient and the therapist).

9. The following extended segment is about the patient's interactions in private school. The allusion to moving in with her father again touches on the unconscious implication of the therapist's inadvertent error. The allusion to smoking and drinking conveys an addictive quality related to the narcissistic (selfobject) misuse of the patient in holding her beyond the allotted time. Dynamically, this is given an incorporative and ultimately self-destructive set of attributes. This segment also contains an encoded perception of the dishonest and mischievous qualities of this erroneous intervention context.

On the whole, these images center on frame issues (carrying out forbidden actions, such as smoking, drinking, sneaking out of the dorm, and getting into mischief), a pathological symbiotic mode of relatedness, the action-discharge mode of cure, disturbance in communicative relatedness, dynamics related to addiction, dishonesty, and aggression, some sense of disturbed identity (the private school friends turned out differently than expected by her parents), and a strong sense of madness (the uncontrolled and self-destructive behaviors). All of these appear to be valid encoded perceptions of the therapist in light of the prevailing intervention context.

The richness of the patient's communicated encoded perceptions of the therapist in light of his extension of the previous hour raises a question. Should the therapist not have intervened by this point in the hour? Both patients and therapists are able to metabolize only a limited measure of derivative communication. Beyond that, one's mind becomes overloaded. Although the patient has not manifestly represented the adaptive context, the therapist's own allusion to it in his initial comment might have served him if he wished to intervene at this juncture. The therapist's manifest reference could have been supplemented by the patient's clearest derivative representation of the adaptive context—here, the allusion to issues of confidentiality and privacy in the treatment situation. With the adaptive context established, the therapist could then have interpreted the most critical of the foregoing derivative perceptions in light of the identified adaptive context of the extended hour, making certain to include the rich genetic and instinctual drive-related images. Validation of an intervention of this kind would be quite likely.

Despite these considerations, the therapist chose not to intervene as yet, and the validity and wisdom of his silence is amply confirmed in the associations that follow. The patient continues to express extremely important encoded perceptions of the therapist in light of the prevailing intervention context, adding significantly to our understanding of the meanings of the incident for both patient and therapist. This would not be considered open validation; instead, the therapist obtained silent confirmation of his burgeoning impressions of the patient's material.

10. The next segment of associations involves a description of the patient's at-home relationship with her father. In the allusion to the mistresses who stayed overnight with her father, there is another sexualized encoded perception of the therapist's deviation. Repeated are the alcoholic-incorporative image and an image related to staying on beyond usual hours (the patient with her girlfriend from school). There are frame allusions, pathological symbiosis, action-discharge mode of cure, incestuous dynamics, and a possibility of madness in this material.

11. The next section of material pertains to the patient's loss of virginity and her father's attempt to seduce her. The emphasis here is on an unconscious perception of the therapist as inappropriately and incestuously attempting to seduce the patient, having been overstimulated by her sexual material (represented by the talk between

the patient and her father about her boyfriends). The patient's comment that she wanted to go to sleep also embodies a derivative perception of the therapist's failure to notice the time, and the cigarette smoking touches again on the incorporative aspects of the deviation. Here, too, there is a frame deviation, a parasitic mode of relatedness, the action-discharge mode of cure, a major disturbance in communication, intensely incestuous dynamics and genetics, signs of impairment in identity (the father's confusion as to his relationship and role with his daughter) and pathological narcissism (the exploitative use of the patient-daughter as a selfobject), and a moment of considerable madness.

12. The next pertinent image occurs in the dream about Burt Reynolds and Candice Bergen. The allusions here involve loss of control in an automobile (the lapse regarding time), an invitation to bed, again the cigarette smoking, and being out too late. This last is a clear encoded representation of the adaptive context. These images again involve framework issues, pathological symbiotic and parasitic modes of relatedness, cure through action-discharge, disturbances in communication, primal scene, oral addiction, control-loss, sexual and aggressive psychodynamics, identity confusion (the patient expresses concern that Burt Reynolds is really not the therapist, and establishes her own identity toward the end of the dream), likely narcissistic images as connected to the actor and actress in the dream, and a sense of confusion that speaks for madness.

At this point in the session, the patient has alluded directly to the critical adaptive context and provided the therapist with an extremely rich and varied, coalescing derivative complex fraught with selected unconscious perceptions of the therapist in light of his deviant intervention. This is a highly meaningful derivative complex, so rich that it is difficult to sort out and to select those images that are most clear and meaningful. In addition, the therapist must undertake the final task of identifying the patient's major reactions to these perceptions. This effort will further complicate an understanding of the patient's material, but it will ultimately provide additional clarity.

To set the stage for identifying these responses, we may summarize the patient's derivative material as follows: It indicates that the adaptive context of the therapist's extension of the previous hour created within the patient a sense of the therapist as someone (1) who has difficulty managing ground rules and interpersonal boundaries, (2) who is especially invested in the pathological symbiotic and parasitic modes of relatedness, (3) who has overriding needs for cure through action-discharge, (4) who disrupts communicative relatedness, (5) who has unresolved and uncontrolled pathological sexual and incestuous needs for the patient, which are tied to highly meaningful genetic experiences, (6) who lacks a clear identity and who misuses the patient as a narcissistic selfobject, and (7) who has had a lapse that speaks for madness. All of these dimensions reflect, then, the therapist's pathology and madness as concentrated in these areas, as perceived through the patient's own madness.

D. Reactions to Encoded Perceptions

In light of these highly disturbing perceptions, the following appear to be the main patient-responses to these selected encoded perceptions:

1. The patient's decision not to take the medication that she felt was inappropriately prescribed for her may be seen as a *model of rectification*. The patient is suggesting to the therapist that he not continue his inappropriate and deviant behaviors.

2. The patient's concern that she became pregnant to get her parents' attention and the allusion to her own naïveté may be viewed as very general, somewhat clichéd, *unconscious interpretation* to the therapist in light of his error. The patient appears on a derivative level to be advising the therapist that his extension of the hour was incorporative and seductive, as well as naïve, and that it may involve some unconscious need to have his patient's extraordinary attention in light of some type of deprivation in regard to parental care.

3. There is another *model of rectification* in the patient's comments about the lack of confidentiality and the third parties to treatment. The patient is proposing an absence of interest in her case on the part of others, an image suggesting that these third parties should be excluded from the situation entirely.

4. Somewhat exaggerated encoded expressions of the actual implications of the intervention context are contained in the patient's images of her father's overinvolvment with her, his use of her as a substitute object for someone else, and his actual attempt to seduce the patient sexually. It must be understood, however, that notwithstanding the exaggerated nature of these images, there is indeed a strongly incestuous and seductive aspect to this deviation, even though it lacks a specific attempt at direct sexual engagement.

In most situations where transference elements appear in a patient's material, this type of mixture will be found: a strong grain of truth that appears to be somewhat extended or distorted. The grain of truth embodies an actual unconscious implication of the intervention. Here, the extension of the session is not sexual in itself, but it conveys strong *unconscious sexual meanings*. Such responses are not distortions derived from the patient's past so much as they are exaggerated readings of actual unconscious implications selectively perceived and communicated by the patient in terms of an immediate intervention context.

5. The allusion to the private girls' school appears to be another *model of rectification* involving the public qualities of the clinic setting. Strikingly, it contains what appears to be encoded perceptions of the therapist's anxieties and fantasies as they influence his decision to work in a private clinic setting. Simultaneously, it embodies the patient's own anxieties and fantasies—her fears of being alone with the therapist in a private office.

6. The patient's allusion to cooking, cleaning, and being the woman of the house for her father may contain an *encoded directive* to the therapist to clean up his act, so to speak.

7. The patient's allusion to her father's mistresses and to his attempt at seduction may well serve as *unconscious interpretations* to the therapist in an effort to help him understand the unconscious basis or meanings of his error. Of course, simultaneously, this material embodies critical early memories, set off by, and similar to, the intervention context.

8. The patient's refutation of her father's sexual advances is a *model of rectification* and the offer of sound interpersonal boundaries to the therapist. Similarly, her later comment when confronting her father—that he was the parent and had

the responsibility to manage his own urges—is both a model of rectification and an unconscious interpretation to the treating therapist.

9. The dream image of being in bed with several people but unable to have any kind of sexual experience contains some measure of *rectification*. The allusions to drinking and to cigarette smoking may be seen as further efforts at unconscious interpretation of the addictive aspects of the intervention context. The brochure about Smokenders is also a powerful model of rectification, as is the image of accountability.

E. The Possibility of Intervening

This material meets the criteria for an interpretive intervention and an effort at framework rectification. The patient has alluded to the most active and critical adapative context on a manifest content level, and she has provided the therapist with an extensive and highly meaningful, coalescing derivative complex fraught with valid, selected encoded perceptions, critical reactions to these perceptions, and important models of rectification. Virtually all seven dimensions of the therapeutic interaction have been touched on, including critical instinctual-drive perceptions and fantasies, madness, and the genetic repercussions of the therapist's deviant interventions. This is a highly constructive communicative response to the errant intervention context. In view of the fact that it meets the specific criteria for intervening (a clear representation of an adaptive context and a highly coalescible derivative complex that can be used to explain the unconscious basis of patient- and/or therapist-indicators), the therapist is well advised to comment at this point.

It should be noted, too, that the patient has not, as reflected in this material, responded to the therapist's deviation with acting-out behaviors or with symptoms. Her reaction appears to be quite constructive and involves an attempt to delineate her encoded perceptions, evoked fantasies and memories, and her other responses to the implications of the therapist's intervention. There are also powerful efforts on her part to be helpful, curative, and rectifying in her response to the therapist. This highly adaptive reaction to a very traumatic intervention context merits a sound interpretive reaction from the therapist. An interpretation would, among other functions, help to support the patient's healthy functioning by providing her with true insight and a positive introjective identification with the now well-functioning, readily recovered psychotherapist.

F. The Best Available Intervention

What, then, is the best intervention available to the therapist in light of this material? In principle, it should begin with the clearest portrayal of the adaptive context, touch on the most compelling encoded perceptions of the therapist and the patient's responses to them, and center on the explanation of an indicator (those patient-indicators that are available, along with the main therapist-indicator). In basic form, the intervention might be stated as follows (again, a second version of this intervention will be presented with comments in brackets to explain the functions of its various aspects):

You mention not staying over in your session tonight, and you seem to be reacting to my having extended your session last week. It is evident from your indirect comments that you see this as a loss of control—much as you saw the automobile lose control in your dream, and much as you have been describing your father losing control with you. My error has led you to see me as behaving very much as your father behaved in the past— inappropriately and sexually seductive, trying to hold on to and misuse you, being virtually addicted to your presence in the sessions, and trying to keep you on as something of a mistress. My behavior has also led you to recall physicians who hurt you, including one whom you saw as a good therapist, even though his efforts to help you were marred by unsolicited interventions and the misuse of medication—qualities you undoubtedly connect to my lapse as well.

The error has touched upon other compromises in the basic conditions of your treatment and my failure to set proper conditions for your psychotherapy, as witnessed by the existence of records and the presence of secretaries here at the clinic. You seem to feel that these matters should be set straight, which implies as well that we should do something to correct the influence of my error. You seem concerned that I will deny my responsibility for what has happened much as your father did in the past. Nonetheless, you are letting us both know that this kind of lapse should not happen again, that I should apologize and acknowledge my error, and that I should resolve my need to misuse you sexually and addictively. In all, you are stating that I should become accountable in sound fashion— and indeed, I will make every effort to avoid such lapses in the future. In addition, we must, if possible, find some means of redressing the error I made by extending the last session.

Before offering an overall comment on the intervention, the following is a repetition of this effort with explanation:

You mention not staying over in your session tonight [the patient's best representation of the adaptive context], and you seem to be reacting to my having extended your session last week [an identification of the main therapist-indicator and intervention context]. It is evident from your indirect comments [a way of telling the patient that she has communicated through disguised derivatives] that you see this as a loss of control much as you saw the automobile lose control in your dream, and much as you have been describing your father losing control with you [beginning efforts to identify the most compelling elements of the derivative complex]. My error has led you to see me as behaving very much as your father behaved in the past [accepting the encoded perceptions in nontransference terms, without attempting to get into issues of exaggeration for the moment—efforts that would be seen as unduly defensive and as conveying the kind of denial that the patient complained about when she confronted her father]—inappropriately and sexually seductive, trying to hold on to and misuse you, being virtually addicted to your presence in the sessions, and trying to keep you on as something of a mistress. My behavior has also led you to recall physicians who hurt you, including one whom you saw as a good therapist, even though his efforts to help you were marred by unsolicited interventions and the misuse of medication—qualities you undoubtedly connect to my lapse as well [continuing to define and accept the best selected encoded perceptions].

The error has touched upon other compromises in the basic conditions of your treatment and my failure to set proper conditions for your psychotherapy, as witnessed by the existence of records and the presence of secretaries here at the clinic. You seem to feel that these matters should be set straight which implies as well that we should do something to correct the influence of my error [the shift now emphasizes the frame deviations and need for rectification]. You seem concerned I will deny my responsibility for what has happened much as your father did in the past. Nonetheless, you are letting us both know that this kind of lapse should not happen again, that I should apologize and acknowledge my error, and that I should resolve my need to misuse you sexually and addictively. In all, you are stating that I should become accountable in sound fashion— and indeed, I will make every effort to avoid such lapses in the future. In addition, we must, if possible, find some means of redressing the error I made by extending the last session. [The intervention ends with a resolution to maintain the frame and an initial comment regarding possible rectification of the error, thereby showing the patient that the therapist intends to both interpret and rectify his error.]

In this intervention, the patient-indicator involving the patient's concern about the conditions of treatment is mentioned and understood in light of the deviant intervention context of the extension of the session. The patient's central unconscious perceptions of the therapist are identified, especially those that involve instinctual-drive derivatives and critical genetics. Considerable stress is placed on the patient's models of rectification and on an *implicit* apology from the therapist (an explicit apology would be too confessional and unnecessary). Of note too is the manner in which the intervention accepts as valid and perceptive the patient's encoded images of the therapist—without denial and without avoidance. The patient's contributions to these perceptions would be delineated in a later session or, if the material permitted, perhaps toward the end of this hour. In all, then, the basic structure of the intervention centers around the patient's critical representation of the intervention context and the most compelling derivative perceptions and responses to these perceptions available in her associations. Both interpretation and rectification are expressed.

The Therapist's Actual Intervention: Exercise 12.3

In the actual session, as already noted, the therapist did intervene at this juncture. The following was his statement to the patient:

Therapist: You have referred to two of the basic conditions of your treatment that have been trespassed: its confidentiality, and just last session, the length of time that we meet. This causes you to experience me as you used to experience your father, as someone who can't establish appropriate boundaries between us, who can't manage his urges and tensions, and as someone who wants to become involved in an incestuous liaison with you. It's as if my office became transformed into a bedroom, with me seated on the edge of the bed in my undershorts, while you lay there in your nightgown. The temptation that this creates for you causes you to have to deny the sexual implications of it for you and places you in a position where you believe that you have to impose the limitations and restraints that I have failed to institute myself. That is, you remind us of a time as in the dream, where the situation for you is nearly out of control, you are lost, and you are in search of someone to help you impose some kind of limits on the situation. As a result, the woman gives you a Smokenders' brochure.

Approaching the intervention from the listening–formulating vantage-point, the reader should answer the following questions:

1. Has the therapist dealt with the main patient- and therapist-indicators in this hour?

2. Has he made use of the patient's best representation of the most critical intervention context?

3. Has he made full use of the derivative complex—both encoded perceptions and the patient's reaction to them?

4. Has he added anything that was not included in the patient's material in this hour?

5. Has he omitted any critical representation of an intervention context or any aspect of the derivative complex in his comment to the patient?

6. Does this intervention have any other major asset or liability?

7. Do you anticipate indirect and encoded validation?

_____

_____

_____

_____

_____

_____

_____

_____

_____

_____

_____

_____

_____

_____

_____

_____

_____
_____
_____
_____
_____
_____
_____
_____
_____
_____
_____
_____
_____
_____
_____
_____
_____
_____
_____
_____
_____
_____
_____
_____
_____
_____
_____
_____

Answer

The following appear to be the best answers to the questions just posed:

1. The therapist has dealt with the main patient- and therapist-indicators in the hour. He has made reference to the patient's concern over the conditions of treatment,

and especially to the issues of confidentiality and the extended session. He has made an effort to explain the unconscious implications of these particular issues.

2. The therapist has made use of the best representations of the two most active intervention contexts. He began the intervention with these representations, which was the best possible strategy available to him.

3. The therapist has made correct use of the central image offered by the patient, expressing her selected encoded perceptions of the therapist in light of the main intervention context—the image of her father's open attempt at incest. The interpretation accepts the image as an expression of valid nontransference-based perceptions. In other words, it is a *genetic nontransference interpretation* that fully accepts the patient's view of the therapist in light of his errant extension of the patient's hour. The intervention falls short, however, of characterizing additional encoded perceptions related to misuse of the patient, addiction, and the attempt to take the patient as mistress. Also, whereas the therapist does make good use of several models of rectification offered in the patient's associations, he omits others, and he shifts very quickly to the patient's own sense of temptation and her use of denial rather than understanding these associations as continuing perceptions of his own difficulties.

4. The therapist does not appear to add any significant image to the material that is not already present in the patient's associations.

5. The important deletions from the intervention have been already noted.

6. The therapist has a problematic tendency in the initial part of the intervention to be rather concrete instead of accepting the broader sexual implications of the patient's encoded perceptions of his error. Further, toward the end of the intervention, the therapist becomes a bit confused and does not sufficiently spell out the implications of the patient's material. On balance, however, the intervention is well-stated and basically sound.

7. Because of the relatively strong characteristics of the intervention, one might well anticipate some measure of encoded validation. Let us now return to the hour and see it through to its end. We begin with the patient's remarks after the therapist completed his comment:

> *Patient:* I'm not sure how the fact that we went over last time could affect me like that. I was going to tell you about my father last hour, but we had to stop. I did think that when I finally realized what time it was that I had really gotten carried away. I felt almost as if I were out of control. I mean, there was so much emotion and everything as I told you about my father in that incident. I did though have to consciously deny that Burt Reynolds might have been you. And I did smoke cigarettes in the dream just as I did when my father invited me to have sex with him. [Patient glances down at her watch] Well, since we're about out of time, I'll pick up there next time.

How would you evaluate this response or commentary in terms of the intervention it followed?

_____

_____

_____

_____

_____

_____

_____

_____

The patient's response begins with a measure of denial. She quickly shifts, however, to an encoded displacement by referring to her own sense of having gotten carried away, almost out of control. This image validates in a small way the therapist's intervention in derivative form. The patient also acknowledges her tendency to deny part of her imagery as it linked up to the therapist. She then offers some tentative additional confirmation by acknowledging the connection between the cigarette smoking in the dream and the smoking that occurred when her father attempted to seduce her.

In all, then, there is only a small measure of cognitive validation in this material; and it is entirely lacking in interpersonal validation. What might well have been the most critical factor in this outcome?

_____

_____

_____

_____

_____

_____

_____

_____

_____

_____

The critical factor accounting for the minimal confirmatory response from the patient was the therapist's failure to propose the evidently much-needed rectification of the frame. The patient's repeated use of rectifying and corrective imagery suggests that it was essential to (at the very least) propose an exploration regarding the means by which the therapist's error could have been rectified.

In all likelihood, this omission is reflected in the patient's initial denial that the extension of her hour affected her to any important extent. This denial is an unconscious perception of the therapist's failure to actually behave in a manner that fully acknowledged the existence of his deviation—that is, to begin to suggest the possibility of an actual corrective by lessening a subsequent session by 10 minutes. This hypothesis obtains further support in the patient's encoded self-perception that she had really gotten carried away and was almost out of control. A small measure of support is also lent this idea by the allusion to the patient's own use of denial and the continuation of her smoking addiction. In all, this material supports the principle of technique that interpretation must always be accompanied by rectification, or at least the initiation of corrective measures to the greatest extent permitted by the patient's material.

CONCLUDING COMMENTS

The main effort in the present chapter has been directed toward developing an integrated approach to listening and formulating. It must be stressed that although a detailed analysis of the material from a session can reveal the richness, depth, and complexity of the patient's communications in psychotherapy, the therapist need not be overwhelmed by the situation. It is quite possible in a given session to pause only once or twice in order to generate as full a formulation as possible; this would be based on a thorough effort to identify the prevailing indicators, intervention contexts, and their representations, and the key derivative responses from the patient.

It is also possible to identify the main dimensions of the therapeutic interaction, which provide the central idiom for the patient's selected encoded perceptions of the therapist in light of the main activated adaptive contexts. The therapist who listens in terms of the patient's own imagery will automatically formulate the material in a way that is consonant with the seven dimensions of the therapeutic interaction. Adherence to sound basic principles of listening and formulating will ensure that the therapist's interventions touch on the influence of the patient's madness as it leads to selected encoded perceptions of the therapist. Intervening in terms of the patient's derivatives will illuminate those areas of the patient's madness that are most meaningful and cogent for the patient at the moment, and will clarify at the same time the influence of the therapist's madness.

13
The Search
for a Missing
Adaptive Context

As we have seen, the adaptive context and derivative complex interdigitate in a manner not unlike an antigen and antibody, or the cogs of two wheels. The derivative complex, constituted mainly by the patient's selected encoded perceptions, is strongly shaped by the conscious and unconscious implications of the most active intervention contexts, as well as the patient's own madness and adaptive capacities. In virtually all of the exercises we have carried out to this point, the main adaptation-evoking contexts have been known, and we have used their implications to shape our understanding of the patient's encoded and disguised reactions.

In the present and final chapter, we will reverse this process: We will listen to the material from a patient without knowing the most critical intervention context, and we will attempt to identify the unmentioned context based on clues generated from the patient's manifest associations—treated as derivatives of underlying encoded perceptions and reactions to these perceptions. In addition, we will continue to search for indicators and to evaluate possible derivative meanings in the material at hand. But the main thrust of this exercise is the pursuit of derivative clues to an adaptive context that will give relatively unified meaning to the material at hand.

DECODING DERIVATIVE CLUES: EXERCISES

The session we are about to consider was actually presented to a study group, who responded collectively to the material. Their comments form the major basis for the discussion to be offered in this chapter. From time to time, the reader should pause and attempt to identify the missing intervention context—perhaps broadly at first, and then, later, as specifically as possible. All speculation should be recorded and compared with the final revelation. In the course of this work, other exercises will be proposed and carried out.

In attempting to identify an intervention context based on a sequence of encoded derivatives, we are, of course, drawing heavily upon the universal implications of a particular intervention. If the exercise itself is successful—as it was with the study group—we gain a small measure of confirmation that there are indeed broad general meanings to major interventional efforts by the therapist.

On a more practical level, this exercise is designed to acquaint the reader with a particular type of listening that occurs from time to time in the course of most psychotherapeutic experiences: namely, the experience of a situation in which the therapist is for the moment not consciously aware of the adaptation-evoking context that is organizing the patient's derivative perceptions and other reactions. Either there is no known immediate adaptive context, or those contexts of which the therapist is cognizant do not appear to meaningfully organize the derivative material. The search then begins for a missing intervention context that will give unified meaning to the unconscious expressions contained in the patient's behaviors and associations. As the therapist develops a silent hypothesis as to the identity of the missing intervention context, silent validation may be obtained through the emergence of encoded material that fits well with the hypothesis and, at times, by the sudden appearance of a direct allusion to the proposed context in the patient's associations. Intervention typically follows.

The Beginning of the Hour: Exercise 13.1a

To place us on a par with the study group members who carried out this exercise, it should be noted that the presenting therapist was asked to select a session for which there was a basic framework issue. This request was made because of the finding that issues concerning the ground rules and boundaries of treatment are among the most powerful adaptation-evoking stimuli for the patient. Because of this, a deviation in the ideal frame would be likely to stimulate highly meaningful, coalescing derivatives—a likelihood that would facilitate the search for an adaptive context.

The patient is a 26-year-old man, who is being seen in once-weekly psychotherapy in the therapist's private office. The patient's main complaint was episodes of severe anxiety. The session to be presented occurred after about three months of a face-to-face therapy.

The patient entered the therapist's consultation room looking rather terrified. He began to speak as follows:

> *Patient:* At college we have three 12-week trimesters. I just started the summer trimester. I found it easy. I'm glad I chose the courses I did. My social life is going well. I went to a party and I got a telephone number from one of the girls.

With the completion of each communicative segment, we will pause and ask the following questions:

1. Is there any manifest representation of a patient-indicator?

2. Is there a manifest allusion to an intervention context?

3. Does there appear to be a derivative representation of an intervention context?

4. What are the main themes which could link the patient's manifest associations with latent contents, derivative representations of intervention contexts, and/or encoded perceptions of the therapist? These themes should be organized in terms of the seven dimensions of the therapeutic interaction.

5. Is there sufficient derivative evidence on which to base a proposal regarding the missing adaptation-evoking context?

The reader should attempt to answer these five questions for the above segment of material.

_____

_____

_____

_____

_____

_____

_____

_____

_____

_____

_____

_____

_____

_____

_____

_____

_____

_____

_____

_____

_____

_____

_____

_____

_____

_____

_____

_____

_____

_____

_____

_____

_____

_____

_____

_____

_____

_____

_____

_____

_____

_____

_____

_____

_____

_____

Answer

The answers to the above questions as they pertain to the initial segment of material appear to be as follows:

1. There are no evident patient-indicators in this segment of material. In fact, there are signs of improved interpersonal and intrapsychic functioning. For the moment, we would concern ourselves with the adaptive context that accounts for this sense of ego enhancement.

2. There is no direct reference to an adaptive context.

3. There is no evident derivative representation of an intervention context.

4. In considering possible themes that link manifest with latent contents, the following seem pertinent:

a. Frame: There is a frame allusion in the patient's first sentence—the reference to the three 12-week trimesters. This touches upon the conditions of school and may well represent a concern with some dimension of the structure of treatment.

b. Mode of relatedness: Healthy symbiosis with possible commensal relatedness.

c. Mode of cure: There is a sense of cure through insight in the patient's ability to get the telephone number from one of the girls at the party he attended. This appears to be a constructive move and not one that involves action-discharge.

d. Communication: Appears to be open and satisfactory.

e. Dynamics and genetics: The dynamic image pertains to involvement with women, though there is little in the way of more specific content. Genetics are not evident.

f. Self and identity: There is a sense of a positive self-image and constructive narcissistic satisfaction that may also involve encoded perceptions of the therapist.

g. Sanity and madness: The material speaks for sanity rather than madness.

Lacking knowledge of the specific adaptive context that accounts for this material, it is difficult to obtain a clear sense of the encoded implications of these initial associations. The session begins with a frame allusion and quickly shifts to a positive and autonomous act—the patient's choosing his summer courses. The theme of involvement with a woman, possibly that of a healthy sexual interest, is also in evidence.

With these considerations in mind, we can attempt to answer the final question: Is there an evident intervention context that accounts for these initial derivatives? The answer for the moment is apparently, no. There is a vague hint of a frame issue, but little else with specificity.

What then could be tentatively formulated at the moment? There appears to be two possibilities: First, it may well be that these associations represent in encoded form an effort by the therapist (or patient) to secure an aspect of a deviant frame. If this were the case, the patient's autonomous choice of courses would constitute a derivative representation of this framework-rectifying endeavor. The associations with respect to the fact that the patient's social life is going well, that he went to a party, and that he got a telephone number from one of the girls would then constitute positive introjective identifications with the well-functioning therapist. This thesis would propose that in response to securing an aspect of the deviant frame, the patient has himself responded with relatively sound functioning.

There is, however, a second, somewhat converse possibility. Here, the frame allusion may be arising from a continuing deviant condition to this treatment. The reference to the patient's ability to choose courses that satisfy him would then be a reaction to disturbing perceptions of the therapist, as yet unmentioned, in light of the deviant context. Rather than an introject of his sound functioning, the response would involve a model of rectification offered to the therapist. The patient's investment in a heterosexual social life would in that sense represent a defense against unconsciously perceived homosexuality within the therapist based on the unmentioned deviation. (Perversions are a common theme under such circumstances.) Further, the party would represent a manic defense against some measure of loss of the therapist based on the intervention. Obtaining the telephone number of one of the girls could express in derivative form a wish to reestablish relatedness with the therapist—this implying that the deviation has in some way disrupted the therapeutic relationship.

To these two integrated hypotheses, we may add a number of additional but separate considerations. The allusion to obtaining a telephone number might represent a deviant intervention context in which telephone contact was made—either between the patient and the therapist (an interaction outside of the allotted time of the session) or between the therapist and a relative of the patient. Allusions to school and/or learning often suggest an unconscious perception of the therapist's ignorance and a corrective model in which the patient unconsciously proposes that the therapist should educate him or herself—for example, by obtaining supervision. Finally, the material may contain an affirmation of therapy in the patient's satisfaction with his choice of courses— but here we would be seeking out a more positive intervention context.

Exercise 13.1b

In the last analysis, for the moment, it would appear that some frame issue is indeed at hand. The main imagery is positive, suggesting the possibility of rectification, or alternatively, the mobilization of powerful manic defenses within the patient and/or unconsciously perceived within the therapist as well. Beyond these speculations, there is little that one can say with certainty; we will therefore turn to the next segment of material:

> *Patient* (continuing): Last week I finally got my parents' boat to New York from Port Jefferson on Long Island. It was the third time we tried. Twice before, the weather prevented us. Like last week, the water was too rough.

Again, we will pause and answer our five basic questions about the foregoing however briefly. Please indicate your responses below.

_____

_____

_____

_____

_____

_____

_____

_____

_____

_____

_____

_____

_____

_____

_____

_____

_____

_____

_____

_____

_____

_____

_____

_____

_____

_____

_____

_____

_____

_____

_____

_____

_____

_____

_____

_____

_____

_____

_____

_____

_____

Answer

To respond in sequence, the following seem pertinent:

1. There is no evidence of a patient-indicator.

2. There is no manifest allusion to an adaptive context.

3. There is no clear suggestion of a derivative representation of an intervention context. The material does suggest, however, a constructive effort to deal with a difficult problem. There is a similar sense in the first segment of material. There is therefore a suggestion that some corrective measure has been undertaken—or at the very least is under consideration. Still, this may not actually be a derivative representation of an intervention context and may simply allude for the moment to a proposed model of rectification expressed by the patient to the therapist.

4. As for the main bridging themes, there is no frame allusion as such, although there is a reference to holding conditions. In this image, the hold is stormy and insecure, but the patient is able to negotiate the anxieties and difficulties involved.

Mode of relatedness is not clearly portrayed, although there are indications of cooperation suggesting either a healthy symbiosis—the patient as symbiotic donor—or the commensal mode. The mode of cure is once again strongly adaptive and therefore points toward constructive insight. Communication appears to be open and good because the outcome of the effort at hand was successful.

There is little in the sense of dynamics and only the vaguest genetic allusion in a reference to the patient's parents. Successfully transporting a boat through rough water may have sexual symbolic attributes, but these are difficult to establish clearly. Similarly, the rough water may represent in some fashion aggression and destructiveness, but its implications are also quite uncertain.

There is once again a strong sense of positive identity and healthy narcissistic satisfaction. Finally, the material speaks for sanity rather than for madness.

5. It still does not appear feasible to fathom the missing intervention context.

Among the more general impressions, we may recognize the theme of a journey that had failed twice, though it is now successful. Does this suggest again that a break in the frame has at last been rectified?

Danger has been overcome, though its nature remains unclear. Positive functioning certainly predominates, so the search must continue along the lines of attempting to identify either a validated interpretation, or as proposed before, a constructive effort at framework rectification. At the same time, the alternative must continue to be entertained—that the patient is proposing the need to overcome a danger in light of the therapist's failure to correct a deviant frame issue.

Note should also be made regarding the passing reference to the patient's parents. Not surprisingly, they seem to be the genetic figures pertinent to this interlude. Their specific role and the meanings of the patient's allusions to the parents remain cloudy however.

At this juncture, certain additional speculations—silent hypotheses—were made by the study-group members who examined this material in sequence. It was proposed that there might have been telephone contact between the therapist and the patient's parents. The question was raised as to whether they were involved in the treatment situation in some other way. Based more on inferences and guesses then on a decoding of derivatives, there was speculation that they might be supporting the therapy in some fashion—perhaps by paying the fee. The question was raised as to whether this deviation, if actual, had been rectified or whether it was continuing to be in effect, providing the patient with manic-like defenses. The possibility that the therapist had seen the entire family or had held a separate interview with one or both parents was also entertained.

With the therapist maintaining his silence, the patient continued as follows:

> *Patient:*   They had this man on board. He's an old salt. Last week he tried
> to convince us to go ahead, but we didn't. This time, on the way to New
> York, the [Long Island] Sound was rough. I was confident piloting the
> boat. I felt responsible for the others on board. I never felt that before, with
> this boat or when I was on any other boat. I had a very great concern for
> the safety of those on board.

Again, we will attempt to answer the five basic questions in response to
this sequence of material and to comment broadly as well.

_____

_____

_____

_____

_____

_____

_____

_____

_____

_____

_____

_____

_____

_____

_____

_____

_____

_____

_____

_____

_____

_____

_____

_____

_____

_____

_____

_____

_____

_____

_____

_____

_____

_____

_____

_____

_____

_____

_____

_____

_____

_____

_____

_____

_____

_____

Answer

To respond:

1. Again, there is no evident patient-indicator.

2. Also, there is no manifest allusion to an adaptation-evoking context—to an intervention by the therapist.

3. There appear to be no clearly decodable derivative representations of an intervention context.

4. As for the main themes here, there is a general framework-management allusion in the image of the patient's responsibility for piloting his parents' boat and in his concern for the safety of those on board. The mode of relatedness is primarily a healthy symbiosis with the patient as the symbiotic donor, though there is a hint of

some type of disturbed relationship in the pressures placed on the patient and his family by the passenger alluded to at the beginning of the segment.

Mode of cure continues to be insightful and adaptive, but there is a shift to disturbed communication in the dispute between the old salt and the patient and his parents. Dynamically, there is a sense of conflict in the initial part of this segment although its underlying basis is unclear. There is also a sense of an intruder into the relationship between the patient and his parents. Genetically, the parents continue to be the critical figures; there is no specific definition of their role or images, however; in the main, they appear to rely on the patient for care and guidance.

Again, there is a sense within the patient—and therefore, by implication, the therapist—of a healthy form of narcissistic gratification and a strong identity. Sanity continues to be uppermost.

5. There is as yet no clear sign of the underlying intervention context. Certain clues appear to be repeated in different guises, however. Thus, the man on board, the old salt, repeats the image of another intruding figure who again suggests the possibility of a third party to treatment. This person seems to be a disruptive force. Through condensation, his image may also relate to an encoded perception of the therapist as having intervened erroneously or inadvisably—this, however, the first such allusion in that particular direction. On the other hand, positive imagery continues to prevail: Where the patient had not been especially responsible for others before, he was now both fully responsible for them and self-confident. Repeated here is the theme of prior difficulty and new adaptive resourcefulness.

For the first time, then, there are suggestions of a split image of the therapist: acting inappropriately on the one hand and nonetheless gaining a new sense of confidence and responsibility. It may well be that the therapist has done something to endanger the patient while doing other things that render the patient safe and responsible.

Once again, if a deviant framework condition still exists, this material may well convey a model of rectification. In effect, the patient is proposing to the therapist that whatever his prior difficulties, he should take responsibility for the safety of the patient and the conditions of treatment.

Another possibility is that the therapist may have attempted a pressured intervention with the patient. It is striking, however, that there is as yet no direct representation of an adaptive context, nor the presence of any bridge to therapy—that is, the appearance of a nonspecific allusion either to the therapist or to the treatment situation.

Still other considerations present themselves. Is the old salt a third party to treatment in the sense of the patient having discovered the presence of a supervisor, perhaps through the observation that the therapist takes notes during the patient's hours? Is there a model of rectification here in regard to the patient advising the therapist to take on greater responsibility for treatment, or perhaps some suggestion that the patient himself should become responsible for the fees for treatment? There is also the vague possibility that the intruder into therapy is an insurance company, a third-party payer. Still another common implication to material of this kind is an unconscious realization within the patient that the therapist has intervened in erroneous fashion—whether verbally or in terms of the ground rules—and the patient has found it necessary to become the functional therapist to the designated therapist.

The Session Continues:
Exercise 13.2a

In all, the preceding formulations appear rather scattered. Instead of a coalescing derivative complex, we are faced with a series of uncertain and fragmented images. It remains impossible to determine whether a ground-rule deviation does exist, whether it has been recently rectified or, instead, is in acute need of correction. It also remains impossible to determine whether the patient is introjecting aspects of the therapist's positive functioning, or is holding himself up unconsciously as both a model of a well-functioning therapist and someone capable of proposing the necessary rectification of a deviant frame. Clearly, the material does not yet point toward a specific intervention context and lacks a sense of integrated meaning. It therefore behooves us to return to the session:

> *Patient:*   I don't care about my own safety. I was nervous at times. Things got rough at times. But I knew everything would be okay. The boat had some mechanical problems, so I couldn't push it until we got to the City. I was afraid we'd break down in the middle of the Sound. There were some transmission problems.

Again, we must respond to this material by answering the five basic questions and proposing additional observations regarding these associations. Please respond in the following space:

_____

_____

_____

_____

_____

_____

_____

_____

_____

_____

_____

_____

_____

_____

_____

_____

_____

_____

_____

_____

_____

Answer

1. This segment contains the first allusion to patient-indicators—the patient's lack of care regarding his own safety, his nervousness, and his fear of breaking down in the middle of the Sound. The allusion to transmission problems suggests an encoded patient-indicator that remains unidentified for the moment.

2. There remains no direct representation of an adaptive context.

3. The material continues to fail to organize as an evident representation of an intervention context.

4. As for the main themes, there is a small measure of frame allusion in the basic mechanical problems of the boat, including the transmission problems. The image of going down in the middle of the Sound also suggests a poor therapeutic hold and therefore an insecure frame.
Mode of relatedness is not well represented in this material, although there is a minimal sense of autism—the patient appears rather isolated at the moment. Such an

autistic image may be related to an unconscious perception of the therapist's continuing silence in this hour, a silence that is, however, probably appropriate and necessary. The manifest imagery here also suggests an isolated (healthy/autistic) form of concentration necessary for navigating the boat under difficult conditions.

The image of transmission problems suggests communicative difficulties. Dynamically, mechanical problems in the boat may have some qualities of bodily anxiety, though the material remains striking for its lack of dynamic imagery. And the segment lacks any manifest genetic allusion.

In the realm of identity, there is some sense of uncertainty and, narcissistically, a lack of self-concern. Madness does not appear to be present, and sanity appears to be represented in the patient's decision not to push the boat until he was in safe waters—that is, until they got to the city. On the other hand, the patient's concern that the boat would break down could refer to some emerging anxieties regarding the expression of madness. The imagery once more suggests a split view of the therapist—as someone who has functioned in sane fashion in certain areas, while expressing himself through some form of madness in another sphere.

5. It is still not possible to offer a clear formulation of the missing intervention context. This material suggests, however, that there is some fundamental difficulty with the conditions of treatment; this is represented by the mechanical problems in the boat. The deviation involved appears to be such that it could lead to a breakdown of treatment and to a view of the therapist as mad—as having decompensated. The deviation also appears to have created problems in communication between patient and therapist.

Perhaps most striking about this segment is the patient's shift from the previously positive imagery and sense of confidence to the emergence of anxiety, caution, and fear of decompensation. These images now suggest that the deviant conditions to treatment are still in existence and are causing both patient and therapist a significant measure of difficulty. Perhaps the most integrated formulation involves the split images that emerge: It appears that the ground rules of treatment are secure in some areas while deviant and modified in one or more specific ways.

The allusion to transmission problems may help to illuminate the difficulties experienced to this point in the hour in sorting out the unconscious implications of the patient's associations. It could be proposed that the deviant condition to treatment has created a significant level of communicative resistances within the patient, who fears the decompensation of both himself and the therapist if he were to express himself meaningfully regarding the ground-rule issue at hand.

Not pushing the boat for fear of a breakdown could allude to an unconscious perception of the therapist's reluctance to secure the frame, or conversely, to a response by the patient to efforts by the therapist to undertake such measures. In the latter instance, the patient would be conveying his own fear of a secure therapeutic setting in which he would be relatively alone with the therapist. Tracing out this particular line of thought, the earlier positive images would then be seen as defensive attempts by the patient to reassure himself with regard to his ability to function in a secure frame setting, and to similarly reassure himself in this regard as to the therapist's continued sound functioning.

At this point, we remain faced with contradictory and confusing images. The shift to qualities of anxiety, mechanical problems, fear of breakdown, and transmission problems suggests that the initial part of the hour contained a significant measure of manic-defensiveness. It appears that these defenses have now diminished to the point where the patient begins to reveal both patient-indicators and unconscious perceptions of the therapist with distinctly negative qualities. For this reason, it is well to begin to suspect that a basic deviation in the conditions of this treatment remains in existence and that it has formed a basis for negative images of the therapist and anxieties in the patient.

Another continuing sign of the patient's communicative resistances is the lack of a general bridge to therapy and the absence of a direct representation of an adaptive context. In the absence of a known intervention context, we continue to experience the indefinite qualities of the derivative meanings contained in this material. We can see that there is no such entity as material qua material, and no inherent single meaning to a patient's cluster of associations. It is possible to develop a number of image derivatives, but there is little certainty to any of these formulations. We continue to be faced with derivative material that is difficult to organize and coalesce in meaningful, consistent fashion. We see, too, the potential for several meanings to be suggested by a particular communicative element and the consequent importance of identifying a known intervention context in order to select the meaning most pertinent to the patient's communicative intentions.

Perhaps above all for the moment we can recognize the critical role played by the correct identification of an activated adaptive context in ascertaining the most important *functional meanings* contained in the latent aspect of the patient's associations. If we may be permitted a small pun, perhaps the patient will not keep us at sea for very much longer. We therefore return to the session:

> *Patient* (continuing):   There have been situations where I was uncomfortable on a boat. One time I was on a friend's boat and it was docked on the Sound. The waves rocked the boat and I got queasy and a little green. The unstable water got to me and got me upset. When I'm at the helm, I worry. If I'm not careful, I could cause harm to people and to other boats. Father's boat is made of steel. If it hit another boat, it would cut it in two.

Again, respond to this segment in terms of the five basic questions, and make additional observations:

_____

_____

_____

_____

_____

_____

_____

_____

_____

_____

_____

_____

_____

_____

Answer

The following appears to be the best available evaluation of the foregoing segment of material:

1. These associations do not reflect an immediate patient-indicator, though the material does touch on background (past) symptoms. These could well represent as yet unmentioned (latent) presently cogent patient-indicators.

2. There is no direct allusion to an adaptive context or any general bridge to therapy.

3. Although there is no indication of a derivative representation of a specific intervention context, there is a strong sense of a poor hold and therefore of some type of basic framework deviation.

4. As for the main bridging themes, the frame imagery continues to be rather prominent. There is the docked boat that does not hold the patient well, and the unstable water beneath it. There is the framework-management image in the allusion to the patient at the helm, as well as concerns about handling the boat and damaging others. As for relatedness, this area is not well represented in the material, but there is a hint of parasiticism in the patient's image of possibly hitting another boat and cutting it in two. Being on a friend's boat may have a quality of healthy symbiosis.

Mode of cure is poorly represented here, but there is a suggestion of action-discharge in the image of hitting another boat and cutting it in two. Communication does not appear to have been represented here. Dynamics on the other hand, seem to center again on issues of aggression—harming others and cutting another boat in half. There are also other dynamic possibilities hinted at in this material: perhaps something latently heterosexual or homosexual in respect to being on the friend's boat, continued signs of bodily anxiety in the patient's physical upset when the waves rock the boat, and the possibility of sexual symbolism in the image of father's boat cutting another boat in two—this latter a possible latent homosexual or primal scene image involving a highly destructive (castrating) paternal phallus.

Genetically, there is only the indefinite allusion to the patient's father. While narcissism and identity are also not portrayed especially well in these associations, there is a negative narcissistic image in the patient's sense of sickness and a concern regarding his identity when at the helm—the worry of causing harm and damage to others. Neither sanity nor madness is especially prominent here, though the stronger scene of the material involves an image related to loss of control and doing violence to others, both of which suggest possible expressions of madness.

5. As yet, the specific deviation does not appear to have been portrayed in derivative form, nor is there evidence of a deviant intervention context that would meaningfully organize this material as a coalescing derivative complex.

Perhaps the best that can be said for this material is that there appears to be a distinct shift from early images of sound holding and framework management to those of poor holding and even the potential of loss of control—of a violent deviation that would do damage to the patient and/or others. The images suggest that the therapist is not holding the patient well, and there is the notable clue that in some way the patient's father is involved—possibly as a third party to treatment.

Perhaps the clearest proposal of an adaptive context at this moment is that the therapist has in some way permitted the father to intrude upon the therapeutic space and to do violence to both participants to treatment. The specific form that this intrusion might have taken seems to be uncertain, though we have already considered the possibility of telephone contact and speculated regarding the father's support of the patient's therapy. (This last was not based on decoding the patient's encoded derivatives, but on deductions drawn from the patient's circumstances and the allusion to the father.) The image of being on a friend's boat lends some support to these propositions, in that the holding environment does not belong to the patient, but to someone else—the friend and the father, and perhaps the latter in some real sense. Similarly, the earlier allusions to being in his father's boat may have comparable implications.

As for the additional impressions, the docked boat could represent a stalemated therapy. The patient's caution regarding the care needed in steering the boat could well be an unconscious warning to the therapist regarding the management of the frame. As for the patient's own psychopathology, concerns with bodily disturbance and harm (castration and other forms of bodily anxiety) seem prominent as a determinant of the patient's communicative idiom and his selective unconscious perceptions of the therapist. Unresolved and violent unconscious perceptions and fantasies also seem prominent. Notable, too, is a disturbed sense of identity, whereas the remaining implications of the material appear to be far more tentative.

In principle, an effort at formulation of this kind must concentrate on the search for an actual adaptive context and, therefore, on the unconscious implications of the therapist's interventions—on latent meanings of actualities rather than primary fantasies. The theme of needing to take responsibility may suggest a deviation that requires rectification, such as the patient's adopting full responsibility for his fee for the missed sessions. There is a sense here that the patient's autonomous functioning is being disturbed, as is that of the therapist. There is a plea for rectification, though danger follows there as well—if the patient is at the helm, he must be careful not to harm others and to not hit another boat.

The patient's choice of the boat and the sea as metaphors for the therapeutic setting and environment is of interest. His stress is notably nonhuman rather than on a mixture of nonhuman and human qualities. Human relationships are present, but shadowy. This is in keeping with the patient's failure to allude directly as yet to the treatment situation and in particular to the therapist himself. There is an autistic quality to the patient's sense of relatedness, although it must be stressed that within the session, this attribute must be taken first as an unconscious perception of the therapist before being located as well within the patient. We may therefore wonder if the therapist has indeed failed to intervene properly, especially in the form of a much-needed effort at rectification. When the therapist does not intervene in terms of an adaptive context (i.e., to fully understand the patient) and/or does not carry out a rectification to which he is directed through the patient's derivatives, there is a break in the important meaning-link between the two participants to treatment. The absence to this link is tantamount to the absence of the therapist who is not experienced as meaningfully present when other links are active, such as love and hate (Bion, 1962).

Exercise 13.2c

It may well be that we have not been sensitive enough to detect an intervention context to which the patient's material is actually directing us. If this is not the case, however, we are faced with a session in which there are notable communicative resistances—which themselves may be a product of the deviant conditions of the treatment situation. It remains to be seen whether the patient will overcome these defensive obstacles. The session proceeded as follows:

> *Patient* (continuing): I've always felt that way about getting angry and hurting people. When I was in junior high school I fought with a kid and I got him into a headlock. The other kids kept telling me to hurt him, but I couldn't. I would rather hurt myself. When I hurt someone, I feel guilty and it lasts a long time. I saw this handicapped Vietnam veteran selling something. He asked me for money. I didn't give him any. I felt bad afterwards.

Once again, answer our five basic questions and comment as needed:

_____

_____

_____

_____

_____

_____

_____

_____

_____

_____

_____

_____

_____

_____

_____

_____

It is well to note that the material of this session, is, in the main, constituted by narratives and images. Associations of this kind are certainly the best carriers of encoded meaning. The patient has not as yet shifted to generalizations, intellectualizations, and rumination. Thus, the following may be stated about this last segment of material:

1. There is a rather minor patient-indicator in this set of associations, reflected in the patient's "feeling bad" after not buying something from the Vietnam veteran. There are also background indicators in the patient's recollection of getting angry and hurting others in junior high school; these may serve to reflect in derivative form existing patient-indicators not yet manifestly expressed.

2. There is still no direct allusion to an intervention context.

3. Perhaps now we have our first definitive clue regarding a deviant intervention context—the allusion to asking someone for money. Based on hints from the patient's circumstances and on impressions from well-disguised derivatives, we have entertained for some time the possibility that one of the main deviant adaptive contexts for this patient involves the fact that someone else is paying for his treatment—in all likelihood, his father.

4. As for bridging themes, there is little here regarding frame issues. Mode of relatedness is initially parasitic—getting angry and hurting people, and being encouraged to hurt others; it is also autistic in view of the patient's thought that he would rather hurt himself than others and in view of his not giving the veteran the money that he asked for.

As for mode of cure, there is now a stress on action-discharge both in the fighting with and hurting others and in not giving the veteran any money. Communication now appears impaired in the patient's early relationship with his peers and in his interaction with the Vietnam veteran.

Dynamic issues regarding hostility and aggression remain prominent. There is a clear and strong superego expression in the patient's sense of guilt and in his preference to hurt himself rather than others. The bad feeling after not giving the veteran any money also suggests a guilt-ridden response. Depressive dynamics are suggested by the patient's wish to hurt himself rather than others, as well as in the image of the veteran who was deprived of money. This last image also contains within it a further expression of the patient's bodily anxieties and those unconsciously perceived in the therapist—all conveyed through the allusion to the veteran's handicap. It is to be stressed again that each of these themes and qualities must first be formulated as an encoded though selected unconscious perception of the therapist before being applied to the patient.

There is a genetic quality to the patient's allusion to junior high school, but its specific implications are not clear. There is also an impaired sense of narcissism and identity in the reference to the handicapped veteran and in the patient's struggle with his impulses to hurt others. There is a sense of inconsistency that suggests madness, but this quality is not especially prominent.

5. The direct allusion to money may well be a key surface theme that links up to the underlying framework deviation issue—the patient's fee. Clustered around this theme are images of being handicapped, of not giving money free and clear, and of

feeling bad afterwards. If the therapist is indeed accepting the patient's fee from a third party—for example, the father—the patient sees the therapist on the basis of this adaptation-evoking context as handicapped, needy, and impoverished. The patient responds with an encoded model of rectification in not giving money to the veteran. The image implies that the therapist should not obtain his fee in this fashion. The guilt of the patient then becomes the guilt of the therapist who is accepting a fee from a third party and thereby hurting the patient—this is also the earlier theme of this segment.

This tentative formulation is further supported by the allusion to third parties in the images related to the fight with a kid in junior high school. Here, the patient perceives the therapist as engaged in a battle with him and deflecting his own aggression onto himself—perhaps, again, by accepting payment from a third party. The images also suggest a perception of the therapist as accepting others into the treatment situation in an attempt to deal with his own hostility. Still, the third parties involved are provocative and are geared to increase the level of aggression; they do not therefore serve a helpful or modulating function. They are in all a rather negative and destructive influence.

The deviation also appears to be linked to images of losing control and the struggle to maintain these controls despite such pressures. On the first level, this is an encoded perception of a struggle within the therapist, though it undoubtedly also corresponds to a comparable difficulty within the patient. The model of rectification appears here when the patient says that he was unable to hurt the other young man and that he would rather hurt himself. The message to the therapist is to control the aggressive qualities of the deviation and, furthermore, if he does indeed have hostile impulses, to turn them against himself rather than the patient.

It is also possible that the damaged frame has mobilized the patient's bodily anxieties, and has led to a particular unconscious perception of the deviation in terms of bodily impairment. Finally, there is a sense that the patient unconsciously perceives anxiety within the therapist who fears the rectification of the frame, an anxiety that he himself shares with the therapist as well.

The Final Segment:
Exercise 13.3a

An intervention is now made by the therapist who was, of course, familiar with the background intervention context:

> Therapist: In this session you are talking about responsibility and the stability of an environment, the boat. There are allusions to anger and guilt in connection with money, and to someone who is not able to make a living. It seems that you are saying that the treatment situation is unstable and this has to do with money. There is something here which is causing you to feel angry and guilty.

Though we are still as yet not entirely certain that we know the critical adaptive context, we may nonetheless evaluate this intervention from the vantage point of the listening–formulating process. We will therefore ask and answer the six questions we have developed for an appraisal of an intervention:

1. Does it deal with the main patient-indicators in the session?

2. Does it make use of the best representation of the adaptive context?

3. Does it make full use of the derivative complex, beginning with encoded perceptions of the therapist?

4. Is anything added that is not conveyed by the patient in the session at hand?

5. Is anything of significance deleted?

6. Are there any other general comments, and is validation anticipated?

The reader should attempt to answer these questions in the following space:

_____

_____

_____

_____

_____

_____

_____

_____

_____

_____

_____

_____

_____

_____

_____

_____

_____

_____

_____

_____

_____

_____

_____

_____

_____

\

————————————————————————————
————————————————————————————
————————————————————————————
————————————————————————————
————————————————————————————
————————————————————————————
————————————————————————————
————————————————————————————
————————————————————————————
————————————————————————————
————————————————————————————
————————————————————————————
————————————————————————————
————————————————————————————
————————————————————————————
————————————————————————————
————————————————————————————
————————————————————————————
————————————————————————————
————————————————————————————
————————————————————————————
————————————————————————————
————————————————————————————

Answer

As best as seems possible, the following answers to the above questions are pertinent:

1. As noted previously, the patient-indicators are quite weak here, a phenomenon that may occur, as discussed, in the presence of a major and active deviant intervention context, one that constitutes a traumatic therapist-indicator that is active in the session. In substance, then, when the therapist's madness is in its ascendency, up to a point, patient-madness recedes. This may well be the case in this particular hour, where the main known patient-indicators are indeed the patient's recent sense of guilt and the images of his earlier anxieties and difficulties in managing his aggressive impulses. In this light, the therapist does attempt to touch upon the patient's current disturbing affects—his anger and guilt.

2. If the patient's father or someone else is indeed paying the fee for this treatment, or if there exists some other issue and deviation with respect to the fee, the therapist appears to have selected the best encoded representation of the intervention context in his comment.

3. As for the use of the derivative complex, the therapist interprets the patient's unconscious perception of the instability of the treatment situation, though he makes little use of the specific images from the patient that convey this quality. In addition, there is a rather quick shift to the patient's sense of anger and guilt without first accepting these qualities as encoded perceptions of the therapist in light of the deviant intervention context. Thus, the therapist seems to have made rather limited use of derivative material as far as the patient's unconscious perceptions of him are concerned. The patient's multiple models of rectification are also underused, although the therapist does indicate that the material reflects some concern about responsibility and the stability of the therapeutic situation.

4. The intervention, on the whole, makes use of the patient's material in this particular hour, but the therapist introduces the bridge to therapy on his own.

5. As noted, the intervention overlooks a great deal. Especially lacking is an allusion to the patient's encoded perceptions of the therapist's uncertain identity and his possible bodily anxieties, the existence of dangers for the patient, and destructiveness. It is important for the therapist to include these images in his intervention, because they touch on both the patient's critical unconscious perceptions and the madness within the patient that has led to these selected images. The therapist might also have spelled out the material from the patient indicating an unconscious view of the therapist as badly managing the ground rules of treatment.

6. Based on this highly tentative evaluation, we might expect a rather mixed response from the patient to this intervention. We have here a playback of selected derivatives organized around the best representation of an unmentioned intervention context. As noted, the major flaw in the intervention is the fact that the therapist himself introduced the subject of the treatment situation at a time when the patient's communicative resistances and defenses had led him to avoid any direct allusion to the psychotherapy. Thus, we have a situation in which the therapist was attempting to modify the patient's denial defenses (the denial barrier), but doing so in an area that is undoubtedly fraught with meaning.

Speaking for validation is the fact that the therapist has in all likelihood intervened around a critical and urgent deviant intervention context. The patient may therefore provide additional derivative material that will clarify his unconscious perceptions in light of the deviation; he may also offer clearer models of rectification.

On the other hand, speaking against validation is the therapist's premature direct mention of the treatment situation, his omission of several important derivative encoded images, and his ultimate focus on the patient's anger and guilt rather than his own. Further, although the therapist hints at the need for rectification, the intervention conveys this element in far weaker form than exists in the patient's associations. As we have seen, failure to move toward rectification in the presence of a major deviation will decrease the likelihood of validation when an interpretive intervention is applied in such an area.

In all, then, there is some reason to expect confirmation, though many reasons to anticipate further communicative resistances. The latter possibility is reinforced by the fact that the intervention has qualities of a projective identification and dumps into the patient: The therapist seems to hold the patient primarily accountable for the fee problem, rather than centering the intervention around the adaptive context of the therapist's own failure to constitute a treatment situation in which the patient may well not have been responsible for the fee.

Exercise 13.3b

This last segment contains the patient's response to the therapist's intervention:

> *Patient:* Yes, I do feel badly that my father is paying for treatment. I feel like I'm hurting my father even though he says it's not a problem. No matter what he says, it bothers me. I would feel a lot better paying my own bill. I can't do that until after I finish with graduate school. I know I did feel better paying for my own clothes when I could.

We are left now with one final exercise:

1. Is there any measure of validation for the therapist's intervention? If so, what form does it take?

2. What is the patient's unconscious perceptions of the therapist in light of his intervention—as best as can be determined by these brief associations?

3. Is there any last comment you wish to make regarding this session?

_____

_____

_____

_____

_____

_____

_____

_____

_____

_____

_____

_____

_____

_____

_____

_____

_____

_____

_____

_____

_____

_____

_____

_____

_____

_____

_____

_____

_____

_____

_____

_____

_____

_____

_____

_____

_____

_____

_____

_____

1. In answer to the first question, we must take as validation of the therapist's intervention the fact that the patient now provides the therapist with the specific missing adaptive context—the fact that his father is paying for the treatment. This revelation clearly confirms the working hypothesis developed by the study group members—that the deviant adaptive context was the payment of the patient's fee by his father.

The material, however, does not offer much in the way of additional derivative support for the therapist's intervention. The patient's thought that he felt better paying for his own clothes when he could is too simplistic to constitute major encoded validation. For the moment, then, there is a measure of validation without additional encoded images that would lend unique understanding to the intervention context.

2. As for the patient's commentary on the therapist's intervention, the patient perceives the therapist as feeling bad that the patient's father is paying for his treatment. The image that the patient is hurting his father is a likely encoded perception of the hurtful qualities of the therapist's intervention—qualities the patient believes the therapist would deny. There is, however, little else in the way of encoded commentary for the moment.

Before offering a final commentary on the session, the reader may wish to read through the hour in its entirety. It runs as follows:

Patient: At college we have three 12-week trimesters. I just started the summer trimester. I found it easy. I'm glad I chose the courses I did. My social life is going well. I went to a party and I got a telephone number from one of the girls.

Last week I finally got my parents' boat to New York from Port Jefferson on Long Island. It was the third time we tried. Twice before, the weather prevented us. Like last week, the water was too rough.

They had this man on board. He's an old salt. Last week he tried to convince us to go ahead, but we didn't. This time, on the way to New York, the [Long Island] Sound was rough. I was confident piloting the boat. I felt responsible for the others on board. I never felt that before, with this boat or when I was on any other boat. I had a very great concern for the safety of those on board.

I don't care about my own safety. I was nervous at times. Things got rough at times. But I knew everything would be okay. The boat had some mechanical problems, so I couldn't push it until we got to the City. I was afraid we'd break down in the middle of the Sound. There were some transmission problems.

There have been situations where I was uncomfortable on a boat. One time I was on a friend's boat and it was docked on the Sound. The waves rocked the boat and I got queasy and a little green. The unstable water got to me and got me upset. When I'm at the helm, I worry. If I'm not careful, I could cause harm to people and to other boats. Father's boat is made of steel. If it hit another boat, it would cut it in two.

I've always felt that way about getting angry and hurting people. When I was in junior high school I fought with a kid and I got him into a headlock. The other kids kept telling me to hurt him, but I couldn't. I would rather hurt myself. When I hurt someone, I feel guilty and it lasts a long time. I saw this handicapped Vietnam veteran selling something. He asked me for money. I didn't give him any. I felt bad afterwards.

Therapist: In this session you are talking about responsibility and the stability of an environment, the boat. There are allusions to anger and guilt in connection with money, and to someone who is not able to make a living. It seems that you are saying that the treatment situation is unstable and this has to do with money. There is something here which is causing you to feel angry and guilty.

Patient: Yes, I do feel badly that my father is paying for treatment. I feel like I'm hurting my father even though he says it's not a problem. No matter what he says, it bothers me. I would feel a lot better paying my own bill. I can't do that until after I finish with graduate school. I know I did feel better paying for my own clothes when I could.

SOME FINAL PERSPECTIVES

In retrospect, it appears that the patient had indeed begun this hour with powerful communications regarding the need to rectify the deviant frame and to provide a secure therapeutic space that would promote his autonomous functioning. The presence of the patient's father as a third party to treatment has evident unconscious homosexual implications, although the patient represents these in heavily disguised form. The allusion to a party conveys the manic defense offered to the patient in having his parents pay for treatment, and getting the telephone number of one of the girls appears to represent a defense against the latent homosexual implications of the payment arrangement.

The patient's wish to navigate his parents' boat continues to express his wish to have his own therapeutic space, and his concerns about harming others or cutting another boat in two reflects his anxieties of damaging others or being damaged himself within such a contained treatment situation. Simultaneously, and of prior importance, these same images express the patient's unconscious perceptions of these very same needs and anxieties in the therapist. It is these fantasies and anxieties that the patient believes to have motivated the therapist to accept him into treatment under deviant conditions.

Only the fact that the patient cannot indeed afford to pay for his own therapy will soften these perceptions and render them analyzable in this treatment situation. This same fact will provide a perspective to the patient who will tolerate his unconscious perceptions of the therapist in light of the deviation in better fashion than would be the case if the patient could in fact afford to pay for his own treatment.

Thus, while a deviation will indeed interfere with open communication between the patient and the therapist, it will have a less destructive effect than otherwise because of the modifying conditions involved. The absence of rectification will not entirely destroy this treatment relationship and experience, and it will remain possible to work meaningfully with the patient with the implications of this particular deviation—all of this in light of its inherent necessity.

The man on board the parents' boat is clearly a representation of the patient's father—the third party to treatment who is having a destructive influence. This particular image is repeated again in the allusion to the kids who told the patient in junior high school to hurt the young man whom he had in a headlock. The destructive influence of the fee arrangement is quite evident in these derivative communications.

The patient feels unsafe with his father as a third party to his psychotherapy. His presence has caused problems within the treatment and transmission difficulties—issues in regard to the openness of communication between patient and therapist. The therapeutic hold is unstable and making the patient sick, causing him significant bodily anxieties. Simultaneously, the therapist is perceived as damaged and as coping with bodily anxieties of his own. The model here is that the therapist should take over the helm and create a secure framework for the patient's treatment experience. The patient perceives both himself and his therapist as fearful of this possibility.

The damaged frame is seen as having been created by a handicapped therapist, arranged for a handicapped patient. Both should experience guilt for having created these conditions to treatment. The therapist's decision to accept the patient's fee from the father has qualities in the patient's eyes of parasiticism, pathological symbiosis, cure through action-discharge, homosexuality, impaired narcissism and the use of the patient and father as selfobjects, disturbed identity, and a measure of madness. Interpretations of these unconscious perceptions of the therapist in light of the deviant intervention context could help this patient to resolve his measure of madness quite well, though up to a point. Efforts to intervene in other areas would undoubtedly be met with nonvalidation, and certainly would preclude the insightful resolution of the patient's psychopathology (madness).

Some additional information sheds further light on this discussion. The therapist reports that because the patient is in graduate school, it would be possible for him to work part-time and to pay the fee for his single weekly session. This fact may help to account for the strong models of rectification present in this material. This is, then, a deviant situation that could be rectified through interpretive efforts by the therapist, acknowledgment of the patient's models of rectification, and an *implicit* attitude within the therapist that would indeed encourage the patient to assume a responsibility for his treatment—a course adumbrated here in the patient's own opening associations.

In addition, the therapist has made it a practice to accept through the mail a check made out by the patient's father. In view of the fact that the patient has his own checking account, this accentuates the deviant conditions and creates an image of the therapist as wishing to avoid the entire issue. This, too, may help to account for the intensity of the patient's models of rectification and for his encoded pleas that the issues involved be explored and resolved—dealt with rather than avoided. In principle, even when a parent provides a patient with money for treatment, the therapist should only accept a check from the patient. To do otherwise is to more powerfully accept the third-party payer as a presence in the treatment situation—much as reflected in the encoded images in this session.

We see, then, that it becomes much easier to assign definitive meaning to this material once the specific adaptive context is known. In terms of working over the representations of the intervention context itself, the context is possibly latent to the patient's initial comments about school, given that his father also pays for this undertaking. It appears next in the patient's presence in his father's boat and in his allusions to the old salt. It is present too in the images of a poor holding environment, though it emerges in specific form—the allusion to the veteran's request for money—only toward the latter part of this session.

It would require further knowledge of both the patient, the therapist, and the transactions of the therapeutic interaction to account for the communicative resistances that led to the heavy disguise of these portrayals. In part, these obstacles appear to stem from the therapist's original decision to accept the patient under deviant conditions and, further, to accept the check directly from the patient's father. Another element appears to involve the patient's unconscious perceptions of anxiety in regard to the secure frame in both the therapist and himself.

It has been the main goal of this exercise to demonstrate the manner in which the patient's manifest material, decoded as derivative communications, are sufficiently organized by a compelling deviant intervention context so as to eventually render that context detectable or decodable from the patient's associations. It is to be hoped that the reader has gained both a sense of the difficulty in deciphering derivative material without a known intervention context, as well as a sense of the clarity that emerges in the latent material once such a context is known.

CONCLUDING COMMENTS

With this last discussion, we come to the end of this second workbook. The reader, it is hoped, is now in the position to create additional listening exercises for use on his or her own or in small study groups. Once we move beyond manifest content and self-evident implications, there is an enormous richness to the patient's encoded and derivative communications. Staggering at times to behold, the realm of unconscious communication is nonetheless both understandable and manageable.

The sensitive therapist weaves in or out as he or she listens, attending loosely and without aim at one moment and formulating at a furious pace at another. In time, the experienced therapist develops an ease of listening with which he or she works at a relatively slow pace when faced with intellectualized and relatively empty communicative material, only to shift to a relatively automatic but emphatic organizing process and analysis when the patient's associations move toward rich narratives and images. Familiarity with the implications of prevailing intervention contexts, whether deviant or frame secure, greatly facilitates the efforts involved.

Sound listening is a creative process for the therapist. It involves an ability to tune in to the marvelous unconscious creativity of the patient. Together, these two resources—one in the patient, the other in the therapist—are ultimately the basis for the cure of the madness of the patient—and in a smaller way, of the therapist as well. Through this means, the three factors in cure are joined: sound holding and containing, which provide the patient with general ego strength and broad coping abilities; true cognitive insight produced by validated adaptive context-oriented interventions, which assist the patient in resolving intrapsychic and narcissistic conflicts, and other internal disturbances; and positive introjective identifications with the well-functioning therapist, who is capable of appropriate silence, essential interpretation–reconstructions, and the management of a secure frame. At bottom, all of this and more depends on sound listening and formulating.

Appendix A

The Seven Dimensions of the Therapeutic Interaction

I. **The Ground Rules, or Frame**

   A. *The secure frame*—offers basic trust, clear interpersonal boundaries, support for reality testing, sound holding and containment. Sources of anxiety: responsibility and confinement that produce claustrophobic anxieties, fears of losing control—of unbridled sexuality, aggression, including fantasied rage toward the therapist, and dread of annihilation by the therapist.

   B. *The deviant frame*—offers basic mistrust, impaired interpersonal boundaries, disturbances in reality testing. Sources of inappropriate gratification: serves as a basis for pathological defense via merger, offers counterphobic and manic-fusion defenses, and the escape from experienced subjective madness.

   C. Other implications center on the nature of the specific deviation, the moment at which an aspect of the frame is secured, ramifications of the ongoing therapeutic interaction, and the specific meanings for both patient and therapist.

II. **The Mode of Relatedness**

   A. *Healthy symbiosis*—for the patient, accepting the conditions of treatment, free associating, attending to the therapist's interventions, and being prepared to analyze all proposed deviations from the ideal frame. For the therapist, securing the frame and adopting a basic interpretive-reconstructive stance.

   B. *Pathological symbiosis*—for the patient, the search for or achievement of frame breaks and noninterpretive interventions that are inappropriately gratifying. For the therapist, the offer of such interventions, as well as obtaining inappropriate satisfactions from the patient beyond the fee and evidence of the patient's improvement.

   C. *Healthy autism*—for the patient, expressions of nonmeaning at a time when there is no pressing adaptive context to which to respond. For the therapist, silence in response to material that is without meaning and therefore requires no intervention.

   D. *Pathological autism*—for the patient, the absence of meaning in the face of an activated (disturbing) intervention context. For the therapist, either a failure to intervene in the presence of meaningful associational material or an intervention that does not properly construe the patient's associations, thereby introducing images and contents that derive primarily from the therapist.

E. *Pathological parasiticism*—the exploitation and harm or frustration of one participant to therapy by the other.

III.   Mode of Cure

A. *True insight*—generated by interpreting an expression of the patient's madness in a given session in light of the implications of an intervention by the therapist that has activated the madness. The effort is carried out in terms of the patient's derivative complex—encoded perceptions and reactions to these perceptions, which reveal the unconscious meanings of the pathological expression.

B. *Action-discharge*—constituted by a noninterpretive intervention or any effort other than those which interpret or secure the frame, including the dumping aspects and erroneous use of verbal interventions.

C. The additional consideration as to whether the patient's material expresses basic *curative or harmful wishes* directed toward the therapist and similar consideration of the therapist's work with the patient.

IV.   Mode of Communication

The degree to which derivative expressions are implicitly supported by the interventions of the therapist: the openness and freedom with which the patient is encouraged to express him or herself; considerations of communicative style (the presence of meaning or its absence): and a study of whether the patient's associations and behaviors reflect quiet communication or dumping (the use of projective identification and efforts to arouse the therapist).

V.   Dynamics and Genetics

The vicissitudes of the sexual and aggressive instinctual drives; issues related to id, ego, and superego; problems of intrapsychic and interpersonal conflict and of psychosexual and aggressive development; reflections of all forms of psychodynamics; and the pertinent history of the patient and, secondarily, of the therapist.

VI.   Identity and Narcissism

Implications that pertain to self-serving needs, the use of the other as a selfobject, tension regulation, ideals and values, self-esteem, and the like—for both patient and therapist.

VII.   Madness and Sanity

The vicissitudes of the psychopathology of both patient and therapist.

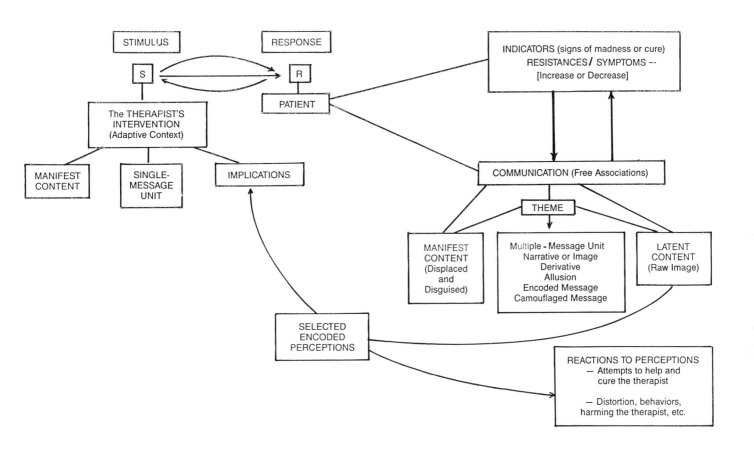

EXPLANATION:

The Therapeutic Interaction is circular. If we begin with an intervention of the therapist, we see it is a single-message communication. It has surface meaning and *implications* (it is not usually an encoded message).

The patient responds on two important levels, First, through vicissitudes of madness — intensification or diminution of symptoms and resistances. Second, with communications, mainly free associations. When there are narratives and images, they are usually multiple-message expressions (derivative in nature). They have both manifest and latent (encoded) meaning; the two levels are linked through shared themes.

The latent meaning of the patient's associations is constituted as *selected* (according to the patient's own madness and other interapsychic factors) *unconscious perceptions* of the *implications* of the therapist's interventions. Secondary reactions then follow.

References

Bion, W. (1977). Learning from experience (1962). In *Seven Servants*, New York: Aronson.

Bion, W. (1967). Notes on memory and desire. *Psychoanalytic Forum*, 2:271–280.

Freud, S. (1900). The interpretation of dreams. *Standard Edition*, 4–5:1–627.

Freud, S. (1908). Hysterical phantasies and their relation to bisexuality. *Standard Edition*, 9:155–166.

Langs, R. (1973). *The Technique of Psychoanalytic Psychotherapy, Volume 1*. New York: Aronson.

Langs, R. (1978). *The Listening Process*. New York: Aronson.

Langs, R. (1979). *The Therapeutic Environment*. New York: Aronson.

Langs. R. (1980). *Interactions: The realm of transference and countertransference*. New York: Aronson.

Langs, R. (1981). *Resistances and interventions: The nature of therapeutic work*. New York: Aronson.

Langs, R. (1982a). *Psychotherapy: A basic text*. New York: Aronson.

Langs, R. (1982b). *The Psychotherapeutic Conspiracy*. New York: Aronson.

Langs, R. (in press, a). *Madness and Cure*. Emerson: Newconcept Press.

Langs, R. (in press, b). *A Workbook for Psychotherapists, Vol. I: Understanding unconscious communication*. Emerson: Newconcept Press.

Little, M. (1951). Countertransference and the patient's response to it. *International Journal of Psycho-Analysis*, 32:32–40.

Searles, H. (1975). The patient as therapist to his analyst. In Peter Giovacchini (Ed.), *Tactics and Techniques in Psychoanalytic Therapy, Vol. II: Countertransference*.

Index